# A Pedagogy *of* Place

# A Pedagogy

## *of* Place

### Outdoor Education for a Changing World

Brian Wattchow and Mike Brown

MONASH University
Publishing

Monash University Publishing
Building 4, Monash University
Clayton, Victoria 3800, Australia
www.publishing.monash.edu

This book is available online at www.publishing.monash.edu/books/pp.html

ISBN: 978-0-9806512-4-9 (pb)
ISBN: 978-0-9806512-5-6 (web)

**Design**

Les Thomas


**Cover images**

Courtesy of the authors.
Front cover, Waikato River, New Zealand.
Back cover, Nooramunga Marine Reserve, Australia.

All images were supplied by the authors except for the images on pages 98 and 179, which are courtesy of Te Rūnanga o Ngāi Tahu and Arthur Curl respectively.


**Printer**

Griffin Press

# Dedication

This book is dedicated to *all* educators who wish to explore new ways of practice in order that they may enrich the lives of their students, their communities and their places.

> *The most profound satisfactions are to be found in living a life in accord with the natural world, exercising the human capacity for friendship and altruism, engaging in creative and purposeful activity, and experiencing an allegiance to one's origins ... But it is insufficient to hear such a message; one has to experience it to know that things are so.*
>
> Michael King (1999, 240)

# Acknowledgements

Beyond the debt owed to the many writers whose works we have drawn on in this book, we would specifically like to thank the following individuals and organisations:

The participants in the four case studies, both anonymous and named, thank-you for your willingness to share your insights and stories.

Professor Alister Jones, Dean of the Faculty of Education, University of Waikato, for his support to utilise the King Residence as a writing retreat.

The Teaching and Learning Research Initiative (TLRI) Fund for supporting the work from which the case study in chapter seven is drawn.

A particular thanks to Jane Burnett for her diligent proof reading and editing work.

To Dr Nathan Hollier and the team at Monash University Publishing. A heartfelt thanks for taking on the project and handling it with the highest standards of professionalism.

Mike would like to thank Paula for her support and patience and for helping to keep things in perspective. Finally, his heartfelt thanks to Brian for his support, insight, wise words and enduring friendship.

Brian would like to thank Katrina, Bess and Kate for tolerating his many journeys and making 'home' such a wonderful place. Also Mike, thanks for your sustained energy and passion for this book project. Also, for your ongoing sense of humour and your generosity and friendship.

# Contents

# Preface

The American heritage farmer and poet Wendell Berry once said; 'If you don't know where you are, you don't know who you are.' This statement has a special resonance in countries like Australia and New Zealand. These post-colonial societies continue to wrestle with important questions and issues that relate to land, identity and community. There is a palpable sense that many of us are still searching for ways to connect with where we are, in both our personal and professional lives. Many people may experience a sense of placelessness in the hyper-mobility of present times where 'globalising' agendas are not conducive to gaining a sense of place in a constantly changing world.

We believe that it is vitally important for outdoor educators to understand and foster a sense of connection with the places where they live, learn and teach. These outdoor places are much more than mere sites for human activity. They make us and we make them. They are the sources of our identities.

Why is this important for outdoor educators? First, it involves an important step in participating in the ongoing process of reconciliation with the indigenous peoples of both countries. It includes becoming reconciled to the unique characteristics of the 'land' and learning to live in harmony with the ecological systems that sustain our communities. Second, it compels us, as professionals, to question taken-for-granted approaches to outdoor education that have often been based on ideas and practices imported from abroad. Finally, it is likely that the 21st century will bring extraordinary challenges to how we all live on the Earth. Climate change and social and economic instability will force individuals and communities to react and evolve. Even though these phenomena are global, their impact will be experienced locally. Outdoor education has the potential to play a significant role – but only if it can respond to these changing conditions.

Why place? Because place refers to a participatory and experiential phenomenon. Our experience of a place is always a combination of a specific physical location, our embodied encounter and the cultural ideas that influence the interpretations we make of the experience. This provides rich potential for outdoor educators who are already well-versed in experiential pedagogies. A participant learning about the significance of a place, and how their beliefs and actions impact upon it, will be well positioned to reflect on how their community may need to adapt to the challenges ahead.

Why Australia and New Zealand? The focus in this book on these two countries is not only a result of the fact that the authors live, work and call these respective countries 'home'. It is also a recognition that we are located in specific places, with their own 'identities'. It is important that discussions of this nature be located and grounded rather than abstract and generalised. Another reason is that a substantial body of material challenging 'traditional' approaches in outdoor education has come from Australia and New Zealand; perhaps because there is ongoing public debate about land and identity in both countries. We will discuss these contributions in the light of international developments throughout the book. As far-flung former British colonies, the countries share similar origins. But the fact that the different indigenous cultures and environments encountered there by the colonisers have elicited very different responses in terms of land practices and cultural identities is instructive when it comes to considerations about the centrality of place in our lives. Drawing on literature, cultural images, and outdoor education practices provides a richness and diversity in the book that encourages greater reflection and contemplation about what may be possible in outdoor education. But we certainly hope that outdoor educators in other countries will be receptive to the ideas we present. We have kept in mind the international character of our profession when planning and writing the book.

In the pages that follow we provide an overview of some problematic aspects of contemporary practice. We then provide examples of how some educators and participants are working and learning in quite different ways that respond to the particularities of their outdoor places. We do this via four research case studies of programs, each one revealing something different about the concept of place-responsiveness. Finally, we offer a series of signposts to a place-responsive outdoor education philosophy and practice that we hope will provide useful guidance to others considering the need for change in how they work with young people in outdoor places.

Our approach here is to invite reflection and consideration about why outdoor education and outdoor places matter. We want to encourage a subtle shift that takes the best that our profession has developed to date and then adapts and readies it for the challenges ahead. Our work here is inspired by the Australian academic John Cameron's call for a place-responsive society: 'because the word "responsive" carries with it the impetus to act, to respond' (Cameron 2003a, 180). When we look to the challenges ahead, we see the potential for outdoor educators to make a significant contribution in developing an optimistic view for future generations of learners.

*Brian Wattchow*
Trafalgar, Gippsland, Australia

*Mike Brown*
Cambridge, Waikato, New Zealand

# Introduction:
# Towards Place-Responsive Outdoor Education

Many outdoor educators have been asked 'What is outdoor education?' It is not a question that educators in mainstream curriculum areas such as mathematics, history, science or literacy are likely to have to answer about their own disciplines. Established school subjects are seldom required to justify their place in the curriculum. But outdoor education is a relatively new form of educational practice and can appear, to the uninitiated at least, to function outside the usual norms of the educational setting. When faced with the 'What is …' question, many of us may have replied with the rather formulaic 'It's about helping people learn about themselves, how they relate to other people and the environment'. This is often met with a nod and a story from the person based on their own experience: 'I went on an outdoor course in 1990 and it was amazing'; 'We did some of that outdoor team building stuff at work a couple of years ago'. Our inquirer might tell the story of a friend or relative, 'My nephew is into all that camping stuff at school', or comment, 'That's what these kids need today; get them out in the bush, that'll straighten them out'. One gets the impression that, at a popular level at least, participation in an outdoor program will be good for a person, help them to work with others, and give them an appreciation for the 'great outdoors'. Stories told by participants often recount long days doing things they never thought possible, the majestic views from the mountaintop, friendships made, the food cooked on fires or simple camp stoves, and a sense of accomplishment. But occasionally you will hear stories of people being pushed to do things they did not want to do or of being placed in situations that, years later, seem to have left a lasting negative impression.

If the conversation continues discussion may extend to different forms of outdoor education, such as residential camping, expedition programs, leadership training, personal development courses or environmental education projects. We might, should our listener still feign interest, talk about industry training, tertiary courses or formalised curricula within schools where outdoor education may be subsumed into other discipline areas (typically within health and physical education), or where it exists as a specialised subject of study (as it does in the senior years of secondary schooling in some states of Australia).

We may go on to describe to our listener how outdoor education has always proclaimed the importance of program participants having direct experiences that make learning 'real'. 'It's about hands on learning,' we say. 'It's about learners having to make decisions for themselves and then having to work through the consequences. It's about taking responsibility!' We may even begin to discuss how outdoor education uses an experiential approach to learning where challenging tasks are set for a group of participants, how their progress is facilitated by an outdoor education teacher or guide and, finally, how that experience is reflected upon or debriefed so that learners may be able to generalise useful knowledge that transfers back to school, work or home.

This is often about as far as we have to go in our attempts to justify outdoor education practice. In this book we are interested in going deeper than this. We will call into question some of the taken-for-granted 'truths' and underlying assumptions about what outdoor educators do and the nature of the educational experiences that are provided for their students. However, we want to do more than critique. We will also offer alternatives to the dominant forms of contemporary outdoor education practice. In this introduction we briefly introduce the main areas of concern which we feel require consideration and necessitate a reappraisal of the foundations of outdoor education, its aims, ideals, and pedagogical practices.

We hope that our views will be of interest and relevance to those training to become outdoor education instructors, guides and teachers as well as experienced practitioners. We have sought to be as inclusive as possible and to address the considerable diversity of forms of outdoor education practice; from school-based programs to camps and outdoor centres, from youth intervention programs to expeditionary learning, from outdoor guiding to those involved in nature interpretation, and from industry-based training providers through to postgraduate students and academics. Obviously we cannot please all, it may be considered too intellectual by some and not rigorous enough by others. We use case studies, anecdotes and personal narratives as ways of posing questions and teasing out, exploring and amplifying some of the more theoretically 'dense' sections of the following chapters.

We believe that outdoor education has now moved beyond its infancy. From time to time, however, outdoor educators may still need to justify their position and programs and the role outdoor education provides in enhancing the quality of life of individuals within their communities (e.g. via youth groups, formal and informal networks of clubs and volunteer organisations). We suggest that there is a poor collective understanding about the legitimacy of what we can reasonably claim outdoor education programs achieve and how outdoor educators go about their work. In this book we propose to take you, the reader, on a searching journey through some of the profession's most 'heartfelt' beliefs about outdoor education and, in finding some of them wanting as appropriate forms of educational theory and practice, to propose a renewal of outdoor education for a changing world.

The old truism that nothing is more certain than change is perhaps more apt than ever. Surely there are few left, even in the realms of politics and corporate business, who would deny the magnitude of global environmental issues such as climate change or the challenges posed by international social and economic instability. We are not going to spend much time discussing the history, economics or politics of these issues directly; there is plenty of good material available written by others more versed in the topics. The idea of educating for a changing world, however, is an important one. The effects of global phenomena like climate change, shifting populations, economic disruption and so on, are always experienced locally. It is local individuals and communities that will grapple with understanding these changes and developing appropriate responses. Today's youth will need to know both how to understand local conditions and how they are connected to global changes. Rather than a 'doomsday curriculum' we think that this can be done in a way that encourages resilience and optimism. Typically outdoor education is an endeavour that is focused on youth and young adults. In this book our focus will be on outdoor education within the broad educational context, from all levels of schooling through to tertiary education and its use in community settings. It is worth noting that many vocational and university programs now support curricula incorporating the philosophies and practices of outdoor education. Some of these tertiary students may have had minimal exposure to outdoor education through their schooling. Hence it is possible for a student to be in the process of learning about outdoor education for the first time while simultaneously developing the skills and knowledge needed to lead and teach as an outdoor educator. Graduates from these tertiary education programs have the potential to be significant catalysts for change as they take on instructing, guiding, teaching and management roles within schools, community-based youth programs and commercial outdoor education providers.

**"Today's youth will need to know both how to understand local conditions and how they are connected to global changes."**

Though this book draws extensively on international literature it is also strongly focused on the Australian and New Zealand education and environmental contexts. Our intent is to remain cognisant of international debate about outdoor education theory and practice but to concentrate mainly on home-grown conceptual understandings and programming initiatives. As we hope to demonstrate, developments in outdoor education on both sides of the Tasman have the potential to make a unique contribution to the field locally, nationally and, we believe, internationally.

There is ample evidence to suggest that the ecological environments of both New Zealand and Australia have been significantly degraded and damaged through the process of European colonisation (Lines 1991; Park 1995). It is also evident that these settler societies have yet to adapt to local conditions in terms of establishing sustainable land management practices, which in turn suggests that we have yet to develop a set of sustainable values and ideas about the land. Yet both nations have established stable, and many would argue, successful, democratic societies. A critical awareness of the ideas and practices imported from abroad, those of which are worth adopting or adapting in the local context and those which are not, and recognition of where we need to develop more indigenous, home-grown knowledge, is a crucial challenge facing both countries. We suggest that the same challenge now confronts outdoor educators. Our overall aim then, in this book, is to discuss and argue for a place-responsive philosophy and form of practice in outdoor education. At this point it might be helpful to go into a little more detail about the struggle over the last few decades to find a common understanding of what it is that outdoor educators collectively believe defines outdoor education.

## What is outdoor education?

Some may argue that debate around finding a universal definition for outdoor education, one that could apply in all learning contexts, is a futile one. It is not our intent here to seek the 'Holy Grail' of defining precisely what it is that outdoor educators believe and practice. However, we do feel that it is worth briefly summarising some of this debate to provide background to our arguments for an alternative set of values and practices. There are some quite detailed accounts of the historical development of outdoor education in the United Kingdom (Nicol 2002a, 2002b, 2003), Australia (Brookes 2002; McRae 1990) and New Zealand (Lynch 2006). For the purpose of this introduction we pick up the debate in the 1970s, where we see the emergence of outdoor education in its contemporary form. Since the mid-1970s outdoor education has developed as a recognised form of educational practice, both in formal schooling and in the community. Typically outdoor education has been presented in the professional literature as being concerned with personal and social development of young people across a range of areas of interest, such as: 'self-awareness, teamwork, decision-making, environmental awareness, spiritual and aesthetic awareness, relationship-building, taking responsibility, communication skills and physical awareness' (Gair 1997, 27). Writers from diverse international backgrounds, such as Mortlock (1984) in the United Kingdom and Schoel, Prouty and Radcliffe (1988) in the United States, claim that the aim of outdoor education is to facilitate the achievement of human potential through outdoor adventure experiences.

These oft repeated aims of outdoor education – to heighten awareness of and foster respect for self, others and nature – originated in the discussions and resulting publications from the Dartington conference in outdoor education in 1975 which was convened by the United Kingdom Department of Education and Science (Nicol 2002b). Gair (1997) credits this conference with introducing the three commonly accepted components of the outdoor adventure experience (self, others and nature) to the discourse of outdoor education professional practice. In this context, argues Gair, 'the self' is concerned with the prospect that increased self-awareness and enhanced self-concept may stem from a positive response to experiences of a challenging and adventurous nature. 'Others' extends this concept to one that maximises the potential for group development and cohesion via experiences such as 'the expedition'. From this viewpoint it is argued that physical challenges and a degree of emotional stress contained in adventure will demand that the group forges effective underlying social structures. Finally, 'the natural environment' is considered to be the arena for challenge in a physical sense. In addition, environmental awareness is considered an outcome of direct experience in the natural world.

The reason we introduce the debate about outdoor education for self, others and nature is that these foci have come to be repeated like a mantra in many outdoor education curricula and programs. Robbie Nicol (2002a, 2002b, 2003) has provided a detailed critique of these foundational concepts.

> These aims were a formulation of what conference delegates already perceived their job to be. However, the aims were not arrived at as the result of empirical analysis and so there is no evidence to suggest, for example, that by 'heightening awareness' 'respect' would be fostered for any of the three aims. (Nicol 2002b, 89)

Nicol goes on to quote Cheesmond who stated that 'maybe each strand has a distinct philosophical underpinning; the mountaineer, the group worker, the biologist for example, but they have proved to be uncomfortable bedfellows in achieving something overarching' (Nicol 2002b, 89).

In very general terms, part of the confusion surrounding attempts to define outdoor education may be characterised by Ford's (1981) early attempt to provide a catch-all concept for the nexus (or tension) that exists between outdoor education and environmental education. Ford's (1981, 12) 'in, for and about the outdoors' definition of practice is characteristically broad in scope and ambition, and preceded several attempts to establish universal definitions that claim outdoor education as an experiential process, located in outdoor places, and that the subject matter is 'relationships' (Priest 1986). Simon Priest (1986) provided a definition that serves as a good summary of attempts to encapsulate both the aims and pedagogies of this relatively new form of educational practice. Priest's (1986) definition of outdoor education was founded on six major points: that outdoor education was a method; that it draws upon a heritage of ideas about experiential learning from the likes of Comenius, Rousseau, Pestalozzi and Dewey; that the outdoor setting is vital to learning; that learning in outdoor education occurs across the three domains (cognitive, affective, and motoric); that the curriculum is interdisciplinary in nature; and that learning is a matter of many relationships (see Priest 1986, 13–14).

Some of these claims appear to be, if not grandiose, at least overly ambitious. There does not appear to have been much left off the rhetorical wish list surrounding the rise of outdoor education and what it claims to achieve. In some ways this is understandable. Outdoor education writers and practitioners, particularly in the early decades of its development, have had to quite deliberately practice a proactive and assertive form of advocacy for what has typically been seen as a fringe subject or an extra-curricular activity within educational programming.

Even so, given these efforts to define outdoor education, we might ask ourselves the following questions. Is outdoor education a curriculum or a form of pedagogic practice, or both? Is there anything distinctive about its educational aims, its content, or its pedagogic methods? How, specifically, do participants experience learning in the outdoor education context? We suggest that at times the rhetoric of the enthusiastic outdoor educator does not necessarily mirror the reality of what outdoor programs might actually achieve, nor how outdoor educators go about their work.

There is a growing body of literature which questions the underlying philosophical and pedagogical assumptions upon which much outdoor education practice is based. We will examine this literature in detail throughout the book. But, in broad terms, Alison Lugg (1999) traced a major shift in outdoor education discourse led by Andrew Brookes (1993) and Peter Martin (1992) in Australia, and Geoff Cooper (1994) and Peter Higgins (1996) in the United Kingdom. She argues that these authors have presented an alternative 'that sees the primary purpose of outdoor education as educating for an environmentally sustainable future' (Lugg 1999, 26). Chris Loynes (2002) has provided a paradigmatic overview of contemporary outdoor adventure education practice that brings some order to an otherwise broad and sometimes confusing professional discourse. He juxtaposes the influence of military, modernist and algorithmic (or formulaic) paradigms with alternative moral, ecological and generative paradigms for outdoor education. He focuses largely on differences between outdoor education's origins in the United Kingdom and the United States, and is critical of the masculine and hierarchical tendencies of militaristic and expedition-based programs in Britain and of 'production line' approaches to learning in the outdoors that have become established in the United States. He contrasts these with the Scandinavian tradition of 'Friluftsliv' (as a cultural approach to outdoor living) and, in the UK, an emerging local 'generative approach', where he defines outdoor experiential learning as radical practice:

> a journey of discovery of a personal ontology and epistemology for the participant. It incorporates actions based on the experiences inspired by learners choosing for themselves how to make a difference. The individual moves through the role of participant and narrator, and becomes an agent in their world. (Loynes 2002, 121)

It is clear that outdoor education is a term attached to activities and pedagogic approaches as disparate as adventure therapy, corporate training, outdoor pursuits, recreational camping, and elements of formal schooling. Yet the significance of the local outdoor places, the sites where outdoor education is actually practised, can be lost in the diversity of this educational landscape. The geographical locations where programs run can all too easily come to be seen as clinical sites, obstacle courses, testing grounds, venues, or curriculum resources. Philip Payne (2002) provides a useful summary in the Australian context, though the quotation could probably apply in most countries where outdoor education features as a component of schooling and community development.

> Undoubtedly, outdoor education in Australia is a 'set' of social and cultural constructions, whose activity base borrows from diverse histories and has numerous aims that now tend to stress the development of adventure recreation skills, personal therapy and spiritual growth, social or 'community' development, profit-making or, more recently, environmental relations. (p. 5)

As we have already suggested, outdoor education is no longer in its infancy. Yet attempts by theorists, writers and researchers to define and qualify the profession's scope and ambitions are made increasingly difficult by the proliferation of these multiple forms of practice, each with its own educational, therapeutic or economic agenda, yet each claiming an allegiance to outdoor education and the outdoors itself. Given the historical basis of the three aims of outdoor education, that participants will learn something worthwhile about self, others and nature, and the small but growing number of critiques of contemporary approaches and practices, we suggest that it is timely to consider recent literature, both from wider disciplines and from within outdoor education, concerning the concept of 'place'. Place, we feel, has the potential to provide a renewed philosophical and pedagogical basis for outdoor education. A shift towards a stronger focus on a place-responsive outdoor education stands to serve youth and young adults well in a rapidly changing and, all too often, abstracted world.

## Introducing the concept of place

The concept of place has to do with how people develop and experience a sense of attachment to particular locations on the Earth's surface. It also has to do with how people are affected by and effect those places. Therefore, place is suggestive of both the imaginative and physical reality of a location and its people, and how the two interact and change each other. In this book we bring a fresh perspective to the growing interest in the meaning and significance of place-responsive experiences in education. Rather than harking back nostalgically to 'the good old days when life was a lot slower and simpler', much place literature is inspired by a desire to develop a realistic response to the many social and ecological challenges that individuals and communities face in different locations around the world, from rural town to city suburb, from industrial district to national park.

Whilst the late polymath and 'scholar of everything', George Seddon is probably responsible for introducing the phrase 'a sense of place' to Australia, it is John Cameron (2001, 2003a, 2003b) who has most clearly articulated the case for a pedagogic response to place. Both Seddon and Cameron were keynote speakers at the 12th National Outdoor Education Conference held at La Trobe University in Bendigo, Australia. Interestingly the conference was titled 'Education Outdoors: Our Sense of Place'. In his address, Cameron (2001) suggested that 'the task of the educator is how to foster an inclusive sense of place in students so that their love of wild places can extend to care for all places, even neglected city spaces' (p. 28). Cameron's quiet but hopeful challenge to the audience was to overcome the dualistic divide between wilderness, the prototypical site of much outdoor education, and home, the place where educators and students alike actually live most of their lives. This book is, in part, a response to that challenge.

There are a number of approaches to the notion of place that we could have drawn upon as a conceptual guide for this book. The Australian eco-philosopher Val Plumwood (2003) has argued that we need 'a place-sensitive society' whilst the American educator David Gruenewald (2003a) calls for 'place-consciousness' in education. However, the concept that we find most compelling is Cameron's call for a place-responsive society which necessarily draws upon a place-responsive pedagogy.

In this book we consider how a pedagogy of place may reinvigorate both debate and practice in outdoor education. Initially we do this by drawing upon the extensive scholarship of place that has developed across a range of disciplines. Much of this scholarship has focused upon notions of home-place and dwelling, and we consider how it may apply to regional, residential camp and expeditionary style outdoor education programs. In addition, we couple this with a reconsideration of experiential learning pedagogies and how they may best serve renewed forms of place responsive outdoor education practice. The final part of the book reports upon a series of case studies that offer empirical evidence for alternative forms of place-based and place-responsive outdoor education programming.

## The structure of the book

In chapter one we start the book with two personal narratives. It is not intended that these autobiographical accounts be complete. Rather these narratives aim to highlight some of the experiences that we feel have shaped our interest in the outdoors and raised important personal and professional questions about the purposes and practices of outdoor education. Our intent here is to inform readers about our personal histories in outdoor education so that they may have a sense of our preferences, our biases and the types of outdoor places and programs where we have worked and developed our ideas. We also use these narratives to forecast significant themes and issues in the book that we write about deliberately later on. We draw on anecdotes throughout the book from a range of sources, as we believe that this style of writing about outdoor education is important. It signals to the reader that context, situation and story matter. Much of what we have to say in the book relies upon the reader considering how it may or may not apply in their own personal and professional circumstances.

In chapter two we discuss some of myths, dubious claims and problematic assumptions we find evident in the professional literature and contemporary practices of outdoor education. The focus here is not on disproving claims about the documented outcomes of participation in outdoor education programmes. There is a large body of empirical evidence supporting the benefits of outdoor education on a number of psychological constructs (Cason & Gillis 1994; Hattie et al. 1997). The majority of quantitative studies seek to measure changes in various psychological variables using pre- and post-test questionnaires or validated measurement scales (e.g. self-esteem, locus of control, self-efficacy). The battle lines between quantitative versus qualitative methodologies and psychological approaches versus sociological studies have on occasions been well defined, fought over, blurred somewhat, or completely circumvented. We opt for the latter approach. In this book we are interested in asking questions of a different nature. So, we will deftly sidestep issues and debates about quantifiable educational outcomes at this point. Instead, our intent here is to question, describe and discuss the pedagogical and philosophical basis of an alternative outdoor education philosophy and practice, one that is based upon the principles of place-responsiveness.

In this chapter we also explore how outdoor nature as 'wilderness' has been valorised as a place in which it is argued that one's true self will be revealed or where one can truly be free from the corrupting influences of society. The belief in the purity of the wilderness and the concept of naturalness serve to mask the particularities of the local and create a universal notion of the wild as a backdrop for human action. We also cast a critical eye on the taken-for-granted belief that adventure is a natural human condition and the taking of risks is not only desirable but a necessary component of learning in outdoor education. Drawing on a broad base of literature we seek to highlight the problematic aspects of placing young people in risky situations as a means to facilitate learning. The focus on the provision of risky activities as a means to learn has, in a New Zealand context at least, caused one outside observer (Andkjaer 2009) to suggest that outdoor education has developed as a 'paradoxical spiral' (p. 5) where activities involving risk and the ensuing search for safety constantly fuel each other. Risk taking and risk management as a pedagogic strategy in outdoor education reflects changing societal values. As Caplan (2000) noted ten years ago risk is a topic that is increasingly difficult to ignore. Hope (2005) has argued that Western society has become obsessed with the probability of accidents, illness or death. He has stated that 'concern about such things as spread of disease, food production and global terrorism have encouraged individuals to increasingly think of everyday activities in terms of danger and risk alleviation' (p. 3). We only need to think of recent media images which allude to the heightened risks of air travel and the necessary security measures put in place or the seemingly innocuous TV commercials warning mothers of the risk to their children of household germs and the need to use product x to sanitise surfaces and door handles. Hope (2005) has also suggested that many people believe that today's society is much more dangerous than the one that existed even a few decades ago. Drawing on Giddens, he argues that it is not necessarily that society is more dangerous, but rather that people have become risk obsessed.

As Hope and Oliver (2005) have rightly observed, perspectives of what is risky are culturally constructed and differ across time and cultures. Thus opinions as to whether risk is likely to have positive or negative outcomes will also differ. Thus various interpretations of the benefits, or dangers, of a particular risk will change, reflecting the dynamic nature of risk discourses. In chapter two we discuss these complex concepts of risk as it applies to outdoor education. A recent tragedy (April 2008) at a New Zealand outdoor education centre, in which six students and their teacher died, has brought the issue of risk taking in an educational context into sharp focus once again. We discuss how the educational aspect of outdoor education can be overshadowed by an emphasis on risky pursuits and the associated safety management policies and procedures that must then be put into place in an increasingly risk averse society.

The final issue to come under the spotlight in chapter two in is a critique of the promotion of a stylistic or simplistic version of the Experiential Learning Cycle which is often deployed in outdoor education programs, possibly in the place of more localised approaches to teaching and learning. We believe that the idea that a challenging activity followed by a debrief, in which participants are coached to articulate what has been learnt, so that it may be applied in other contexts later, is too neat and tidy a product to explain the complex processes of learning. Drawing on a range of critiques from a variety of disciplinary areas we suggest that this formulaic model overlooks the nuanced embodied, social, cultural and geographical components of the learning process.

## The case for place

In chapter three we begin the argument for a consideration of an alternative place-responsive form of outdoor education. According to David Orr (1992), educators have failed to see much significance in understanding, or attempting to teach, about place. He explains that 'place is nebulous to educators because to a great extent we are displaced people for whom immediate places are no longer sources of food, water, livelihood, energy, materials, friends, recreation or sacred inspiration' (p. 126). The typical curriculum, according to Orr, is based upon abstraction, which disconnects people from their tangible experience and from day-to-day problems and issues where they live and work. Outdoor education participants' experiences can be based at or near their homes, or occur nearby within their region. But outdoor education is also often practiced in remote locations, far from where participants live most of their lives. In either case, we argue, it may be taught in a way that is responsive to place or in a way that it is not. There are environmental and cultural consequences that flow from any form of practice that does not respond carefully, and we will argue empathetically, to place. It is possible for educational practice to function as a form of placelessness and to encourage a sense of detachment from local conditions as much as it is possible for it to encourage a sense of attachment to a place.

In chapter three we introduce and discuss concepts from clearly articulated theories of place that have been developed in other disciplines. The focus here is on how places are encountered and experienced by people and how people develop relationships with particular places, and how these relationships are influential in the creation and maintenance of their identities. We argue that this scholarship of place has considerable potential to provide new perspectives and possibilities for outdoor education. The outdoor places where outdoor educators work are so close to them that it is possible that they may fail to carefully consider how place(s) contribute to and shape the educational experience. Equally it is possible that outdoor educators may not often think about how their actions while working in a place, shapes and changes the place itself. Leaders, teachers and participants may all too easily project certain desires upon the place for what they want it to be, such as: a wilderness, an adventure gymnasium, a therapeutic refuge, an arena, or a playground. We peel back these different cultural constructions for outdoor places and reveal how they shape what we do as outdoor educators. It is possible that educators and outdoor leaders may be guilty of projecting their desires for what they want a place to be in order that it appears to neatly match the learning goals and intents of their program. When this happens educators are really claiming that it is only the learners' experiences that matter. The leader's role becomes one of facilitating the learners' construction of worthwhile knowledge and a sense of personal development while simultaneously silencing or dismissing an alternative experience of the outdoor place that is possibly rawer, deeper, more sensuous and more connected to the past, present and possible future of that place.

## Place-based and place-responsive approaches in education and outdoor education

In chapter four we explore how the theoretical understandings about place and identity have been interpreted and applied in place-responsive educational initiatives. First, we discuss how the development of teaching for positive relations with nature in outdoor education has proved a false dawn in terms of a place-responsive form of practice. Here we discuss examples of how, despite the best intent, the goal of developing relationships with nature is problematic for a pedagogy of place. Next we discuss what writers and educators have had to say about placed-based imperatives and initiatives in education generally. Though it may not initially seem that this is directly related to outdoor education programs that tend to provide experiences away from the more 'formal' learning environment of the school, we feel that there is much of value here.

Many of the theoretical arguments and case studies of place-based programs in schools and local communities, which focus on how participants experience the places where they live and learn, provide compelling role models for outdoor educators and practitioners to consider. There are opportunities for place-responsive outdoor educators to work as an extension of these place-based approaches in the school and local community, and also to be a distinctive form of educational practice that sometimes occurs far away from the learners' homes.

The final section of chapter four considers the work of outdoor education writers and researchers who have begun to explore the significance of place in participants' outdoor education experiences. There has not been a great deal of work yet published on this topic. That this is the case is not altogether surprising. Perhaps outdoor educators are, as David Orr suggests, a displaced people. Yet seasoned outdoor educators and guides are often acutely aware of how local tides, weather, river levels and so on dictate to them what they may or may not do within a program. They know which campsites will be sheltered from a shift in the wind and which will catch the morning sun, and how important this knowledge might be for participants to have a good experience. They also often know a lot about local flora and fauna, even in which forest tree a particular bird or animal might be spotted. They may be interested in the local geology, history and ecology of the places where they work, and often know about the threats to the ecological stability of the place. They may also have collected anecdotes and stories about the place's cultural history, and they usually have a good feel for when it is appropriate to either pass these understandings along to participants or how to craft learning encounters that make it seem as though it is the experience of the place that is revealing this knowledge to learners. So, why is there so little of this evident in the professional literature of outdoor education? Why is it that undergraduate students training to be outdoor education teachers, or trainee guides, or even current practitioners, when reading outdoor education textbooks or journals, or attending an outdoor education conference, may well get the impression that this kind of local knowledge and sensitivity does not really matter? Why does it seem that many of the practices and principles of our profession are presented as being 'place proof' rather than place-responsive?

No place-responsive pedagogy for outdoor education that is based upon empirical evidence has yet been proposed, enacted or evaluated. But a small number of important research studies have been completed that begin to illuminate the complexity of place-oriented teaching and learning in the outdoors. We focus mainly on research writing which presents empirical evidence. In Canada, Brent Cuthbertson (1999), Bob Henderson (1995) and James Raffan (1992), while not specifically researching place-responsive outdoor education, offer some very interesting insights. Similarly, in Australia, Alistair Stewart (2003a; 2004b), Brian Wattchow (2006; 2007; 2008) and Marc Mullins (2007) have begun to address this gap through researching outdoor education expeditions and outdoor educators working as river guides. In each case the researchers were examining existing programs and seeking to establish how participants experienced those outdoor places. Similar to John Cameron's work, Lou Preston and Amma Griffiths (2004) used an action research project to work with students to establish connections to their local landscape through repeated visits. In New Zealand, Mike Brown (2008b) has written of his experiences on a program with a strong *Ngāi Tahu* cultural influence; Dave Irwin (2007/08) has commented on educating for change in the tertiary sector; and Jocelyn Papprill (2009) and Arthur Sutherland (2009) have written about secondary school programs that link outdoor education with sustainability and ecological activism. We plan to draw upon this research and these narratives for inspiration in this book as we advocate both a philosophy and form of practice that sees local places as a vital partner in educational endeavour.

## The case studies

Having completed the theoretical underpinning of our argument for an alternative focus upon the significance and educative power of place in outdoor education in the first four chapters, we continue the book by presenting a series of case studies. Each of these case studies addresses a different set of problems and issues regarding place and outdoor education philosophy and practice. In each case study we describe recent research projects that we have completed into outdoor education practice and what they reveal in terms of the challenges and possibilities of a place-responsive approach. These research projects have not necessarily been framed as resolving what a place-responsive outdoor education program should look like. Rather they represent attempts to keep adding to the empirical evidence base for outdoor education and especially, in this instance, to contribute knowledge and insight into a place-responsive outdoor education.

The first case study focuses on Australian university outdoor education students' responses to extended river journeys on the River Murray that they completed as part of their studies. The study sought to reveal the complex responses of the participants and how they represented both a sense of place and placelessness. As a phenomenological study it highlights how often it is the mundane, embodied, everyday qualities of outdoor experiences that are rich in potential for place-responsiveness. The second case study reports on New Zealand tertiary students' experiences of outdoor education in their own backyard. As part of a second-year paper entitled 'Learning in Adventure and Outdoor Environments' students embark on a three-day journey from their university via bicycle, on foot and river travel. This mini journey (approx. 125 km) starts and finishes at the university campus. This outdoor education experience takes them through countryside that many of the students pass through as they commute to and from their classes; yet it opens up a different way of seeing the landscape and understanding the significance of everyday taken-for-granted places. In the third case study we report on a localised outdoor program that is being developed in a secondary school in the North Island of New Zealand. Here we seek to gain insights into and understand why teachers in a local secondary school sought to move away from a traditional activity-focused outdoor education program and what it was like for them to make that transition. The final case study is based on a series of interviews with a Victorian outdoor education teacher who has developed a place-responsive outdoor education program in his school over the last 15 years. It presents and reflects on what it is like for a teacher to develop a deep affinity with a number of outdoor places, what these places mean to him, and how he works to develop an appropriate pedagogy for his students and staff colleagues that responds to the particularities of those places.

These stories of current programs – the ideas of the educators and guides who have designed and worked on them, and the responses of the participants to them – are not intended to be exhaustive. We have already stated that outdoor education is a diverse field of practice, and it would not be feasible to try to audit how place is incorporated into all forms of outdoor education in every possible location. Rather we hope that each case study reveals insights for the reader and provokes discussion about outdoor education philosophies and practices. We hope that it will encourage reflection about how current programs are already responding to place, or may be modified to become more place-responsive, or to stimulate outdoor educators into designing alternative programs and to think about emerging pedagogic strategies that respond to both the best traditions of outdoor education and the local conditions where teachers and learners engage meaningfully with local places.

## Designing place-based and place-responsive outdoor education experiences

The final chapter summarises and concludes the book. We are cautious about being seen to provide prescriptive advice about outdoor education programming. To do so would be hypocritical given the emphasis we have placed on the importance of geographical situation, cultural context and the experiential education encounter with place. Only the local educator who has actively developed a sensitivity to the interaction of these phenomena can know what kind of experience may best provide learners with opportunities for a successful educational experience. As we suggest in our autobiographical narratives and much of the content of the book, place experiences are unfolding in their character. A nuanced, local, place-responsive curriculum and pedagogy is likely to evolve over time, through repeated efforts. Even so, we do feel that it is appropriate to provide a series of signposts for other educators and outdoor education programmers to consider. These might best be thought of as design principles in crafting place-responsive outdoor education experiences. We hope that the discussion of theory, the presentation of stories of practice, and the reflections that follow provide food for thought and some inspiration about the power and potential of place in outdoor education.

# Chapter 1

## Personal Narratives: A Place to Start

This chapter aims to highlight important formative experiences of the authors, Brian and Mike, which have raised professional questions about the purposes and practices of outdoor education. It strives to give the reader enough insight into our backgrounds in outdoor education and about some of our preferences and biases. Place, and our senses of it, is inevitably personal and subjective. As we mentioned in the introduction, place results from interaction between the geophysical reality of a location, cultural values and practices, and individual experience and interpretation of those experiences. So, why start with the personal?

We feel that telling these stories is important. It indicates our intention to take seriously the connection of lived experiences with reflection upon the role of outdoor places in peoples' lives, and with the creation of a written text about those experiences. We do not write as disembodied academics sitting in our offices abstractly disengaged from daily life. We want to demonstrate that our own outdoor education, through work and recreation, has shaped our writing of this book. The following narratives signal that context and personal and professional histories matter. Professional issues, questions and paradoxes arise for all of us. What we are suggesting is the need to reflect critically on these issues to ascertain how they interact with our ideas and beliefs, in this case, about place-responsive outdoor education. This kind of auto-ethnographic work can reveal much about ourselves and our profession. It begins to break down the false dichotomy, which often occurs in western societies, between personal and professional life. We have all, no doubt, heard sayings such as: 'Don't allow the job to impact on your home life,' or, 'Don't bring your personal issues to work'. Yet, place and place education inevitably deeply intertwines the two in a way that, we argue, is much more natural and realistic. So, let us begin. We start with Brian's narrative.

**"Professional issues, questions and paradoxes arise for all of us."**

## Brian's story

The following four short, personal stories – 'The smell of woodsmoke / the sound of the sea', 'Franklin River story', 'The river dreams', and 'Place-responsive pedagogies: Early attempts' – aim to provide enough detail to enable you to judge the intentions and background that I bring to this book. I hope that they will also assist you in reflecting on the significance of your own life history and how the places where you have lived and worked influence your beliefs and practices as an outdoor educator or guide.

### The smell of woodsmoke, the sound of the sea

I was lucky enough to have the kind of free-range childhood that seems unthinkable these days. My father was a teacher and later a principal in the South Australian education department. This meant that I, along with my mother, older brother and sister, would be relocated every three to four years to another school posting. As Dad gained increasingly senior positions we gradually moved from the far west coast of South Australia (where I was born in the south coast fishing town of Port Lincoln), to the Flinders Ranges in the north, and then the mid-north town of Riverton. By the time I was in the final years of primary school we had moved to Blackwood, a suburb of the state capital in the Adelaide hills, where my father had taken up the principal's position at the local secondary school. We lived in a house with large windows that seemed to let a lot of the outside world in. Gum trees, flowering plants and the chattering birds of the hills surrounded the family home throughout my years of schooling and undergraduate studies.

Due to the influence of my mother's parents we were caravaners. Every school holiday would see us packing the van and hitting the road. Most often we would be returning to campgrounds that we knew well, either in the Flinders Ranges in the north, or along the South Australian coast. With grandparents and cousins in their caravans the extended family would set up a base at Port Vincent on the Yorke Peninsula, or at Port Elliot on the south coast. The vans and annexes served two purposes. They were our home away from home, as familiar to us children as the houses we had left behind in suburbia, and they served as a base for many day expeditions spent driving, walking, picnicking and generally exploring the surrounding countryside and coastline.

For much of that time we, the children, were left to amuse ourselves. This meant a lot of time swimming, fishing, reading, writing, drawing and playing improvised games or sport on the beach. If possible, my older brother David and I would cook breakfast over a small campfire – eggs and bacon, toast and sweet billy tea. There is a very particular smell to the woodsmoke given off by those small fires of eucalypt twigs and leaves. It lodges itself in deep memory. Not only does it conjure memories of childhood activities, it is highly evocative of the places themselves.

I feel this phenomenon is also true of the sounds that were ever present on those formative camping experiences. We had a beachfront campsite on Horseshoe Bay for six weeks every summer, in the small south coast township of Port Elliot. The sound of the surf and the squawking sea gulls has called to me ever since, and these annual camping trips are, no doubt, the source of my love for the south coast of Australia. The ozone smell of the ocean, the pungent rotting seaweed, the sound of waves, wind and current, the feel of sand beneath bare feet, or the crystal hardness of the granite boulders along the coast; all of these combined to form a world of sensual saturation. A young child's flesh and mind soaks it up like a sponge.

My father's teaching specialities were in the humanities and my mother was an artist and art teacher. So both our house and the caravan were always full of books, writing pads, pencils, pastels, paints and sheets of white cartridge paper. I never had to look very far to find a book of Australian poetry or a novel by Ivan Southall or Colin Thiele. It was Thiele's many stories about children my own age at the time, and the various adventures they had growing up in regional South Australia, that resonated with me most. It was so easy for me to put myself into the shoes of his characters for

I'd already experienced the same landscapes where many of the stories were set. A feature of much of the fictional literature of Australia is that local landscapes are often presented as characters, equal in status to the human characters, rather than as a mere backdrop against which the human drama unfolds. The land's character may be a malevolent one, such as in Thiele's story of summer bushfire in *February Dragon* (1965), or it may be that the landscape is presented as a friend and provides companionship, as it does to the young lad in Thiele's best known novel, *Storm Boy* (1963): 'When Storm-Boy went walking along the beach, or over the sandhills, or in the sanctuary, the birds were not afraid. They knew he was a friend' (p. 17).

My association with these familiar places remained stable right through my schooling and undergraduate studies. Significant life experience research (Palmer et al. 1999; Tanner 1980) into the formative experiences of environmental educators indicates that many of the elements present in my own childhood (family interest, regular visits to a 'natural' place, access to 'environmental' literature) are all key indicators in the development of an interest in environmental education and activism.

My interest in sports saw me complete a teaching degree in physical education at the South Australian College of Advanced Education. It was while studying this degree program that I had my first encounter with more formalised outdoor education. Lynton 'Daisy' Day ran a two-year sequence of electives in outdoor pursuits. Bushwalking, sailing, sea kayaking, canoeing, rock-climbing and skiing were all taught with a strong skill-base and leadership orientation. There were also units of study in conservation and national parks. As a part of one of these units I distinctly recall Daisy giving a lecture-slide show about the Franklin River, an expedition he had completed the previous summer. The Franklin is a remote, wilderness river in south-west Tasmania that, at the time, was under threat of being dammed by the state's Hydro Electric Commission. I was captivated by both the river and the possibility that it may be lost in the rush towards economic development.

## Franklin River story

After graduation in the early 1980s I moved interstate, far away from the familiarity of home, to take up a teaching position in the Gippsland region of Victoria. I ran many outdoor programs in the mountains and countryside surrounding the schools where I worked. These included bushwalking and cross-country skiing trips, geography camps and other outdoor field trips. Through these years I was climbing, walking, skiing and paddling a lot, not just for work, but in almost every spare moment I could find. But I will focus here on one particular experience. The following story highlights my earliest recollection of an inner conflict and confusion about my experience of outdoor places. This experience had a compelling mixture of danger, fear, politics and the way that wilderness images may be presented and manipulated.

I had only been kayaking for a few years when I first paddled the Franklin River with my brother and a small group of friends, at the end of my first full year working as a teacher. The Franklin River trip varies between eight and 16 days depending on how long you have to wait for floodwaters to recede if there is heavy rain. The river is steep-sided, remote, and has many difficult rapids. The Franklin had been saved from being dammed under the voracious development imperatives of Tasmania's Hydro Electric Commission only months earlier on July 1, 1983, as a result of a decision in the High Court of Australia. The High Court ruled that Bob Hawke's Federal Labor government's legislation to protect the region on the basis that it had been listed as 'world heritage' overrode state legislation to build the dam. Many argued that Hawke's Labor government had won office on the back of the 'green vote' at the 1982 federal election, and that this victory for the environment was attributable to the Tasmanian Wilderness Society who ran a well-orchestrated anti-dam campaign and the thousands of 'blockaders' who impeded construction of the dam through non-violent protest. The Franklin River campaign marked a profound shift in public opinion in relation to preservation of wilderness in Australia (R. Brown 2004).

Most of our expedition party had prepared themselves for this remote, wild river trip by training in their one-person rubber rafts in the surf at the local beach! There is a sense on a long wilderness journey that every traveller is exploring a wild place for the first time. We had a rudimentary set of river-notes produced by the Tasmanian Wilderness Society. The notes, compiled by wilderness campaigners Bob Brown and Fred Duncan (1980), provided little knowledge of the river's history. We gleaned no insights into the indigenous inhabitants, or what the lives of the early timber-cutting 'piners' who worked the lower reaches of the river might have been like. We did not even know who had made the first descent of the river. Perhaps this absence, or erasure, of historical knowledge was an important ingredient in the quality of our wilderness adventure at that particular time. We had been lured by the river's endangered status and the prospect of adventure.

> Rafting on the Franklin is one of the world's great outdoor adventures. It requires you to be fit, adventurous and self-reliant in the bush … Rafters should be aware that the remoteness of the area – so much a part of its attraction – means help in the event of an emergency can be several days distant. If an accident occurs in the Middle Franklin gorges, or if floodwaters force a retreat from this area, considerable bushwalking skill and endurance would be required before civilisation is reached. (Brown and Duncan 1980, 3–4)

The sun shone and the river levels stayed low on that first 11-day trip and we completed the expedition without significant incident. The closest we came to harm was in the streets of Strahan, the small west coast town where paddlers finished their journey. We were easily spotted as a group of 'greenies' from the river, and copped some abuse from pro-dam locals. The community of Strahan had split along pro-development or pro-preservation lines, with the latter still in the minority.

Two years later I returned to run a commercial rafting expedition and experienced a very different river. On this 16-day expedition it rained for 15 days. On the other day, it snowed! We encountered high floods and were trapped in campsites for several days. We lost and later recovered one of the rafts. In the Great Ravine section of the river, we completed high and risky portages around long sections of boulder-choked rapids that were too dangerous to paddle. The trip involved exposure to many risks and there was an element of good fortune in our survival. It is one of the few experiences of working with people in my care in the outdoors that left me with bad dreams for some years to follow. Here, perhaps, beneath the wilderness ideals that were broadcast as a political slogan 'to save the river' – the quiet solitude, the pristine remoteness, the evocative renaming of river features, and the stories of reconnection to the natural world – was a more visceral or embodied wild experience. Here was intuition and fear, movement as habituated reaction, and I found hauntingly dark and swirling water sliding beneath the popular images of Australia's most celebrated wilderness river. It was a stark lesson about the 'nature' and 'place' of river experiences and added a layer of complexity and ambiguity to the sunny adventure of my first encounter.

My combined Franklin River experiences left me with an inner tension, a conflict between the romantic images of a pristine river and the harsh realities of losing control to a wild river in flood. Coming home from the river the second time, I would carry an image of the magnificent wild river, like a wilderness template, with me to other places and into my teaching. Yet in my body, my flesh, I also sensed that I carried something else: an embodied feeling of a wild force I struggled to articulate. It was knowledge of something deeper, something darker.

## The river dreams

Not long after the second Franklin River expedition Katrina, my wife, and I left Australia so that I could study for a Master of Education degree at the University of Calgary in Canada. I majored in experiential education and outdoor pursuits and was introduced to new and very different ideas and outdoor places. I studied under the mentorship of Bill March, a renowned mountaineer, writer and deep thinker about the need for adventure in modern life. I became familiar with the emerging professional discourses of experiential education and adventure education, and with the history of the North American preservation movement. I read John Muir's *My First Summer in the Sierra* (1911) while backpacking in the Rockies, Henry David Thoreau's classic *Walden* (1854) while watching the Canada geese foraging along the banks of the Bow River, and Aldo Leopold's (1987) *A Sand County Almanac* as the winter snows built their layers, like sedimentary stone, on the window sill of our university apartment. This introduction to the genre of North American nature writing provided inspirational although, romantic, transcendental and ecological interpretations of the outdoor experience.

When we returned to Australia in 1990 I took up a position with the Department of Outdoor Education lecturing in environmental studies and outdoor education at La Trobe University's Bendigo campus in central Victoria. During my time in Bendigo the department offered two degree programs, a three-year Bachelor of Arts (Outdoor Education) and a one-year Graduate Diploma of Outdoor Education, and had developed a distinctive approach that might best be described as critical outdoor environmental education. Many members of the department are well published and we have drawn upon some of their work in this book. As a new staff member I had several academic units to teach and a heavy fieldwork load and considered myself to be an all-rounder in outdoors. The gaps in staffing saw me become the coordinator of paddling programs and I spent most of my time in the field, on and around many of the rivers of south-eastern Australia. All students in both programs completed flat-water canoeing instruction and a journey on a section of the River Murray. Groups of students from the Bachelor of Arts degree could also take a paddling elective sequence, which mainly involved white-water kayaking, in the last two years of their degree.

When I started at La Trobe University, Bendigo, I inherited a fleet of plastic kayaks and a much worn set of poorly designed, semi-enclosed plastic canoes. Among the canoes, however, were two even older and much repaired, traditional-style fibreglass open canoes (often called Canadian canoes). I began experimenting with paddling techniques in these craft. In Australia the open canoe was considered an anachronism, and a dangerous one at that, as there had been several notable fatalities in school groups attempting open-water crossings using these type of craft. The practical push for adventure with controllable risk seemed to include a desire for the newer, 'unbreakable' plastic kayaks. Canoes tended to be either fully decked competition-style craft for the elite paddler, or cheaply built and poorly designed craft for the average member of the public or school groups. These canoes were considered only suitable for flat-water instruction or perhaps a modest journey on a sheltered inland waterway.

The degree courses espoused philosophical values and ideals not dis-similar to those I had been reading in Thoreau, Muir and Leopold's writings. Yet some of these concepts did not seem to be well matched to an outdoor practice of encountering the slow-moving inland waters in the fleet of cumbersome and uncomfortable canoes, nor the faster and more violent rivers of the mountains in the plastic kayaks. I began to recognise significant gaps between outdoor education theory, or at least the literature that it frequently drew upon, particularly in relation to the presentation of environmental values, and the way that I was practicing outdoor education in the field.

I continued to develop my self-taught solo canoeing skills, based largely on the series of photographs in Bill Mason's book *The Path of the Paddle* (1984) and was delighted to discover a well-articulated philosophy of canoe travel in Mason's sequel, *Song of the Paddle* (1988). I also began a search for a fibreglass canoe mould with more aesthetic lines than the fleet of craft I had access to in the equipment shed. It took nearly two years to find what I was after, a canoe mould with lines similar to that of a Chestnut Prospector. I wanted a boat that could be paddled solo and double and was large enough to carry a decent load, but still small enough to be agile and a joy to paddle. The fibreglass hulls that I built using the mould were finished with gunwales, seats, thwarts and decks made from timbers and fittings bought from the local hardware store. I used the tools my grandfather had left me and the rudimentary skills I found I somehow remembered from the many informal woodworking lessons he gave me in his backyard shed. After a summer of canoe building we had a sleek new fleet of canoes for the program. They opened up many new possibilities. All students were then taught to paddle solo, with a range of traditional (Canadian) techniques. Fifteen years later I am still trying to perfect the single-handed cross-bow draw and the silent Indian hunting strokes.

I developed a five-day canoe journey for students along a stretch of the River Murray, which was about an hour's drive north of Bendigo. The Murray and Darling Rivers combine to form one of the most important river catchments in Australia. The Murray-Darling Basin covers more than a million square kilometres, one-seventh the surface area of the Australian continent, and is the country's most significant source of agricultural production. There is almost no section of these waterways that could be called a wilderness. Instead there is a complex and rich history of Aboriginal occupation, European exploration, colonisation and environmental modification. The Murray is known simply as 'the River' by those who live within its catchment and the section we paddled most often followed the meandering path it took through the Barmah State Forest. I was aware that ancestors on my father's side of the family had pioneered a family farm on the banks of the River Murray far downstream, and that my father had lived on the farm as a boy. We'd even had a couple of caravanning holidays to the River during my childhood. But my sense of connection to the river landscape at that stage was more immediate and to do with the programs I was running at Latrobe rather than intergenerational and historical. Even so, I felt an almost immediate affinity with the River. I developed a strong sense of attachment to the Barmah during my time at Latrobe. This was to be heightened even further years later when I completed a descent of the River from headwaters to the sea and told that story through a book of poems, drafted along the way, titled *The Song of the Wounded River* (2010).

During my years at Latrobe I completed about twenty-five journeys with students along the Barmah section of the river (roughly between the townships of Tocumwal to Echuca) and developed an affinity for the river and red gum forest which extends across almost 30,000 hectares of natural floodplain, the result of a geological uplift known as the Cadell Tilt Block. An extensive network of anabranches leave and return to the river and in times of high water they flood the forest completely, triggering its regeneration. The canoe journeys began by driving to the old timber-milling site of Morgan's Mill. We would arrive at night so that students would first get to know the River through the slivers of moonlight reflecting from its surface and its gentle sounds in the darkness. As students awoke on the first morning the River would slowly materialise in the dawn light – first a silvery thread, then an emerging scene in the heavy, fragrant eucalyptus air.

These canoe trips attempted to shake off some of the conventions of the normal outdoor education experience. No tents were taken and students shared their shelter under a large tarpaulin or slept around the campfire embers if the weather was fine, or made a simple shelter for themselves out of a groundsheet and a canoe. Camp stoves were left behind and cooking was done on red gum campfires using the plentiful fallen timber. Students were also required to purchase food locally and prepare it communally. Food purchased had to have minimal processing and no individual food was brought along. If students wanted bread it would have to be baked in camp ovens on the fire (three to four loaves would be needed for the group each day, requiring two to three hours of preparation). Perhaps, like David Orr (1992), we were trying to rediscover the 'art of living well in place' (p. 126).

Part of the experience included drifting slowly along sections of the river either solo or with a partner in a canoe. At other times multiple canoes would be tied together to form a raft and I would introduce stories of how, despite appearances, the Barmah was heavily modified landscape and a fiercely contested place. The indigenous Yorta Yorta peoples of the area had entered a native title claim for the region at the time and the media was being used by timber cutters, cattle graziers, bee keepers, horseback tour operators and to a lesser extent by recreators, to voice their own allegiances and perceived rights of access to the forest and the River.

I will admit that I was experimenting with these programs somewhat, in the best sense I hope, striving to find a balance between crafting an outdoor experience that elicited an emotional response from participants and one that also encouraged them to learn something about the River's history, its current environmental challenges and its possible future. The ecological and economic future of Australia is very much reliant on a healthy Murray-Darling basin, which in current times of sustained low inflows and the over-allocation of water for irrigation is far from the case. While the Barmah trips continued, I also coordinated and taught many other aspects of the paddling program in a more conventional skill and leadership training style. Many other faster-flowing rivers were utilised and an emphasis on skill development and safety was often paramount.

Re-reading my old journals and writings I wonder about aspects of the student experiences of river places that I was inattentive to at the time. Did they experience the Murray as simultaneously beautiful and ecologically damaged? Did students take on board the culturally contested nature of the places that they were experiencing – their history, politics and economics? How much was the romanticism, transcendentalism and wilderness ideology of the nature writing I had begun to read while studying in Canada and was still using in my teaching shaping my interpretations, and those of my students, of the river places we encountered? How much did the ideas that we carted to the rivers that we paddled influence our experiences?

At this time I was beginning to reflect more seriously and critically on the connections that existed between people, place and pedagogy. Using Aldo Leopold's *Sand County Almanac: And Sketches Here and There* (1987 edition) as a guide and a teaching text, I sensed the importance of combining both a rational story of the experience (as often found in historical, geographical and ecological accounts of places, as well as in students' own retelling of events in essays and field trip logs) with a more poetic sensibility. Leopold's seminal contribution to the development of environmental ethics, his eloquent modelling of descriptive prose for outdoor encounters, and his analysis of much that is taken for granted in the outdoor experience, continues to raise questions for both students and myself about the ecological integrity of human values and actions.

Leopold's book, first published posthumously in 1949, is presented in three distinct sections. In the first part of the book Leopold describes in intricate and intimate detail his observations of nature made on weekend visits to on his farm property in the derelict sand counties of Wisconsin. In the second section, he recounts a number of stories and insights about nature experiences gathered through a range of outdoor journeys. In the final section, Leopold draws his professional conclusions on topics such as ecological consciousness, land as community, the role and value of perception, wilderness and recreation and, famously, the land ethic. Leopold's poetic and allegorical style makes his writing both readable and searchingly provocative. Daniel Berthold-Bond (2000), reflecting on the lasting legacy of Leopold's writing as a bioregional poetics, suggests that his 'essays attempt to "rebuild … what we are losing elsewhere," which is precisely a love and respect for place' (p. 20).

Subsequently both students and I often wrote and shared poetic and reflective responses to those experiences. I had begun to develop an interest in the different possibilities for students (and myself) in representing the character and nature of their outdoor experiences. During these years at Bendigo I employed one of the pedagogic practices I had experienced as a postgraduate student at the University of Calgary in a subject taught by Dr Jean Clandinin. At the end of the sequence of paddling experiences, I asked each student to write me a letter that reflected on some personally significant learning discoveries or issues that arose as a result of their paddling and river experiences. The letters were not an assessment task and I wrote back to each student. They provided highly useful insights into the complexity of student experiences. Reading them and responding to them at the time provided important feedback about student experiences and responses to the various paddling programs.

But the greatest value of the letters for me as a young academic was the questions they posed about the 'match' or 'mismatch' of outdoor education theory and practice and, of course, about the strengths and failings of my own teaching. Students from the same trip would tell dramatically different stories of their river experiences. These ranged from fear to exaltation, accelerated or stalled learning, and they presented anecdotes that seemed to portray either a connection or ambivalence to the river. Similarly, it was possible to interpret from the letters how individual students would respond very differently from one paddling or river experience to another. In 1997 one student proffered:

> The best trips I've been on during the duration of the course have been canoeing up and down rivers where there's no pressure to perform. Perhaps kayaking allows one to become intimate with a river in a different way than canoeing does, but I find that I don't have much of a chance to take in my surroundings like I do when I'm in a canoe.

Sometimes successes on the river were retold in such detail that it was possible to interpret many aspects of the experience: risk taking, skill development, peer pressure and, perhaps, the thrill of success.

> There we were at the top of the Amphitheatre [a long and difficult rapid] on the Mitchell [River], stories of carnage from the other group still fresh in our minds. But we weren't going to become better paddlers by portaging around: in fact you were going to gain nothing more than a lot of 'shit hang' from the rest of the group. So we checked our lines, we prepared for carnage, we were quite prepared to swim most of this one … and we had a deadest crack! … And we there we were coming backwards through a monster hole, water up to our waists, but we kept upright and worked our way into the top eddy … Then came the last section, a small drop and sweeping bend. It doesn't look as hard as the

rest, but many a great paddler has come unstuck here ... We watched a couple of boats go down, pounding into the rock on the far bank, a couple of swims. Then we went, adrenaline flowing, we could do this ... and we did ... We were the best paddlers in the world!

Another student recalled the vivid memory of a cold dawn paddle on the Murray River. Leaving camp in the dark before the other students, he experienced the gradual awakening of the river, yet wondered what the experience might mean if he could not capture it in words.

The problem that I've been contemplating revolves around the fact that because I can't define the good in what I feel, I find I can't therefore trust in it. I've stumbled across a range of experiences that have felt intrinsically special. In reflection though, doubt creeps in, undermining their importance, leaving me hollow inside.

Another student wrote eloquently about her emotional response to the experience, yet also worried about what would happen if it became necessary to neatly articulate her encounter with the river.

It can be like being with somebody you love – overwhelming, intense and moving. The sun and wind on my skin, my senses alive and alert and aware, when my mind is at peace or racing, my breath catching in my throat with fear or exultation, or flowing easily, when my heart beats steadily or pounds furiously, when my chest tightens with emotion I cannot express and I feel I might explode with the enormity of my feelings, when I am brought to tears by the ecstasy and beauty of a place, of just being there, of experiencing it, of sharing it or keeping to myself. I don't know what these feelings symbolise or mean. In many ways I am afraid I might destroy them by analysing them and reducing them to words.

Even this small sample of examples from the letters begins to indicate the array of responses that students were expressing in relation to these paddling programs on Victorian rivers. Different river places and different styles of paddling seemed to result in dramatically different student responses. The thrill and fear of the whitewater rapid seemed so utterly different to the calm reflections evoked on the Murray River journeys. Yet my own experience at that time was of a continuity of experience from the river in its headwaters to the river meandering across its floodplain. What could explain such clear differences between one student and another, one place and another, and between my experience and interpretation of rivers and that of many of the students? Was it even possible to plan for some of these highly subjective and emotive encounters between participants and the outdoor places I was working, and how should they be considered educative?

While I was still wrestling with pedagogic approaches to teaching paddling that might better accommodate the range of responses I was reading in the letters, I took up a position at Monash University, in Victoria's Gippsland region, late in 1998. I had previously lived in Gippsland early in my secondary school teaching career and was happy to return to its greener, moister hills on the southern flanks of the Great Dividing Range. The Bachelor of Sport and Outdoor Recreation / Bachelor of Education (BSOR/BEd) double-degree program I and colleagues developed at Monash University provided opportunities to contribute to the establishment of a tertiary program for physical and outdoor education teachers, and to teach in a more diverse range of subjects, activities and environments.

## Place-responsive pedagogies: Early attempts

The Monash program soon expanded to include a suite of undergraduate degrees, postgraduate supervision opportunities, and a stronger emphasis on research. I commenced my doctoral candidature early in 2000 while continuing to write new study units for the program as the first group of students progressed through the degree. My reading and research focus had progressively highlighted 'sense of place' and 'place experiences' as a potential alternative experiential and theoretical foundation for outdoor education. Like the Canadian, James Raffan (1992), I was beginning to accept that 'land' (or 'river' or 'coast') could be a teacher in its own right, and that there seemed a good fit, potentially at least, between 'place' and the experiential pedagogies of outdoor education. This research led me into the multi-disciplinary scholarship that has developed around the theme of place – from phenomenological philosophy to human geography and to cultural studies of identity and land in Australia. It also led me back to fiction and poetry, literature that seemed capable of capturing a sense of the highly subjective quality of encounters between people and Australian places. It has made me reconsider the educative power of interactions between place, experience and reflection in outdoor education practice. Some of this research is presented as one of the case studies later in the book.

My teaching focus was wider at Monash, encompassing both sport and outdoor recreation subject offerings, and also teaching methods subjects in outdoor education. We had a strong sequence of undergraduate units in outdoor education and utilised outdoor places in the Gippsland region to program camps and journeys. Mike Brown joined the academic team for some years during this crucial establishment phase of the program. There has been an emphasis among colleagues at Monash to develop a local pedagogy for the outdoor places we were working with students – a process that remains ongoing. At the same time we remained committed to students experiencing what we have called Expeditionary Learning (a term I have seen used elsewhere), where they travel to locations that appear remote from the campus. On almost all of these outdoor education program experiences I have encouraged, and usually required, students to learn not only the outdoor travel skills required for safe participation, and knowledge about outdoor leadership, programming and risk management, but about the place we would be experiencing. Each place we go to is presented to students as a place rich in natural and cultural meanings. Assessment work requires students to research, interpret and present an understanding of the place through their own encounters.

Sometimes this can still feel like a bit of a struggle, even a disheartening one. A number of our undergraduate students anticipate novelty and excitement on field trips, and are attracted to programs like the Monash course, at least in part I'm sure, by the cultural images of sport and outdoor activity that they are exposed to on a daily basis in the media. It is hard sometimes to motivate these students to be interested in subtle things going on in the landscape, like shifting tides, the first arrivals of birds from the annual northern or southern migrations, a historical narrative from the area, or the fading marks of aboriginal occupation or early European settlement. But I feel it is a struggle worth continuing. I keep searching for pedagogical strategies that provide students with the opportunity to get past the popular image of outdoor activities and a romantic view of nature, so that they can gain a deeper understanding of, and feeling for, the place.

On both a personal and professional level the move to Monash has given me the opportunity to reconnect with the southern Australian coastline in a deeply meaningful way. I have now done more than twenty, week-long programs in the Nooramunga Marine Reserve region and feel the beginnings of a strong affinity with this area. I miss its tides, wind and shifting sands when I'm away from it. As I begin to learn more of its history and ecology I feel as though it is slowly revealing itself to me. I feel this at both the embodied and intellectual levels, a mix that it I do not feel it possible or even necessary to disentangle.

## Mike's story

Note: The first draft of this chapter was written while sitting at the desk of the late Michael King[1] at his former home overlooking the Wharekawa Inlet at Opoutere on the Coromandel Peninsula. The property now belongs to The University of Waikato and is available as a retreat for staff to write and complete research projects.

On the bookshelf in the room is a collection of works authored by Michael. One, *Being Pakeha Now*, features a photo of Michael superimposed over the view that I can see from the house. Glancing up from my computer I can take in the vista that includes the inlet, sandspit and the ocean beyond. Being able to use this property to write arouses mixed feelings. On one hand it is a privilege, on the other it is tinged with a sense of sadness that the original owners are no longer here. In 1990 I purchased an earlier version of Michael's book *Being Pakeha* which proved to be influential in how I thought about my place, as a descendent of European immigrants, in Aotearoa/New Zealand. Themes of belonging and identity, which were discussed at length in the book, have developed greater resonance for me in recent years. It is through my current teaching and researching position at The University of Waikato that I am able to utilise the King House. Prior to my appointment at Waikato I had spent several years as an instructor at Outward Bound in the Marlborough Sounds. There were a number of reasons why I found myself at Outward Bound, but not least amongst them was a desire to return home.

'Return home'. In 1998 I left New Zealand on a yacht for a six-month cruise in the Pacific. In late 2004 I returned. Somehow six months had become six years. On the return leg of the original voyage I had stopped over in Brisbane to avoid the cyclone season and turned a six-month brief stop-over into what appeared to be permanent move. Three-and-a-half years were spent at The University of Queensland completing postgraduate studies and two-and-a-half years researching and lecturing at Monash University in Victoria. I was employed and had established a home but something did not quite feel right. It was difficult to define this sense of unease as I had lived overseas before for extended periods. In a somewhat serendipitous conversation with a colleague I was asked if I had read a book by the New Zealand author Geoff Park, *Ngā Uruora: The Groves of Life* (1995). Park's book examines the intersection between history and ecology, with a particular focus on the effects of colonisation and the ensuing ecological devastation wrought on New Zealand's lowland areas. I vividly remember the following phrase, 'a sense of place is a fundamental human need' (p. 320). Those words resonated deeply. Obviously during my time in Australia I knew where I was geographically. Having made the voyage to Australia I knew I could navigate, so the question was not one of spatial location but of belonging – Australia (for all its good qualities) was not my place.

I am a Pākehā[2] New Zealander, this is my home, my place in the world. My understanding of being Pākehā has evolved over time and through my involvement with, and engagement in, New Zealand's peoples, culture(s), history, landscape, and briefly glimpsing my family's roots in Scotland. This brings me back to King's *Being Pakeha* which I first purchased when I was teaching at a school in Auckland. This book has had an enduring influence. I remember taking it with me in late 1990 as I headed off on my big OE.[3] I'm not altogether sure why I took this book when all my belongings had to fit in a backpack. Not surprisingly it got lost, or left with someone along the way. I have subsequently replaced it with the newer edition, *Being Pakeha Now*.

So I now find myself sitting in Michael King's former home surrounded by his works writing a book on place and outdoor education theory and practice. Unsurprisingly these topics intersect with King's interest in identity and belonging. In the next room I can hear the rapid tapping of fingers on a keyboard (he obviously uses two fingers rather than my feeble attempts with one). It's that ex-colleague who pointed me in the direction of Geoff Park's book and ultimately home. I'm not sure if Brian has regretted recommending *Ngā Uruora* or was secretly pleased not to have to put up with my hassling every Monday morning when his footy team lost. I suspect he merely advanced the inevitable: it is hard to deny Park's call to locate oneself in a place which meets a 'fundamental human need' – knowing where and who one is.

In academic books and journals we are often required to regulate our writing to conform to various guidelines; be they matters of referencing style, word length, or the need to rigorously substantiate assertions with research findings. As a consequence the motivations and biases of the writer become largely hidden though they can never be completely removed. An underlying theme of this book is the importance of the social, cultural, historical and geographical dimensions of lived experience. We are who we are because of where we are and the experiences we have had. The meaning(s) we give to events, possessions (our cars, homes etc), places and people are bound to situation and context. No matter how strongly we try to present an image of objectivity and rationality we cannot escape the futility of such an endeavour.

As a reader you have every right to wonder why Brian and I may seem to have headed off on a tangent of personal storytelling so early in the book. Why, you may ask, have they chosen to write about place and outdoor education? Surely, you might add, outdoor education is fine as it is, why the need for change? In this chapter we have the opportunity to partially fill in some gaps to explain how we arrived at the decision to detail our case for a renewal of outdoor education. The case we make here should not be interpreted as a final destination nor something that won't be modified in the future. Similarly we would anticipate that readers of the book who feel compelled to make changes to their own outdoor education philosophy and practice, would adapt rather than adopt much of what we have to say. That is a crucial part of our argument. Local conditions, local histories and community values will play a significant role in any place-responsive program. Part of the purpose for this chapter is also to signal to each reader the importance of reflecting upon their own history, or narrative if you like, and how it is influential and formative in the professional decisions that they might make.

## Influence of the sea

My youth was spent in the middle-class, predominantly Pākehā, suburb of Pakuranga, Auckland. From my room I could look out over the Tāmaki River and see boats travelling up and down the waterway out to the Hauraki Gulf. I attended a local boys' school, competed successfully at provincial level in athletics, performed adequately academically and participated in sea scouts and church youth group activities. Nothing special or unusual except for the fact that, for many years of my secondary schooling, instead of a front lawn we had a big grey, partially-completed boat. I'm sure it caused the neighbours no end of concern when it arrived and towered over the house. You could actually step off the deck of the boat onto our roof.

My father had an engineering business and had decided to build a steel launch. The hull and cabins were completed at Dad's factory and we finished it off in the front yard. So my teenage years were spent painting and assisting Dad to finish the boat. It was a fantastic way to share time with my father and learn invaluable skills. My father is a highly skilled tradesman, a fitter and turner who worked with fine tolerances. I, however, would invariably break a saw blade, mount something out of square or lose nuts and bolts into the deepest recesses of the hull. Fortunately for society I didn't become a car mechanic or a surgeon.

My sailing career had actually started a lot earlier. I had my first boat at about the age of five. It was built out of an old machinery packing case Dad brought home from work and was fitted with a broomstick for a mast and a bed sheet for a sail. It was loaded on to a neighbour's trailer and taken to the beach along with the other kids 'boats'. We carried them to the low tide mark and I proudly sat in it until the tide rose and flowed through the boat. It was an inauspicious start to my sailing career.

Several years later Dad and a couple of friends decided to build a number of 12-foot sailing dinghies. One of the family's homes became the boat yard and the three men and various kids would gather on Saturdays to work on the construction of these two-person plywood yachts. I don't remember helping out too much but I do remember playing war games in the backyard. Maybe it was more helpful if four or five hyperactive boys kept out of the way. Hulls completed it was time to finish each boat off individually at the respective owners' homes. I learnt to sail, soon became sick of being the crew, and persuaded Mum and Dad to let me buy my own boat, a small single-handed boat known as a Starling.

Sometime during this period we were invited out onto larger boats of various family friends, a neighbour's launch or another friend's yacht. Dad seemed keen to jump at any opportunity to get out on the harbour. He had grown up in Dunedin and his first experience of Auckland had been in the navy as part of compulsory military training. Those experiences in the Hauraki Gulf were sufficiently powerful and positive for him to transfer north with his company some years later. After a few years of caravanning and sailing dinghies Dad had a motor boat designed which he built slowly over a number of years. Eventually the 'ark' moved off the front lawn and into the water. Throughout this period I can remember visiting people with boats in various stages of construction. There must have been some sort of informal network into which you were invited to visit other people's projects or follies. Some, I'm sure, never made it to the water, the fun was in the dreaming and the building. There would be long discussions about the intricacies of CQR anchors compared to Danforths, or some other obscure marine topic.

I remember quite clearly visiting a couple, who had become friends with one of Dad's work colleagues, on their yacht at Half Moon Bay Marina. He was Hungarian and she was French. They were based in Canada and sailed the world on their yacht. Their poodle would respond to instructions in both French and English. If you asked it if it would rather be dead or married it would roll over on its back and lie very still resulting in much laughter. I remember sitting in the cabin listening wide-eyed to stories of how one of the boats' owners had fled Hungary during the 1956 revolution and the freedom of the cruising life. I looked at their charts of far-flung islands and imagined what an adventurous life they led. I wanted this adventure for myself. For the next few years books by the Hiscocks (a famous cruising couple) were high on my Christmas and birthday wish list.

In retrospect these early experiences were laying down a foundation of possibilities, dreams and practical skills that, though I didn't know it at the time, were to prove important in later years. I'm not sure that I have an innate love of the sea but I was immersed in stories and the culture and history surrounding seafaring. Every morning when I opened my curtains I looked at the sea and I would walk to school along the edge of the estuary. If I was in the right classroom I could look out over the boats swinging on their moorings.

My university years were spent at Otago University in the southern city of Dunedin. Boating was restricted to holiday breaks back in Auckland or whitewater paddling with friends during term time. This was a time of youthful bravado and endless enthusiasm for the next adventure. I hung out with a group of paddlers who were always working out how to buy the latest kayak or planning the next trip away. It was a period of pushing boundaries and living in the moment, we were young and bullet-proof, or so we thought.

In late 1990 I set off on my OE. During this time I worked for Outward Bound Scotland (OBS) at Loch Eil and the Ocean Youth Club (OYC), a sail-training charity whose head office was in Gosport in Hampshire. In Scotland I had the opportunity to kayak and sail with groups of students on Loch Eil and Loch Linnie. Camping with students near the ruins of castles was very different to cruising the Hauraki Gulf in New Zealand. From OBS I took a position with OYC and progressed from mate to skipper. The club was established to provide opportunities for young people from all sections of society to be integrated in a small community aboard a purpose-built vessel.

The club operated ten 70 foot yachts around the British Isles and provided me with a unique opportunity to master the intricacies of seamanship. The skippers were a bunch of unique characters from a variety of backgrounds, but one thing linked them, their high standard of seamanship. Imagine turning a 72-foot yacht in an estuary only 90-feet wide; drop the anchor just enough to drag on the muddy sea bed and then hoist the mizzen (small sail on a second mast near the back of the boat) to 'weather cock' the boat and turn it on a dime. All this was done without fuss and bother and usually performed by a group of teenagers from somewhere like Newcastle. It was an incredibly steep learning curve from the relatively benign, deep, traffic-free waters of home.

Learning to navigate the shifting sands and strong tidal streams of the Thames estuary, locking in and out of marinas in the Netherlands, drying out against a pier in places with large tidal ranges, sailing across the Bay of Biscay, crossing the English Channel, operating in heavy fog within submarine exercise areas, dealing with armed Royal Marines boarding the vessel, were all part of a rapid and thorough apprenticeship in the art and craft of handling a large vessel with a novice crew (14–18 year olds). It was torrid and exhausting work albeit with plenty of laughter and some very satisfying moments. A strong northerly bringing snow and steep waves in the Irish sea isn't most people's idea of fun … and it wasn't mine after a couple of years either. Long hours, a constant stream of novice crews each week and missing my new wife eventually took the gloss off being at sea.

We spent the first year of our married life in Suffolk, on the east coast of England. Grey skies, changeable weather and less than rewarding jobs meant a decision to set up home in New Zealand wasn't difficult. Samantha had visited New Zealand on travels several years earlier and, apart from leaving behind family, wasn't at all fazed by travelling half way across the world to begin a new life. I don't recall any great sense of a 'pull home' at this time – it was mostly a desire to leave another grey United Kingdom winter behind. We arrived back in New Zealand in 1994 and began the 'yuppie' phase: two incomes, no kids, and professional jobs. In the following three years we sailed extensively around the Hauraki Gulf and ended up with a 38-foot steel cruising yacht of our own. We spent about a year getting the boat ready with 101 jobs to do (some of which were still not done after the voyage) and left New Zealand in 1998 for Tonga, Fiji, Vanuatu and Australia. The idea was to summer over in Australia and return via New Caledonia during the next cruising season. The space and time provided while cruising gave us an opportunity to think about future work options. I didn't fancy going back to sports administration so took the opportunity to begin postgraduate study. So began six years in Australia, a marriage break-up and the sale of the boat.

Apart from sailing with students at Outward Bound New Zealand my sea-based activities have recently been restricted to sea kayaking. Yet the pull of the sea is still strong. Recently boating magazines have been falling off the shelf into my supermarket trolley and I find myself looking in the classified section at the boats for sale. I suspect another yacht isn't far away. The images and memories that are alluring include being tucked up in the corner of a bay at anchor, swimming off the back of the boat, or the smell of bacon and eggs wafting across the water at breakfast time. The desire for a long ocean passage is no longer there. Rather it's the sense of being 'placed' in the familiar, in the bays and islands of the Hauraki Gulf – places that reverberate with meaning and significance.

## Mature appreciation or am I just getting old?

I now live in the small landlocked town of Cambridge, a twenty minute drive from the university. The closest ocean is just over an hour's drive east or west but I have the Waikato River running through town whenever I need a dose of water. I am enjoying discovering the river and sharing time on it with my students as part of their fieldwork.

I no longer have a great desire to sail offshore. Thoughts of cruising closer to home, revisiting the places that are etched in my memory, and sharing the delights of boating with my partner and her children are far more appealing. The lure of the sea and the desire to participate in other outdoor activities is still there. However, how I engage in them has changed over time and in some ways reflects my changing perspectives of outdoor education. Gone are the days of trying to prove myself in the outdoors by kayaking over a technical drop, scaring myself witless on a poorly protected rock climb, or crossing oceans. Perhaps I am getting old (well I know I'm getting older) or maybe it is a realisation that the thrill of personal risk-taking is inconsequential compared to larger issues facing society. Issues such as ecological degradation, educating in a manner which promotes pride in mastery, authentic choices and decision-making, connecting learners with their community and understanding who they are is more challenging, and possibly more beneficial in the long term, than providing quick fix fun activities in the outdoors.

The things that used to drive me and provide a buzz have changed. Taking my time, understanding my companions, and thinking about the educational significance of what it is I'm trying to achieve are the new challenges. How do I introduce new students, or for that matter friends and their children, to the outdoors? Do I push them outside their comfort zone so that they will learn? Do I make sure they are completely worn out at the end of the day so that they realise that they are capable of more than they imagine? How do you engender a love for the outdoors in the young? I'm sure there are many parents and grandparents who instinctively know the answer (just go to any wharf and watch the intergenerational transmission of knowledge through fishing). I am particularly interested in the *education* in outdoor education, for I fear it is overlooked in many courses that have a heavy focus on skill acquisition and adventure. There are many good providers of skill training and the acquisition of skills and the pleasure in competent performance is to be celebrated. But what is that skill and competence for? Is it merely to develop a sense of individual achievement or give a person the skills to lead an active, outdoor life (important as these things may be)? Can, or should, outdoor education experiences be about more than this?

As a young practitioner I would have claimed that outdoor education consisted of a series of activities or perhaps, in more contemplative mood, I might have suggested it was a teaching methodology involving reflection on experience. Yet I now find that simple descriptions and formulaic approaches fail to do justice to the complexity of life, nor do they help in answering the question about what constitutes a meaningful life.

I frequently think back on working with students at Monash University (on the ropes course, for example). I sometimes felt like I was looking through a window at an image of myself at their age – gung-ho and keen to be seen as the outdoor guru. What always amused me was the manner in which many of the students would, after the first session, purchase their own equipment. They did this in spite of the university having its own store of near-new equipment that they could freely access. On the second or third session the 'arms race' was in full swing: who had the latest helmet, most colourful harness, most gear clanging on their gear loops (much of it irrelevant), and who had the biggest rescue knife? They, like many of us, had contracted the virus of outdoor consumerism, a bug that led invariably to the incurable condition of 'gear freak-itis'. Technology and the look of being a real outdoor instructor had subsumed the role of the educator. I sometimes ponder what image outdoor educators convey to their students, with their rescue kit, technical jargon and well-practiced banter? Sometimes this image seems to be saying: 'This is risky business – but look at me I'm kitted out for scaling cliffs and rescuing you from certain calamity!'

Where once I would have uncritically bought into this discourse, I am now a little more circumspect. What message does this send about power and knowledge? About who knows best? How egalitarian is our profession? The focus on technical competence is based on certain notions of how people learn, the necessity for risk, and creating an image of otherness. But is this what outdoor education should be about? These are questions we hope to discuss and stimulate reflection on in this book.

Although neither Michael King nor Geoff Park were necessarily concerned with outdoor education pedagogy their insights into the importance of connections to land and belonging have enriched my understanding at both a personal and a professional level. I'm not entirely sure why I took King's book overseas with me all those years ago, or why Park's simple statement that 'place is a fundamental human need' triggered a series of events that sees me sitting here now. Perhaps part of the answer lies in King's later statement that 'The most profound satisfactions are to be found in living a life in accord with the natural world, exercising the human capacity for friendship and altruism, engaging in creative and purposeful activity, and allegiance to one's origins' (1999, 240). I have been drawn home because of a realisation that who I am is intimately connected to where I am – something which Māori, and other indigenous peoples, have never forgotten. The waters of the Hauraki Gulf, the motion of a boat at anchor, and the contours of the land are not only embedded in my memory, they form part of who I am.

The outdoor environment, the land and seascape of my home provide more than a background to action, be it kayaking, mountain bike or sailing. Viewing the outdoors as merely a site for activity overlooks the historical, cultural, ecological particularities that make a place what it is. It also diminishes opportunities to connect with place(s) and display care and empathy. An adventure ethos, with a focus on activities risks consuming and commodifying places as spaces that are irrelevant except for the resource that they offer (e.g. rapid, climbing crag, peak to bag). In so doing it limits opportunities for people to understand who they are in relation to place and how changes to places impact on individuals and communities. Part of what we are advocating is a localised, modest approach to educating in the outdoors. Understanding what is available locally takes time and effort and requires responsiveness to place and people. In an effort to promote that approach we feel it has been important in this chapter to locate who we are and how we got to be here.

## Conclusion

So now you know a little more about each of us as the authors of this book. You might be thinking that, given our backgrounds, it's a bit ironic or even hypocritical that we are suggesting that outdoor educators should place *less* emphasis on adventure and focus on something else. If so, good. It shows that you are already critiquing the argument we are presenting. But we hope you will bear with us. We are not suggesting that outdoor educators need to abandon all of the ideas, ideals and practices that have brought us to where we are today – a robust, professional and vital part of a young person's overall education. But we are suggesting that it is necessary to adapt to the changing needs of learners and the communities and places where they live and learn. Rather than becoming entrenched within a set of beliefs and practices that have, in many instances, been imported from abroad, we are advocating careful reflection on local conditions and opportunities. We are encouraging a considered pedagogic exploration of both new and renewed versions of practice. This involves a kind of light-footedness – an ability to tread lightly on the local land and in the local community. It involves a willingness to 'sniff the winds of change' in our changing world, and to react. To do this requires educators to have a genuine interest in the places where they live and work. Such an approach might involve giving up on some of the grander visions of outdoor education, and accepting a more humble path ahead. This begins, we feel, in a critical appraisal of some of the philosophical and pedagogic foundations that outdoor educators may hold most dear. For, as we hope to show, much of this bedrock of our profession may well be very shaky ground.

# Chapter 2

# Outdoor Education:
# Myths, Dubious Claims and the Denial of Place

In this chapter we intend to question and discuss some of the underlying beliefs and assumptions about outdoor education that we believe can act as denials of place. As indicated in the introductory chapter this is not an attempt to diminish or undermine the value of quality outdoor education as part of young people's educational experiences. Contemporary practice sees a great number of staff and students getting outside into the environment and, in the main, that is a good thing. Our intent here is to shift the focus towards a more empathetic appreciation of the experience of the learner, the significance of place, and the consequences of certain aspects of outdoor education philosophy and practice.

The emphasis on gaining a greater understanding of oneself and improving interpersonal relationships is frequently deemed to be the primary foci of outdoor adventure education (OAE) programs (Ewert and Garvey 2007; Priest and Gass 1997). A number of Australasian writers (Cosgriff 2008; Payne and Wattchow 2008) have argued that the historical priority given to personal and social outcomes has kept particular outdoor pursuits and adventure activities at the forefront of many programs. This, they suggest, has created a situation where the field has become preoccupied with notions of adventure, risk and challenge, and the personal and social benefits which are believed to accrue from being immersed in outdoor recreation culture. In addition, Mike Brown (2009) has argued that the continuing emphasis on personal development as a key educational objective has led to the use of teaching and learning strategies that are largely based on an understanding that learning occurs via the cognitive processing of experiences. In this view the individual is seen as an autonomous agent who is capable of internalising experiences and applying the new knowledge acquired in an OAE program to other real-life contexts. This set of beliefs about the individual learner's capacity to cognitively evaluate, articulate, transfer and apply learning has, we argue, become entrenched in outdoor education practice. These beliefs now function at the level of taken-for-granted cornerstones of practice and as such are rarely questioned. But there are elements of this approach that are problematic and potentially impoverish opportunities for other types of learning.

While we acknowledge that at both global and local levels outdoor education practices may have evolved differently in response to particular social, historical, geographic, economic and ecological conditions, there are some common characteristics embedded in practice, particularly the repertoire of activities, 'that signal how the identity of outdoor education has been constructed' (Payne and Wattchow 2008, 26). Through our teaching experiences in various settings we have observed that, in some instances at least, there appeared to be vivid examples of 'fabricated' or 'theme-park' elements utilised to facilitate personal or social development. For example, we have seen the use of a number of interconnected shipping containers to simulate a caving experience or, more ironically, the construction of a mock ice-climbing tower (in the tropics) to simulate a mountaineering ascent. These developments illustrate a focus on the novel and the exotic. Such facilities supposedly act as a vehicle for personal and social development, but they can ignore and override local geographies and sensibility to local affordances. The same might be said of the use of climbing gymnasiums, bouldering walls, challenge ropes courses and artificial whitewater rapids in Australia and New Zealand. Each of these constructed environments act as simulations of the outdoors, where nature is supposedly made more accessible, predictable and affordable.

Should similar concerns be raised about outdoor education experiences that are conducted in more 'natural' environs? Take, for example, an overnight bushwalk in a national park. In many instances where one walks is dictated by park management and camping sites are pre-determined. Dangerous sections of tracks have guardrails. Viewing platforms are arranged so that walkers can pause and take in the best views, and facilities such as benches, toilets and so on are often provided. Such are the trade-offs, it is argued, when catering for mass recreation (and education) in an outdoor space whose primary objective is ecological preservation. But how does this managed experience influence the learner and learning outcomes? Once again, our intent is not to suggest that any of these forms of educational practice should be abandoned. Rather they might each require a different pedagogic response and more cautious and humble claims about what can be achieved educationally in particular settings and via certain activities.

The influence of imperial and militaristic traditions on contemporary OAE practice has been well articulated by others (see Beedie 1995/6; Brookes

2002; Cook 1999; Lugg 2004; Lynch 2006; Nicol 2002a, 2002b). The finger prints of these traditions are visible in practises where nature becomes a site for building character or self-development through arduous self-propelled travel, or the development of leadership qualities through the performance of contrived tasks in simulations and role playing. While these influences continue in many programs it has recently been suggested that outdoor education is continuing to undergo fragmentation because of the impacts of increasing middle-class affluence and social hierarchies, technological developments (e.g. in equipment) along with media representations of nature and the cultural images (e.g. extreme sports) associated with recreating in natural environments (Payne and Wattchow 2008). In this chapter we attempt to draw together what we have termed the myths, dubious claims and denials of place evident in contemporary outdoor education.

It is undoubtedly easy to write a provocative critique. Yet what we are striving to do is not to disregard either the socio-historical trajectory of outdoor education or the significant contribution and goodwill of many practitioners and writers that have preceded us. Instead, we want to make a case that outdoor education must adapt and evolve with the social and ecological imperatives of the times. We are suggesting that it has never been more apposite than now for a reconsideration of outdoor education philosophy and practice. We are conscious that there is no universal outdoor education prescription, but we are also aware that the theories and practices that are currently dominant have arisen in particular social, cultural, geographical and historical settings. By exposing what is hidden, or omitted, we hope to open up new ways of thinking about and enacting outdoor education, which is cognisant of the places participants experience via outdoor education, and the places where they live.

The myths, dubious claims and denials that we raise and discuss in this chapter are not based merely on our opinions. Rather they reflect significant changes in thinking about some of the foundational beliefs and practices that underpin our field. We draw extensively on emergent professional discourse about the problems and possibilities of outdoor education philosophies and practices. Perhaps some of the assumptions and claims about outdoor education have 'had good legs' up until now, because as a field our resources are spread thinly. However, as we mentioned in the opening chapter, outdoor education can no longer be considered to be in its infancy. It now requires a sustained and defensible set of values and practices. This process, we suggest, begins by exposing some of our most cherished ideas and ideals to the harsh light of critique.

## Romantic notions of nature

The first denial of place in outdoor education we will consider is encountered through what may be called a Romantic desire to return to wild nature. The Tasmanian geographer and poet Peter Hay (2002, 4) argues that Romanticism was 'a nineteenth century movement of reaction against the values, tastes, ideas of the preceding century'. The Romantic ideal encouraged people to dream of a transformation for all humankind through imagining an alternative to industrial despotism. Hay suggests that Romanticism has been particularly influential in the development of subsequent environmental philosophies and in the greening of an alternative worldview in Western culture. He goes on to say that it was Romanticism that served as the ecological impulse to launch the modern environment movement. It provided the cultural template for a renewed sensibility to nature. No doubt, most of us would see these developments as overwhelmingly positive and it would be frightening to contemplate a world even more dominated by the rise of modern industrialism than the current one.

European Romanticism can be seen as a reaction against Enlightenment empiricism, rationalism, materialism and its offshoots, such as imperial expansion, industrial capitalism, rapid urbanisation and large-scale environmental despoliation. The literary scholar Jonathan Bate (2000) suggests that Romantic writers and artists proposed a number of pathways along which society might travel in a return to nature. One vision was for the formation of small-scale republics of 'free men living amidst the untamed forms of nature' (p. 40). This, it was believed, would model how society should be configured. It was also proposed that periods of self-imposed exclusion from society might provide the solitude necessary so that the human spirit, crushed by a society which was becoming dispassionate to both nature and the spiritual needs of society, could be fulfilled. Many of these ideas grew out of European primitivism and the ideas of the 18th century French philosopher Jean-Jacques Rousseau.

When the Romantic poets (like William Wordsworth or Samuel Coleridge) or artists (such as J. M. W. Turner or John Constable) walked or stood amidst the elemental forces of sun, wind and rain they experienced the 'clearest medium through which God showed His power and excellency' (Nash 1982, 46). Cronon (1996) suggests that it is from Romanticism that we have inherited the idea that by experiencing the vastness and grandeur of outdoor places we truly gain a sense of our insignificance and are reminded of our mortality. Romanticism was a search for the essential, spiritual quality of humanity in a rapid changing world. For the Romantics, 'God was [encountered] on the mountaintop, in the chasm, in the waterfall, in the thundercloud, in the rainbow, in the sunset' (Cronon 1996, 73). Spiritual fulfilment was no longer to be found in the grit and greed of the industrial city, or even in the cathedral. Instead, it was out there in the wilds. Romantic literature abounds with narratives set in the outdoors where nature was deliberately sought out for its health, educational and spiritual benefits (Macfarlane 2003). The artists and writers of the Romantic period sought the sublime experience, a return to nature to rediscover meaning and a lifestyle apparently denied by modern society. It was, writes Australian scholar Kate Rigby in her book *Topographies of the Sacred* (2004, 18), 'the rebirth of nature'.

It was the view of the majestic waterfall or the exhilaration felt in the storm sweeping across the mountain that provided the celebration of the might and awesomeness of nature necessary for the romantic traveller to reconsider his or her relations with the natural world. Such a response to the outdoors has been evident in antipodean writing and art since European colonisation and continues to profoundly influence our attitudes, visions, and physical explorations (Horne 2005; Park 2006). In our times, the quintessential Romantic landscape, in its New World setting, is no longer the rustic cottage set against the high moor or the bucolic scene of the peasant farmer bringing in the barley. Now, it is wilderness.

"Spiritual fulfilment was no longer to be found in the grit and greed of the industrial city, or even in the cathedral. Instead, it was out there in the wilds."

It is not so much the Romantic's return to nature that troubles American landscape historian William Cronon, as it is the modern corollary of nature as a placeless wilderness. Nature, as wilderness, is now 'harvested for a psychic yield' (Price 1996, 190). In so doing,

> we graft meanings onto nature to make sense out of modern middle-class life, and then define ourselves by what we think nature means. Authenticity, simplicity, reality, uniqueness, purity, health, beauty, the primitive, the autochthonous, adventure, the exotic, innocence, solitude, freedom, leisure, peace. (p. 190)

Let us look at some examples. In Australia the emergence of the wilderness preservation movement as a political force – via campaigns such as those to preserve Lake Pedder and the Franklin River – tells much about how cultural preferences for a particular type of nature aesthetic and experience have changed in recent times. The Australian historian Peter Read (1996, 142) concluded that 'since the 1980s, most special places threatened with destruction must, to be saved, be capable of being universalised'. However there is a cost, for as Read continues, 'the Outsiders – the decision makers no longer understand specific localities in relation to their specific meanings' (p. 143). The annual wilderness calendar has become utter distillation of this New World wilderness ideal. A sweeping vista with huge depth of field reveals a crisply focused, lichen-encrusted boulder in the foreground. Our gaze then traces a line to the perfectly lit hills on the horizon. There is not a building, bench, road, or person in sight. It is a perfect view set before us so that we can project ourselves into the scene.

The Romantic sentiment, both in its original form and its more recent manifestations, is persistent and influential. The Romantics launched the ascendancy of outdoor places as desirable destinations. The experiences they sought in nature combined a heady mix of ideas that embraced temporary solitude from society, a search for self-knowledge and personal improvement, ideals about living in the small-scale communities, and a belief in the wilderness experience as a spiritual quest for personal meaning. This then is the original template for the foundation principles of outdoor education as an education for self, others and nature.

Kurt Hahn, the founder of the Outward Bound movement, was a keen reader of Rousseau, in particular his treatise on child-centred and nature-based education in *Emile* (1762). Rousseau's legacy can be seen in the idealised notion of a small band of adventurers heading out into remote country, and in the desire to return home changed and inspired to fulfil one's civic duty in repairing a broken society. These ideas are codified in Walsh and Golins' (1976) description of the Outward Bound process. Rousseau's influence, through Kurt Hahn, is echoed in Outward Bound New Zealand's vision statement 'Helping to create "better people, better communities, better world."' (http://www.outwardbound.co.nz/7.0.html accessed 15 October 2009). In New Zealand a consortium of schools have formed Outdoor Education New Zealand (ODENZ) to attract overseas students. Learning is 'based on some of the world's most exhilarating outdoor experiences' in 'New Zealand's outdoor adventure-land' (ODENZ 2009). Not surprisingly these programs claim to offer students 'challenging practical programs designed to encourage personal and social development' (ODENZ 2009). The universalised nature of the offering, which fits well with New Zealand's (supposed) clean and green image, is a modern iteration of Romantic philosophy. For, as Lynch and Moore (2004, 5) remind us, '"Adventure-land" is no place, a wilderness, a myth, without social and cultural history or meaning'.

Wilderness, as a placeless and universalised wild nature, has come to stand outside of time and space (Gill 1999). Alternative landscapes and histories are erased, argues Gill, as wilderness becomes hyper-separated, 'founded on a logic of otherness ... "defined" by the absence of humanity' (p. 55). It is Romanticism that provides us with the persistent cultural template of nature as a pristine wild space, an idea we run to in retreat from the dehumanising and unnatural influence of the modern industrial city.

In *Nourishing Terrains: Australian Aboriginal Views of Landscape and Wilderness* (1996), the anthropologist Deborah Bird Rose suggests that

> A definition of wilderness which excludes the active presence of humanity may suit contemporary people's longing for places of peace, natural beauty, and spiritual presence, uncontaminated by their own culture. But definitions which claim that these landscapes are 'natural' miss the whole point of the nourishing Australian terrains. (p. 18)

According to Rose, the traditional peoples of Australia lived in reciprocal union with their 'country', each nourishing the other. The two cultures, settler and Indigenous, therefore, developed very different relationships with these places. We return to this theme in the next chapter. The legacy of European Romanticism, and how it influences and informs the philosophy of outdoor education, is not unproblematic. It is cultural baggage that we cart with us on our various journeys outdoors. It may be said that, without the Romantic poets, thinkers and artists, we may have had no outdoors to retreat into at all.

We have only discussed briefly here the legacy of Romantic ideal and its transportation to New World countries such as Australia and New Zealand. It is only part of the broader complex of Imperialism and colonisation that saw settler cultures from Europe confront indigenous peoples and very different ecological systems on the far sides of the world. The collected essays in William Adams and Martin Mulligan's (2003) book *Decolonizing Nature: Strategies for Conservation in a Post-colonial Era* provide a far more expansive debate of the cultural and ecological consequences that have arisen from European colonisation and what may be required to repair some of the damage already done.

What are the consequences of this legacy for outdoor education and a sense of place in New World countries such as Australia and New Zealand? When we promote nature as a wilderness we risk ignoring or obliterating the local meaning of places, including their ecology, contested cultural histories and ongoing politics. Nature as wilderness is seen as pristine, fixed and simplified. But when nature is seen as a place it is messy, contested and constantly changing. Nature as wilderness is only one of many possible ways to encounter and interpret outdoor places. It relies on a sense of cultural amnesia about the reality of places, both their ecological condition and their often troubling cultural history. To borrow again from Geoff Park (1995, 14), a place-based experience, rather than a wilderness one, may help reveal what Naipaul classed "'the wiped-out, complete past below one's feet"; the truths, often unpleasant, about ourselves and our attitudes and perceptions that the landscape divulges along with its native ecology'.

## Adventure and the pedagogy of risk

The second way that outdoor education potentially denies place concerns the promotion of adventure as a radical alternative to normality. This is coupled with the belief that taking risks is inherently positive. Outdoor education pedagogy, based on variations of Colin Mortlock's (1984) model of adventure or Peter Martin and Simon Priest's (1986) Adventure Experience Paradigm, invariably attempts to balance risk and the learner's level of competence with educational benefits. These benefits are typically articulated as growth in various psychological constructs such as self-esteem, self-efficacy, or self-actualisation. In *The Adventure Alternative* Colin Mortlock (1984) proposed that adventure is

> a state of mind that will initially accept unpleasant feelings of
> fear, uncertainty and discomfort, and the need for luck, because

we instinctively know that, if we are successful, these will be counterbalanced by opposite feelings of exhilaration and joy. (p. 19)

He also claimed that a 'journey with a degree of uncertainty in the "University of the Wilderness"' may well lead to 'one of the greatest experiences of your life' (1984, 19). If conditions and state of mind of the participant are right, according to Mortlock, they might experience a 'frontier adventure'. More recently Ewert and Garvey (2007, 22) have stated that 'inherent in adventure education is the inclusion of activities and experiences that often include elements of danger or risk and uncertain outcomes'. An adventurous pedagogy of risk is troubling for place as it has overtones of a progressive and imperial ideology. It is taken for granted that learners must leave the 'familiar, comfortable and predictable world for uncomfortable new territory' (Luckner and Nadler 1997, 28). Luckner and Nadler (1997) draw on a stereotypical image of the American frontier, the band of adventurous seekers, and what they might expect to encounter as they reach the boundary of their known world.

> At the 'edge' is where many explorers turned back because of the lack of water or food, battles with Native American Indians, or an inability to endure and tolerate the continual fears and apprehension. Breaking through the edge into the realm of possibilities and the land of gold was thereby suppressed. It is the journey between the two worlds, where processing the experience is most important. (p. 28–29)

Confronting the risks at the 'edge', the 'frontier' and venturing beyond one's comfort zone is considered something that will be rewarded (at least by the colonisers). In this portrayal the physical location becomes a featureless backdrop for overcoming metaphorical or literal obstacles and challenges. Clothed in imperialistic metaphors, or viewed as a series of psychological hurdles to confront and conquer, this positions the participant's lived experience 'as a type of decontextualised and disembodied dress rehearsal' for later life (Payne 2000, 188). Local stories, legends, myths, the subtle tone of water on stone, the languages of insects and the wind; the 'interpenetrating webwork of perceptions and sensations' (Abram 1996a, 65) are erased. The underlying fundamental assumption, it would seem, that guides how outdoor places are explored by participants, requires those places to be rendered as abstract and emptied spaces in order that they may be colonised by the achievements of the learner. I disagree

While outdoor education texts promote notions of adventure, risk, and uncertainty and extol the virtues and supposedly intrinsic values of a peak experience as a contrast to the humdrum 'anxieties of modern existence' (Mortlock 1984, 19) there have been few attempts to move beyond accepted definitions of adventure or to provide a sound educational justification for the use of risk as an effective learning strategy.

## Paradoxical aspects of adventure

Pip Lynch and Kevin Moore (2004) suggest that the popularity of adventure, both recreationally and educationally, has arisen from the belief that adventure experiences are radically different from those of everyday life. Lynch and Moore highlight two paradoxes about the nature of adventure experiences. First, those seeking adventure utilise wherever possible technological devices (e.g. synthetic materials and fabrics, satellite navigational equipment and communication devices, and so on) to both invent new activities and to minimise risk. Second, there is a tension between adventure as an outlet or fillip from the constraining influences of modern society and 'the extensive centrality of notions and ideologies of adventure in the history, literature and process of economic expansion of those same societies' (Lynch and Moore 2004, 3). They suggest that notions of adventure are

> swathed in paradox. At different times it has been conceived as either the route to securing the future or the means of opening up uncertainty and therefore possibility (Nerlich, 1987); it has been instrumental as an ideology supporting the physical and economic expansion of states and empires (Nerlich, 1987) or promoted as a therapeutic catalyst for intrapersonal self-development. (p. 3)

The modern-day risk taker seeks an adventure as an escape from modernity, not realising that the phenomenon is 'tightly determined and modified by cultural, social and economic settings' (Lynch and Moore 2004, 3). Sociologists' analyses of the 'risk society', in which individuals are required to negotiate risk and uncertainty as they construct their own biographies, have been well articulated (see Beck 1992; Giddens 1991). Thus day-to-day life can be viewed as an adventure involving uncertainty and risk. Outdoor education's promotion of risk, and the stretching of the learner's comfort zone as a means to self-improvement, finds support within this wider discourse. The taking of organised risks at school camps, for example, supposedly prepares students for the risks they will face as they move to adulthood. In this view the idea of adventure has been largely understood as a socio-psychological phenomenon which Lynch and Moore suggest is consistent 'with the conceptualisation of leisure as essentially involving psychological states and processes and social-psychological variables such as perceived freedom and intrinsic motivation' (Lynch and Moore 2004, 4). While uncertainty is without doubt an undeniable aspect of everyday life, the issue we wish to address is the manipulation of risk and the promotion of stressful situations to push individuals outside their comfort zone as a sound pedagogical principle. The elevation of the adventure (and risk taking) as being central to outdoor education pedagogy is well illustrated in the following extract.

> To maximize safety, adventure professionals structure risk in a manner that causes participants to perceive it as being enormously high, while in actuality it is much lower than perceived and more acceptable as a medium for producing functional change and growth. By responding to seemingly insurmountable tasks, participants often learn to overcome self-imposed perceptions of their capabilities to succeed. (Priest and Gass 1997, 17)

While the issues surrounding the first paradox and the implications for outdoor education have been well discussed (see Cuthbertson et al. 2004; Foley et al. 2003; Loeffler 1999; McAvoy 1999; Payne and Wattchow 2008; Wattchow 2001a), it is the second that Lynch and Moore tease out in more detail. They argue that an ideology of adventure has played a crucial role in the development of the modern, industrialised world economy yet it is paradoxically promoted as an escape from that world. They suggest that 'adventure is a reflexive feature of modernity' (Lynch and Moore 2004, 4).

Drawing on the writings of Nerlich (1987) and Zweig (1974), Lynch and Moore argue that risk taking and adventure have underpinned, and always have been, central pillars of capitalist commerce. Bourgeois interests were served by adopting adventures in commerce as a means to gain wealth and social standing. For the merchant adventurer there was the challenge of the physical journey (often involving a sea voyage) and there 'was also adventure (risk, uncertainty) in the investment with money in those journeys for the purpose of trading exchanges' (Lynch and Moore 2004, 7). As affluence grew the merchant was no longer required to physically venture – this became the role of the employee. However, as the ideology of adventure persisted a transformation occurred in which the concept moved from adventure, or taking risks, for material gain to an undertaking devoid of obvious financial gain. The modern adventurer now deliberately seeks out risk. Interestingly Lynch and Moore argue that adventure has three overlapping roles in modern western societies:

- It is a source of continuity and stability in times of change. It links us to the central precepts of capitalism.

- Adventure can be used as an ideological tool to foster the acceptance and naturalness of constant change. Lynch and Moore contend that adventure is valorised as a natural human condition, which is preferable to the supposedly non-progressive traditions of pre-industrialised peoples.

- Adventure becomes available as a tool of personal agency as individuals seek to construct their identity in modern times.

Thus, suggest Lynch and Moore, adventure ideology is both the continuing manifestation of the social and economic relations embedded in capitalism and a means of constructing one's identity – of linking oneself with the broader discourse of Western capitalism. Placing adventure within this wider social, historical and cultural context requires a questioning of assumptions which view adventure as primarily the endeavours and experiences of individuals (or sub-groups) and explanations of behaviour that rely on psychological constructs. To promote adventure as a route to personal development overlooks and denies the socio-cultural and historical explanations of this central tenet. It places an undue emphasis on the learner, as an individual adventurer, to make meaning of their experiences which are invariably bound by, and often hidden within, broader discourses.

## Assumptions concerning the benefits of risk

The taking of risks is seen as an integral aspect of outdoor education programs that promote adventure for personal and group development. Examples of the centrality of risk abound in the literature. For example, John Miles and Simon Priest (1990, 1) have stated that 'Adventure education involves the purposeful planning and implementation of educational processes that involve risk in some way'. Elsewhere Simon Priest and Michael Gass (1997) have asserted that risk is an integral component of the outdoor adventure education model and one of the reasons it is popular and successful. In addition, Scott Wurdinger (1997, 43) has suggested that risk 'is the element that distinguishes adventure education from other educational fields'.

The impetus to use risk as a pedagogical tool in outdoor education is closely linked to the Romantic notions of nature and the cultural ascriptions accorded to the heroic adventurer in Western literature. In a rigorous cultural history of the outdoor recreational pursuit of mountain climbing, Macfarlane (2003) traced the rise of outdoor risk taking as a relatively late development within the Romantic response to nature. According to Macfarlane, it became popular for people to actively seek exposure to 'pleasurable fear' (p. 73) to re-experience the intensity of life that had become dulled in modern society. Paraphrasing Macfarlane, Brian Wattchow (2007, 17) states that 'the pursuit of pleasurable fear required the wild landscape to be culturally constructed as a *testing ground*'. For the first time the sublime vision for nature as awesome and intensely beautiful was extended to embrace the voluntary experience of danger. The notion of 'pleasurable fear' finds its modern equivalent, in the discourse of outdoor education, in the use of risk (creating uncertainty) and challenge to push learners' outside their comfort zone. It is here, in the zone of 'pleasurable fear', that people supposedly learn and grow.

The structuring of risk, so that participants perceive it to be greater than it really is (which is itself is a contentious distinction), is considered 'acceptable as a medium for producing functional change and growth' (Priest and Gass 1997, 17). It is purported that by achieving 'seemingly insurmountable tasks' participants will move beyond their 'self-imposed perceptions of their capabilities to succeed' (p. 17). Thus risk is seen to play a positive role in the growth and development of individuals and teams. From this perspective, personal growth is dependent on the participant being placed in a setting containing an element, or at the very least the perception, of being at risk (Estrellas 1996). However, Brent Wolfe and Diane Samdahl (2005) have questioned whether taking challenges involving risk necessarily leads to positive outcomes. They have suggested that there are several underlying assumptions regarding the value of risk. The first is that learners need to learn how to deal with risk and that this will be of benefit. The second is that the presumed benefits outweigh the potential risks; 'The overt assumption is that participants have the ability to recover from negative situations' (Wolfe and Samdahl 2005, 33). Dene Berman and Jennifer Davis-Berman (2005) have suggested that challenges to a person's perceived sense of safety and security through the promotion of risk finds parallels in some of psychology's early theories and practices. Rather than using uncertainty to facilitate change, Berman and Davis-Berman have suggested that contemporary understandings of change conditions indicate that people are more likely to respond positively when they feel safe, secure and there is a level of predictability in the environment.

Paul Beedie (1994) has also suggested that the relationship between risk taking and learning is more complex than is portrayed in outdoor education literature. Educator Guy Claxton (2002) has indicated that there is value to be gained in being extended 'by the "risky edge" of our experience' (p. 21). However, he also cautions that such risk is highly personal, contextual and often unpredictable. As Berman and Davis-Berman (2005) have pointed out, perception of risk and the associated levels of anxiety are subjective and people's experiences of, and capacity to deal with, perceived risks can vary widely. For some people exposure to risky situations can become debilitating which may be counterproductive in efforts to bring about change (Berman and Davis-Berman 2005). In is worth bearing in mind Lee Davidson's (2008) reminder that the discourses of risk are both complex and multilayered and therefore not easily reducible to a kind of pedagogic formula.

Mike Brown and Deborah Fraser (2009) have argued that not only is risk too often considered as beneficial for participants, but it is also presented in a way that is highly orchestrated and controlled by the instructor. For example, a ropes course abseiling activity requires careful supervision and adherence to established practices. Brown and Fraser acknowledge that the rhetoric of risk is highly appealing. However they urge caution to avoid mistaking the thrill of taking risks with learning. This point is also raised by Berman and Davis-Berman (2005) who have stated that 'when participants are placed in situations with little perceived control and high perceived risk, they may change some behaviors in order to cope and better conform, but these changes will probably not be internalized very well' (p. 20).

A consequence of the use of activities featuring risk is the necessity of stringent safety management strategies (e.g. standardised operating policies) requiring specialist instructing skills and frequent interventions to ensure compliance. The highly regulated nature of such activities (e.g. specialised equipment is mandatory, a unique vocabulary is taught, the body is regulated and policed through a regime of routines and positioning) may function to undermine internal decision-making and individual agency. Regimentation replaces creative participation with others and with place. Brown and Fraser (2009) suggest that

> The contrived nature of many risk-oriented activities that are highly orchestrated provide learners with a 'do' or 'not do' binary … Little in the way of growth and learning opportunities is afforded in such artificial situations that in effect, do not require significant decision-making by the learner, and thus no ownership of consequences … Participation becomes a zero-sum equation whereby the participant is 'enclosed' by a network of technologies (safety equipment, procedural requirements and predetermined and mechanistic sequencing) which potentially prevent the development of autonomy or resilience by the removal of natural consequences due to the need to manage risk. (p. 70)

One of the inadvertent outcomes of favouring activities which are deemed risky is that the educator is required to be increasingly proactive and interventionist to ensure safety. The educator directs proceedings and the participants are required to comply. Failure to comply places the participant at risk of being withdrawn from the program for reasons of safety. Brown and Fraser refer to this approach as a 'transmissive model of pedagogy' (p. 70). In this situation, the relationship between guide (or educator) and participant is one-way. The expert instructs and the participant follows orders. Johan Hovenlynck (2001) made a similar observation when he stated that 'adventure education is increasingly adopting the didactic teaching methods that it set out to be an alternative for' (p. 4).

The commodification of risk in the provision of outdoor education experiences has been critiqued by a number of writers (Beedie 1994, 1995/6; M. Brown and Fraser 2009; Loynes 1998, 2002; Ringer 1999). Chris Loynes has been critical of 'dominance of the voice of this paradigm' which 'gives the impression of only one way or, perhaps a right way to do things' (Loynes 2002, 113). Brown and Fraser have suggested that a less contrived approach to outdoor education might emphasise the social and cultural context wherein decisions are jointly negotiated and the consequences for all (learners and educators) are considered.

> What could emerge is a transformed territory of meaning (Onore and Lubetsky, 1992) in which the elements of place, space and cultural tools combine with interactions between people. This transformed territory stresses the totality of the experience as a shared enterprise; one in which all may be changed. (Brown and Fraser 2009, 71)

An alternative, subtle and more responsive pedagogical approach would be to focus less on activities involving risk, or a thrill, and more upon the opportunities for learners to engage in decisions in which they can exercise autonomy and authentic choices. For example, providing a group with a food budget and a pile of equipment (suitable for an overnight camp) from which they can choose what they wish to take and leave behind introduces a series of realistic decisions and choices. Who is responsible for what, what are we going to eat, who is carrying shared equipment? This places responsibility with the learners. They are required to negotiate, co-operate, and experience leadership/followership and so on. The consequences of actions and choices made are real and obvious – all this without having to manipulate or manufacture risk. The decisions that learners might face after the experience are of a similar nature (e.g. what course should I enrol in? what is the cost of purchasing a new jacket?). Admittedly this may not seem exciting nor much of an adrenaline 'buzz' but it places learners at the centre as decision-makers making choices and compromises that impact at both an individual and group level.

Life is not a fast-scripted movie nor is it a 30-second advertisement of extreme action. It is invariably made up of mundane and ordinary decisions. If we truly wish to assist participants in outdoor education programs to cope with the trials and tribulations of everyday life perhaps we should anchor our practices in the real rather than in novelty and escapism. We should be mindful of Brown and Fraser's (2009) challenge for outdoor educators to 'shift their focus from "what risk activities can I provide?" to "what educational opportunities can I provide?" This question is far more difficult to examine with any certainty yet it goes to the heart of the matter' (p. 69).

## The use of the comfort zone model to enhance learning

The comfort zone model is inherently linked to notions of adventure and risk. This model, and variants of it, is widespread in outdoor education literature (e.g. Exeter 2001; Luckner and Nadler 1997; Prouty et al. 2007). The comfort zone model is premised on the belief that, when placed in a stressful situation, learners will respond to the challenge, overcome their hesitancy or fear and grow as individuals. Interestingly there is no comfort zone theory per se; rather it is a loose amalgamation of ideas (e.g. Piagetian cognitive development theory, Festinger's theory of cognitive dissonance mixed with cultural assumptions about role of adventure and adventurers). Yet it has been accorded foundational status in outdoor education practice. Within this particular model, which is a tangible example of the intersection of the ideology of adventure/risk and pedagogical practice, personal growth or transformation is dependent on the participant being put in a stressful situation (Estrellas 1996). Brown (2008a) has argued that outdoor educators have taken a creative interpretation of Piaget's and Festinger's ideas around the notions of dissonance/disequilibrium and applied them in a rather functionalist or stimulus-response manner.

> Accommodation-assimilation-equilibrium are conceptual descriptions of a child's cognitive development processes (note they are descriptive not explanatory). To take this concept and apply it as a teaching strategy is a simplistic reading of a *descriptive concept*. Using a description of how we learn, modifying it to promote 'stressful situations', and applying it

as an instructional strategy has given rise to a teaching and learning approach which, I suggest, has placed adventure education on an educational limb; a limb that finds us struggling to gain credibility within the mainstream educational discourse. (M. Brown 2008a, 10)

Outdoor educators' belief that participants are required to be placed outside their comfort zones in order to experience the world of risks, results in participants continuing to encounter the outdoors through the values and attitudes popularised by the Romantic travellers of the 18th and 19th centuries. However, as Leberman and Martin (2003) have pointed out, activities in which students had been pushed outside their comfort zones were not necessarily the activities that resulted in peak learning experiences. The adoption of the comfort zone model, and the assumptions that underpin it, has less than desirable consequences in terms of student engagement, psychological wellbeing and emotional safety.

There is an increasingly strong case to rethink the way leaders frame learning vis-à-vis the manipulation of perceived risk to move students out of their comfort zone (Berman and Davis-Berman 2005; M. Brown 2008a; Davis-Berman and Berman 2002; Estrellas 1996; Leberman and Martin 2003; Zink and Leberman 2003). Research suggests that effective learning depends on solid foundations and strong relationships of trust and support between educator and learner and between learners (Vella 2002). Russell Bishop and Ted Glynn (1999) have proposed that the concepts of reciprocal learning and autonomy/self-determination create new metaphors for teaching and learning that reframe the relationship between educators and learners. Learning can be viewed as a gradual and cumulative process rather than a sudden, and quantum, shift in understanding forced by an existential crisis. As Sarah Leberman and Andrew Martin (2003) have shown, learning can and will occur in outdoor activities that do not create a strong perception of risk.

## The rise of individualism/personal development

A focus on the individual as a site of transformation in outdoor education reflects society's wider preoccupation with the self-authoring, autonomous individual. Hugh Mehan (1996) has suggested that one of the hallmarks of American society, and this may be broadened to include most other Western capitalist societies, is the core value of individualism. In this view the causes of human behaviour are primarily explained in terms of states and traits. These individual states and traits are considered to reside 'in the heads and between the ears of people' (Mehan 1996, 265). Individualism attributes a person's success or lack of success to their personal effort and hard work, rather than broader social or structural factors. According to Pip Lynch and Kevin Moore, the focus on the individual in outdoor education is a consequence of the progressive liberal education movement in the late 19th century.

> According to this strand of progressivism, the education system is the agent of the child, to be adapted to meet individual needs rather than requiring the child to adapt to the system (Blake 1973; Brezinka 1994; Hemmings 1972). The Romantic ideal that was incorporated with educational progressivism imbued outdoor environments with educational value. (Lynch and Moore 2004, 5)

The role of outdoor education in personal development has been a taken-for-granted assumption in much outdoor education research. Investigation of personal traits and states has been the basis of many psychological studies into the benefits of participation in outdoor programs (see Hattie et al. 1997 for an overview). For example, Alan Ewert and Dan Garvey (2007) have suggested that 'one of the most visible and advertised outcomes of adventure education programs is personal growth' (p. 29). However, this focus on the individual, as a site of improvement has not been without its critics (although they are few and far between). Richard Kraft (1981) argued that John Dewey ' … would bridle at the extreme individualism of today's experiential educators, who appear to emphasise the individual, the mystical experience of the mountaintop and the narcissistic pleasures of the wilderness, rather than the arduous task of building a just and democratic order' (p. 6). Andrew Brookes (2000) has claimed that an excessive focus on the individual in outdoor education, as the site of meaning-making and change, inhibits outdoor educators' capacity to deal with the social and cultural dimensions of experience:

> In outdoor education discourse individualism exacerbates realist tendencies to treat cultural and social dimensions of experience only as external distortions to experience … (Brookes 2000, 2).

Interestingly the educator and advocate of an ecological consciousness, Chet Bowers, linked the rise of individualism to various versions of constructivist learning theory. He has argued that constructivist agendas have functioned as a powerful form of colonisation, in that the acceptance of individual meaning-making as a universalised approach to learning has become the accepted pedagogical strategy which should be adopted, or imposed, through educational reform. He has argued that the advocacy and primacy of individual meaning-making works to undermine intergenerational traditions and community life that have formed the basis of different cultures and which have provided ecologically sustainable practices. Furthermore he has suggested that constructivist pedagogies, based on the assumption that students learn more effectively when they construct their own knowledge, potentially restrict students' knowledge to what they can learn from their own direct experience.

> What goes unrecognized in this approach is that the cultural resources of the community, which are largely excluded by this individual or peer-group-centered approach to learning, are essential to developing the talents and skills necessary to being a contributing member of the community ... (Bowers 2005, 10).

According to Bowers, modern society needs a more complex set of understandings than are currently made available in universalised constructivist approaches to learning. The embrace of the experiential learning cycle, as a manifestation of constructivism, highlights the rise of individualism in outdoor education. It is to an overview of experiential learning, and the separation of the individual from their experience and situation, that we now turn our attention.

## Experiential learning cycles

The third way that outdoor education potentially serves as a denial of place is found in the application of various cyclic models of experiential learning. John Dewey (1859–1952) is often cited as one of the principal founders of the experiential education movement. Dewey felt that education should provide an emancipatory, democratic encounter with learning rather than a passive and disengaged experience controlled by others (e.g. adults and teachers). Hunt summarised Dewey's belief that 'primary experience' concerned 'the immediate, tangible, and moving world which presents itself to the senses ... the raw materials from which knowledge can begin' (Hunt 1995, 26). Dewey's philosophy of experience and education warns us about the potential dangers of separating the knower from the known and highlights the sensing body in its environment as the genesis of all learning. However, the real *educational* significance of experience for Dewey came through 'secondary experience'. This reflective experience would take the 'gross, macroscopic, and crude materials furnished by primary experience and seek to make them precise, microscopic and refined' (Hunt 1995, 27).

Outdoor education has grasped the principles of Dewey's educational philosophy in the provision of activities coupled with some form of reflection in which learners, often with the assistance of an instructor, teacher or facilitator, endeavour to make sense of their experiences. It is argued that, through reflection, the learner constructs their understanding of the meaning of their experiences. Laura Joplin (1995) has pointed out that although all learning is experiential (i.e. in so far as it is based on experience), not all learning is intentionally planned. She goes on to suggest that experiential education, as opposed to experiential learning, is the intentional planning of learning that requires two components, the provision of an experience for the learner and the facilitation of that experience through reflection. It is the process of reflection that is considered to turn mere experience into experiential education (Joplin 1995; Walsh and Golins 1976). From this perspective the individual learner is considered to be the agent of self-development (Vince 1998).

Tara Fenwick (2001, 7) has suggested that most experiential educators, regardless of their disciplinary affiliation, 'presume the same basic conceptualization of experiential learning: an independent learner, cognitively reflecting on concrete experience to construct new understandings, perhaps with the assistance of an educator, toward some social goal of progress or improvement'. The models popularised in outdoor education literature tend to be drawn from David Kolb's (1984) model of experiential learning, or variants of it. Vince (1998) has suggested that Kolb's cycle is the pre-eminent model 'to express the nature of experiential learning' (p. 304). The four components of Kolb's (1984) model; concrete experience, reflective observation, abstract conceptualisation, and active experimentation; appear in various forms in a large number of outdoor education texts, either cited directly (Exeter 2001; Martin et al. 2006; Panicucci 2007; Priest and Gass 1997) or modified and simplified; for example the three stage, plan-do-review model (Exeter 2001) or Laura Joplin's spiral version (1995). The emphasis in Kolb's model, and its variants, is on individual experience and meaning-making, which arguably places it 'within the cognitive psychological tradition: a tradition that overlooks or mechanically explains the social, historical and cultural aspects of self, thinking and action' (Holman et al. 1997, 135). Holman et al. (1997) argue that experiential learning theory replicates the assumptions, principles and methods inherent in cognitivist accounts of learning; it is assumed that the learner is separate from their social, historical and cultural context and that thinking can be studied as a sequential process of problem solving.

Several writers have taken issue with the metaphors that are used in regards to learning and experience. Take, for example, the following quote on the role of reflecting on experience.

> Processing enhances the richness of the experience … These unique learnings then can be used again and generalized to other settings. When a new experience is processed, integrated, and internalized, individuals are able to grow, and as a result, they have more choices and influence in their lives. (Luckner and Nadler 1997, 10)

The metaphors used symbolise a technical-mechanistic notion of learning, where experience is an object to be internalised, processed and refined to reveal its true meaning. The processing metaphor assumes that learning happens through cognitive reflection, that experience is a discrete object, and that a learner can be separated from his or her concrete experience to process it and generate knowledge (Fenwick 2001). Chris Loynes (2002) has suggested that the use of production line metaphors (loading, sequencing and processing) is indicative of a rationalist, mechanistic, and deterministic worldview in which learners may be 'oppressed rather than empowered by their managed experience' (p. 116). He has also argued that the commodification of experiences, an adrenaline buzz coupled with processing/reviewing intended to elicit rational learning outcomes, is counter to what should be 'the organic and emergent nature of experiential learning as it takes account of environments, individuals, groups, cultures and activities and the experiences that arise from their interaction' (p. 113). Loynes' concerns are evident in outdoor educators' efforts to institutionalise learning to give it credibility. For example, Joplin (1995) has stated that

> It is the publicly verifiable articulation which makes experience and experiential learning capable of inclusion and acceptance by the educational institutions. The public nature of debrief also ensures that the learner's conclusions are verified and mirrored against a greater body of perception than his alone. (p. 19)

According to Joplin it is the teacher's responsibility to ensure that the actions previously taken are not left to 'drift along unquestioned, unrealised, unintegrated, or unorganised' (p. 19). However, the role that the teacher or educator plays in the verification or mirroring process is potentially problematic. The role of the person responsible for facilitating the reflection process has been examined by several researchers who have raised important questions in relation to the exercise of power and the admissibility of 'appropriate' knowledge in these settings (M. Brown 2002, 2003; Stan 2009).

Joplin's (1995) distinction between experiential learning, where the 'debrief may occur *within* [our emphasis] the individual' (p. 19), and experiential education, where learning must be articulated and made public is a crucial point. What counts as experience in Joplin's model are individual cognitive processes coupled with the public acknowledgment (and approval) of experience, rather than the experience *within*. Yet language is not a neutral conduit through which experiences can be fully and transparently articulated. Language can never fully encompass the felt or embodied qualities of experience. A privileging of language and mental processing risks severing the body from its experiences. Thus experiential education potentially limits the possibilities of place-responsive approaches to facilitation and experience. If participants' vocabularies are poor how can their experiences be articulated? Are experiences that cannot be articulated de-legitimised? What is the role and status of silence in the reflective process? A greater awareness of the links between experience, reflection and the representation of those interpretations of experience (possibly in myriad styles and forms) is a vital issue for all experiential educators, particularly those interested in the possibilities of developing a sense of place.

Brown (2009) has suggested that embedded within experiential learning are two problematic binaries that work to silence connections between the individual and place(s) and ongoing engagement in 'communities of practice' (Lave and Wenger 1991). He claims that as currently practised, outdoor experiential education promotes two distinct binaries: 1) abstraction of meaning from the experience; and 2) the learner from the situation in which the experience(s) occurred. It is worth briefly outlining aspects of Brown's argument in regard to the first point: experiential learning cycles' tendency to reinforce the traditional Cartesian mind–body split (reflection separated from concrete experience). Kemmis (1985) has suggested that because reflection is something deemed to occur inside the head we tend to think of it as an internal psychological process. However, he has warned that to view reflection in this light ignores the situational and embodied experiences that give reflection its very character and significance. Tara Fenwick (2003) has argued that too often

> The body has been somehow banished from learning, along with the body's enmeshments in its social, material and cultural nets of action. Then, appropriated by both school and workplace, the learning that is harvested from bodies in action has been forced into normalizing categories, commodified, and credentialed ... (p. 10).

The proposition that an individual can somehow distance him/herself from experiences and reflect or process them oversimplifies the embodied, situated and discursive constituents of experience. As Kemmis (1985, 141) remarked, 'We do not pause to reflect in a vacuum'. All experiences are mediated through our bodies and our cultural lenses; there is no such thing as a pure, immediate or transparent experience (Fox 2008). Holman et al. (1997, 142) have noted that, a person 'cannot stand outside themselves and their history in order to obtain an account of pure experience or pure self'.

Interpretations of experiences are always bound by context, individual histories (M. Bell 1993), and the interconnected webs of culture, history and power which are embodied in who we are (Fox 2008). Jayson Seaman (2007) argues that the recognition that learning is mediated through cultural understandings challenges 'assumptions about the radical autonomy of learners, about "direct experience", and about the centrality of independent, cognitive reflection in experiential learning' (p. 3). The philosopher of place Edward Casey (1993) reminds us that it is only through the body that we experience place(s) at all. It is through our body that we are taken into place(s); 'It is at once agent and vehicle, articulator and witness of being-in-place' (p. 48). We suggest that cyclic pedagogies discussed above do not merely render the body as invisible but they actively deny embodied ways of knowing thereby presenting a hindrance to both the role of the learner's body in experience and to the ability to be responsive to place. The propensity within experiential approaches to regard the social and cultural dimensions of experiences as external distortions (Brookes 2000) reinforces the notion that true meaning is found through individual reflection which removes these seemingly extraneous details.

The second, and more pertinent, binary is the tendency in cyclic models to separate the participants' learning from the context in which a skill, behaviour or attribute was practiced or observed. This decontextualisation (de-placing) is evident in the importance given to facilitating generalisable concepts or principles that can supposedly be transferred across different contexts (e.g. from an expedition experience to home, work or school). The belief in decontextualised knowing and acting is based on the assumption that an autonomous learner is largely independent of social and spatial relationships (Holman et al. 1997). Thus experiential educators may assume that the specifics of a situation are deemed to be of little or no relevance and can be stripped away to reveal a context-free, universal principle. This assumption appears to allow the broadest possible application of a universal principle, but it denies and silences the uniqueness and particularity of local places and communities.

Fenwick (2001) suggests that in Kolb's model little consideration is given to context as part of the learning process. Where context is discussed in experiential learning (e.g. Boud et al. 1985) it tends to be viewed as a space separate from the learner; context is something that influences the learner but is inherently distinct from the learner who maintains a detached autonomy. However, as Jarvis (1987, 11) reminds us, 'learning is not just a psychological process that happens in splendid isolation from the world in which the learner lives, but is ultimately related to the world and affected by it'. Viewing the learner as autonomous casts them adrift from their social, historical, cultural and material existence. Research into learning provides evidence that this separation of what is learned from how it is learned and used is no longer tenable (Hutchins 1993; Lave 1988).

> The activity in which knowledge is developed and deployed, it is now argued, is not separable from or ancillary to learning and cognition. Nor is it neutral. Rather, it is an integral part of what is learned. Situations might be said to co-produce knowledge through activity. Learning and cognition, it is now possible to argue, are fundamentally situated. (J. Brown et al. 1989, 32)

Clearly learning cannot be separated from, and treated independently from the social, political, historical and cultural contexts in which it occurs. By way of example, Seaman (2007) has shown how learners' experiences in a ropes course session are mediated through cultural and institutional tools. He demonstrated that experience(s) and meaning-making are not individual events but rather collaborative processes. What is learned is situated in a specific place, directed to a purpose or goal, with a particular group of people who bring differing knowledge and attributes. Learning is contextualised according to the demands of the task and the resources available in the situation in which people find themselves. What is emphasised, what is discussed or omitted, the tools that are utilised (physical, cognitive, linguistic etc) and the knowledge that is valued, are functions of the culture and social power relationships which are deeply saturated with meaning (Vince 1998). The uncritical and perhaps unwitting promotion of individualism in experiential pedagogy also impoverishes our understanding of the 'mutuality and reciprocity in learning' (Seaman 2008, 12) and denies both social connectedness and connections with place.

## Conclusion

In this chapter we have tried to draw together some disparate themes in the theory of outdoor adventure education that collectively silence or work against a place-responsive approach. As key concepts in outdoor education they underpin the assumptions of the naturalness or taken-for-granted status of adventure, the majesty of the wild, and the apparent obviousness of following action with reflection. The purpose here has been to draw attention to the cultural, historical, social and geographical factors that have contributed to some of our present day understandings of, and assumptions within, outdoor education practice. It is by no means an exhaustive treatise on this matter. But it will hopefully have served its intended purpose of highlighting for the reader the manner in which a focus on the individual as an adventurer in the wild, facing risks and prevailing in a world of uncertainty in the quest for self-realisation, finds its genesis in particular combinations of ideas arising from a curiously diverse array of histories and professional belief systems.

Our aim has been to draw attention to the omission (or outright denial) of the importance of context in learning in the outdoors. Context, from the perspective we are arguing in this book, can be interpreted as an unfolding phenomenon between person, place and culture. Hopkins and Putnam (1993) typify the neglected aspect of place in outdoor education when they state that the outdoors 'is simply a statement about location; it describes where something happens' (p. 5). An over-extended focus on the individual through challenge and adventure comes at the expense of other possible learning agendas and ways of knowing. If we are not careful Payne and Wattchow's (2008) assertion that it is becoming 'increasingly difficult to confidently make the claim that outdoor education is an "alternative" beyond the fact that some of it occurs in the outdoors' (p. 26) may well be our downfall in an educational system increasingly under pressure from competing curricula demands and tighter budgetary constraints.

# Chapter 3

# The Case for Place

Why place? Why should 'place' rather than 'nature', 'environment' or 'wilderness' serve as the central idea around which to organise a book on the philosophy and practice of an alternative form of outdoor education? Place, as a way of understanding how humans live, experience and relate to particular locations on the Earth's surface, has attracted considerable attention in recent decades across a range of disciplines (cultural geography, anthropology, sociology, phenomenological philosophy, architecture, to name a few). We have already attempted to demonstrate that many of the contemporary assumptions, ideals and practices of outdoor and experiential education may actually be silencing or denying the experience of place for participants. In doing so it is possible that local communities and their histories, as well as local ecologies are erased from the educational experience. A shared feature of much of the scholarship and writing about place and sense of place is concern about the cumulative effects of modernity upon our ability to respect and care for the local places we call home and the remote places we encounter when we travel. There is inevitably a sense of loss in much of this writing. The philosopher David Abram (1996a) suggests this loss is profound.

> Today we participate almost exclusively with other humans and with
> our own human-made technologies. It is a precarious situation, given
> our age-old reciprocity with the many-voiced landscape. We still need
> that which is other than our own creation and ourselves ... we are
> human only in contact, and conviviality, with what is not human. (p. ix)

Much of this more-than-human world (Abram 1996a) is under threat as a result of humans' deliberate or unwitting actions. Of course, any cultural world we may inhabit is deeply enmeshed with the ecological systems that surround and support us. Within the incessant motion of life in late-capitalist societies, argues the philosopher Edward Casey (1993), we rush from location to location, rarely getting to know the subtleties of local places, their histories, ecologies, economies. 'We pay a heavy price for capitalizing on our basic animal mobility,' writes Edward Relph (1976, xiii). The price is a loss of a deep experience of attachment to a place that can sustain our sense of a meaningful life. Relph believes that the experience of place, for many, has been replaced by that of a sense of homogenous 'placelessness'.

As we move along freeways, railways or between airport terminals, they can all seem much the same. Our experience of these locations becomes one of feeling that we could be everywhere-anywhere-nowhere. We encounter supermarkets, streetscapes, suburbs and even landscapes that appear and feel remarkably similar to the ones we left behind. Our memory of them soon blurs due to lack of a sense of any distinctive, defining qualities. Doreen Massey (1994) has described this loss of sense of place as a universal aspect of modern life and part of the 'time-space compression' phenomenon of our times. But placelessness refers not only to our perception of our situation in the world. Adopting a focus on place compels us to consider how the particular qualities within local places may be wiped out by modern development and how that loss may be grieved for by those who once lived there.

The Australian historian Peter Read's (1996) moving study, *Returning to Nothing: The Meaning of Lost Places*, examined the effect upon Australian individuals, families and communities who have had their attachment to the places where they lived, and thus how they lived, obliterated by modern development. Read wanted to know what happened to people when they became displaced. In some cases this involved the erasure of whole communities as dams were built and river valleys were flooded, or the expansion of open cut mines that required towns and their people to be relocated. Hospitals where children were born, the schools they attended, businesses, churches, homes, sporting grounds were all re-located or obliterated. He also studied what happened to people living in urban communities when town planners and engineers proposed and then built a freeway that split an old suburb in half (ironically so that commuters living in the new, sprawling estates on the expanding fringe of the city would have a faster commute to work). Read also examined a case where the declaration of a national park changed intergenerational farming practices and eventually resulted in the family losing its farming land and home. In each of these cases the loss of attachment to place was forced upon the people concerned. The change impacted deeply on where and how they lived and how they felt about life. The impact, for most, was devastating.

'We mourn places as well as people,' writes Casey (1993, 198). The rich mosaic of land, people, community and local history that constitutes a place can be swept aside and replaced by homogenised experience, epitomised by the trip to the shopping plaza, the drive down the freeway, the massive dam, the monolithic sporting stadium and the mono-crop. The land and community, and the meaning we attach to them, can shift before our gaze and beneath our feet. The place we had come to believe was stable and gave us an anchor in the world, morphs into something else. Suddenly we feel estranged from the place we had grown to love or, perhaps, had taken for granted. But, equally, change does not need to be quite so devastating. It is possible that planned change can result in a place somehow maintaining a sense of continuity with the past. Things that are crucial and essential to a place might be fought for and celebrated. The integrity of a place may be sustained through times of change. The fate of each place is finely balanced between these futures – obliteration or continuation. The places where we work with our students in outdoor education are no different. The ideals and actions we foster as educators also contribute to what those places are becoming, for better or worse.

The development of scholarship concerning place has arisen around the world in response to concern about how we live and the consequence of our modern lives for the sustainability of places. In Simon Schama's (1995) monumental study of human interaction with the land, *Landscape and Memory*, he strove for 'a way of looking; of rediscovering what we already have, but which somehow eludes our recognition and our appreciation. Instead of being yet another explanation of what we have lost, it is an exploration of what we may yet find' (Schama 1995, 14). Rather than accepting the now common view that culture and nature are mutually exclusive in Western societies Schama searched instead for what bound them together. This linkage, he argued, is there 'beneath layers of the commonplace' (p. 14). We live in place every moment of every day, whether we recognise it or not. Schama is suggesting that we begin our search for the connections that bind nature and culture and people and places together, right here, right now, on the very ground beneath our feet.

In the previous chapter we discussed how key areas of outdoor education theory and practice are based upon myth, dubious claims and false assumptions. In a sense we argued that much of what outdoor educators do has been built on very shaky foundations, and that it may not continue to be defensible in uncertain and changing times. We now begin the process of re-building, or better, renewing those foundations. In this chapter we discuss how scholars from diverse academic fields have established a case for place as a crucial consideration that cannot be avoided when we start to look at how humans relate to the locations where they live, work, learn or recreate. We relate the complex debate about the meaning of place, how place contributes to our sense of identity and how we experience place. These discussions lay an important foundation for the chapters to follow, which focus on pedagogic responses to place.

## What do we mean by 'place'?

In his highly influential book *Place and Placelessness*, Edward Relph (1976, 6) demonstrated how places serve as 'sources of security and identity', but also how the homogenising influence of modern practices (particularly in engineering, agriculture and architecture and, perhaps, we might add in education and adventure programming) can result in the experience of displacement or rootlessness. These days it may be a sense of placelessness that we take for granted. Yet we are constantly recreating ourselves, Relph (1976) argues, and learning our place in the world, through recreating our place. There is an unavoidable reciprocity between people and places. 'The word "place" is best applied', writes Relph (1992, 37), 'to those fragments of human environments where meanings, activities and a specific landscape are all implicated and enfolded by each other.'

Geographers have long had an interest in the concept of place. In particular, human geographers like Yi Fu Tuan, Edward Relph and David Seamon have adapted the insights of philosophers Edmund Husserl, Martin Heidegger and Maurice Merleau-Ponty to reveal the character and quality of the lived-experience of places. They strive to show how people live within subjective lifeworlds that not only influence their experience of life, but which direct much of their actions. These geographers have built their theories on several of Heidegger's key ideas. These include his depictions of what it means to dwell authentically in place; his conception of 'sparing' as a 'tolerance for places in their own essence' (Relph 1976, 39); and his descriptions of 'fields of care' as a 'taking responsibility for place' (see Hay 2002, 161). For Heidegger, 'man's [sic] essential relation to places ... consists in dwelling ... the essential property of human experience' (cited in Relph 1976, 28). In addition, in applying the work of Merleau-Ponty, David Seamon (1979) has considered the role of perception and the body in experience and how people are irrevocably connected to the places in which they live. Together, the works of Heidegger and Merleau-Ponty have inspired much of the scholarly development of 'place' that followed.

Furthermore, given that human mobility is inevitable, it is important to consider how people become connected, remain connected or become disconnected from particular places. Yi Fu Tuan (1974, 102) suggested that '"home" is a meaningless word without "journey"'. Humans have always moved across territorial boundaries and between places, both aware of and subconsciously responding to the similarities and differences they encounter. There are several distinctions to work through here in terms of place. Place can be taken to mean home. Equally, we might experience a sense of place when we travel. Some places we travel to may seem recognisable whilst others seem almost completely foreign. Both of these are important concepts for outdoor educators. Let's begin by looking at place as home.

Despite its obvious appeal, even place as home is a slippery concept. Heidegger privileged a home-dwelling folk-culture that is hard to imagine survives in late post-industrial societies as anything other than a nostalgic desire. The allure of an authentic sense of place as home might also have negative consequences. For Heidegger at least, it was a dangerously short distance between an authentic idealisation of homeplace and Nazi Germany's nationalistic vision for the Fatherland (Berthold-Bond 2000; Hay 2002).

'The search for homeplace' writes Lucy Lippard (1997) 'is the mythical search for the *axis mundi*, for a centre, for some place to stand, for something to hang onto' (p. 27), but the 'centre doesn't hold forever' (p. 23). Judy Pinn (2003) is also wary of becoming caught up in 'the "one true place" syndrome by idealising a particular place and its people, and burdening them … with special meaning' (p. 40). As Lippard (1997) suggests it is unlikely that there can be one 'true' centre of meaning for us. We are destined to experience multiple places – multiple centres of significance. The outdoor places that we visit and teach in may become such places, but only if they become important sources of our identity. Hence, the places we care for may be places where we live most of our life (work places and home places), but equally they may be recreational and pedagogical places that we are destined to know through our visits and travels.

These views of place immediately raise interesting questions. Can we experience a state of dwelling and become deeply connected to places in the modern age of high mobility and globalisation? Ironically Peter Read's stories about the effects of displacement seem to suggest that people can and do form deep attachments to place. Or do we accept, as the geographer Doreen Massey (1994, 121) puts it, that there can be 'no authenticity of place'? For Massey a place always reflects changing social conditions and she suggests that we should consider places as open, porous and in a state of flux rather than as some kind of fixed entity.

One way of thinking about place is as particular moments in such intersecting social relations, nets of which have over time been constructed, laid down, interacted with one another, decayed and renewed. Some of these relations will be, as it were, contained within the place; others will stretch beyond it, tying any particular locality into wider relations and processes in which other places are implicated as well (Massey 1994, 120).

This is why place remains an elusive conceptual construct. Despite appearances, the meanings and experiences of places to individuals and groups are never stable. In general, place has to do 'with the relationship between people and their local setting for their experience and activity' (Cameron 2003b, 3) and is a continually unfolding phenomenon. We need to keep these differing ideas about what place is, and what it may mean to us, open for a time. We need to keep the phenomenon of the experience of place alive as a question we might ask ourselves about our experience of the world. Perhaps a good way to proceed is to consider one of the most fundamental problems that scholars of place have debated about the meaning and significance of place.

## Space or place

The relationship between space and place remains one of the most difficult questions facing those interested in studying the human experience of place. The implications for outdoor education are significant. In this section we explore how humans experience space and place, with particular reference to the Australian and New Zealand contexts. On the one hand there are those who consider that a place is made through the accumulation of human experience in a particular setting (see for example, Carter 1988; Meinig 1979; Relph 1976; Schama 1995; Walter 1998; Watson 1990). On the other, there are those who propose that place has its own inherent spirit and meaning, waiting to be discovered by those who open themselves to a place as attentive students (see for example, Norberg-Schulz 1980; Park 1995; Read 2003; Tacey 1995, 2000). Differences between understanding a place as set of human meanings that result from layers of cultural ideas, beliefs and histories, or as a site of intrinsic meaning are important to understand. These philosophical positions influence the ways in which outdoor educators and learners encounter, locate themselves within, move through, and identify themselves in outdoor spaces or places.

The question arises – which comes first, space or place? This question is of more than theoretical interest. As already discussed in the previous chapter, the adventure and experiential education paradigms in outdoor education practice are largely premised on an assumption that outdoor places are empty spaces on which certain desires and ideologies can be projected and enacted. Walter's (1998) quotation below provides a typical interpretation of the first position, that space precedes place and that place is solely a cultural construction.

> A place has no feelings apart from the human experience there. But a place is a location of experience. It evokes and organizes memories, images, feelings, meanings, and the work of imagination. The feelings of a place are indeed the mental projections of individuals, but they come from collective experience and they do not happen anywhere else. They belong to the place. (p. 21)

Many scholars of place share this view. Relph (1976, 12) believes that 'existential or lived-space is the inner structure of space as it appears to us in our concrete experiences of the world as members of a cultural group'. For Relph, our experience of space is culturally defined. Ian Watson's (1990) book, *Fighting Over the Forests*, is a compelling study of the radically different beliefs held by conservation campaigners and forest industry workers for the same tracts of land in northern New South Wales. He suggested that 'people inhabit cultural worlds' (p. xix), which are summations of a diverse range of elements (work, family, gender, local environment, entertainment and so on). Tuan (1977) hints at the primordial qualities of space and how, as humans, we fashion a place for ourselves from a meaningless void.

> Space is a common symbol of freedom in the Western world. Space lies open; it suggests the future and invites action ... Open space has no trodden paths and signposts. It has no fixed pattern of established human meaning; it is a blank sheet on which meaning may be imposed. Enclosed and humanised space is place. (p. 54)

European explorers of the Australian continent filled the blank sheets of their expedition journals with narratives in which we can now 'discern the process of transforming space into place' (Carter 1988, xxiii), or so it seems. The preference for a view of land as empty space, as opposed to one which was already occupied and brimful of meanings and significance, made it possible to erase or ignore the original and rewrite it with another set of beliefs and meanings. 'The left hand creates the *tabula rasa* upon which the right hand will inscribe its civilisation,' writes the anthropologist Deborah Bird Rose (2004, 62). We recall Seddon's question; whose place was it in the first place? Thus the orientation we assume to the relationship between space and place is fundamental for settler societies like Australia and New Zealand, with their mix of indigenous and imported knowledge systems and practices, as they struggle towards reconciliation not just between peoples but also with places.

If there is to be any hope for a reconciliation between traditional and settler peoples, and between settlers and the land in a country like Australia, it becomes crucial to accept that

> there is no place where the feet of Aboriginal humanity have not preceded those of the settler. Nor is there any place where the country was not once fashioned and kept productive by Aboriginal people's land management practices. There is no place without a history; there is no place that has not been imaginatively grasped through song, dance and design, no place where traditional owners cannot see the imprint of sacred creation. (Rose 1996, 18)

From this perspective Australia was never an empty space for the colonisers to fill with meaning. It was always a place fully invested with significance, reaching far back beyond human history and memory. The late ecological historian Geoff Park wrote compellingly about the impact of the European imagination transposed onto New Zealand landscape. Whereas Australia was imagined as a 'prison-scape' (Park 1995, 13), New Zealand was seen more as a garden or pasture and an opportunity to rebuild the very best of British society in a remote, ideal community. Yet the consequences for local ecology and native peoples has been every bit as damaging as it has been in Australia.

In *Ngā Uruora (The Groves of Life)* Park carefully details the damage done to the lowland forests which covered most of New Zealand when Europeans first landed there and which now have all but vanished. Europeans believed that they had a cultural licence and obligation to clear and improve the forest and replace it with productive farming land and 'civilised' communities.

> The sad fact of New Zealand's lowlands is that they were found, possessed and gutted by a foreign culture at a point in its history when … the mystique of industry entranced it more than the mystique of nature. (Park 1995, 307)

That many scholars of place continue to write from the perspective that space precedes place and that a place develops only as a result of human experience is curious. Yet this belief is deeply entrenched in the traditions of Western thought. Casey (1996) suggests that it was the abstract physics of Newton and the critical philosophy of Kant that resulted in places becoming 'the mere apportionings of space, its compartmentalisations' (p. 14). In his argument for a return to place, Casey (1996) asks us to avoid the 'the high road of modernism ... to reoccupy the lowland of place' (p. 20). Place can then be considered both premodern and postmodern: 'it serves to connect these two far sides of modernity' p. 20).

If we are to find our way back to place we may need to accept that a *genius loci,* a local spirit-of-place, is already residing there. In Norberg-Schulz's (1980) classic work *Genius Loci: Towards a Phenomenology of Architecture,* he reactivates (or re-animates) the ancient Roman belief that every 'independent' being has its *genius,* its guardian spirit: 'this spirit gives life to people and places, accompanies them from birth to death, and determines their character or essence' (Norberg-Schulz 1980, 18). As an architect and designer Norberg-Schulz is imploring us to be quiet, to be attentive to the subtle, local elements at work, combining to provide the essential character of a place. The organic or place-responsive architect is expected to become attuned to these qualities about a place and build in sympathy with them. *Genius loci* is the belief that the land and things within it have inherent meaning; the rock, the tree, the bird each contain a spiritual force that contributes to the totality of the land.

Yet it is difficult to loosen the grip of rationalism. George Seddon (1997) considered that 'it would be dangerous to assume that there really is a genius loci' (p. 106). It is a useful concept, he argues, but it remains culture-bound. Relph (1976) seems even less hopeful (for Western cultures at least). He sees an irreconcilable gulf between 'the existential space of a culture like that of the Aborigines and most technological and industrial cultures – the former is "sacred" and symbolic, while the latter are "geographical" and significant mainly for functional and utilitarian purposes' (p. 15). It is just such a gulf that David Tacey (1995, 2000) suggests settler Australians must cross if they are to have any hope of reconciliation. Yet, he warns, that the '"spirit of place" is by now a cliché of journalism and a cash-cow of tourism, but "spirit place" is altogether different, a powerful visionary claim that smashes almost everything we know' (Tacey 2003, 243).

Despite the fact that it might be severely diminished, 'Any stretch of country, no matter how pervasive agriculture's marks, has an indwelling life force, waning or waxing, which distinguishes it from any other' (Park 1995, 331). But, can we identify with such a spirit-place or life force in the land? It is on just such a quest, to seek out the 'inspirited earth', that Read (2003) embarks and then writes about in *Haunted Earth*, the third book in his study of relationships between people and places in Australia.[1] After conducting many interviews and a great deal of ethnographic fieldwork, Read concludes,

> Almost everyone ... has pointed me to the indivisible continuum, which starts at superstitious, flows to supernatural, spiritual, unexplainable, intuitive, weird, poetic, strange, odd, coincidental, probably coincidental, fairly explainable, testable, rational, repeatable, verifiable, scientifically exact. (p. 252)

Space or place? Perhaps to consider that we must make a choice between one or the other is to fall into the dualistic trap of forming binary opposites. Perhaps it makes more sense for us to consider that we slide backwards and forwards along a continuum between the two.

## Space, place and landscape

One of the barriers to a more sensuous and perhaps even spiritual experience of place is the Western concept of landscape and the belief system that it represents. *Landscape* entered the English vocabulary at the end of the 16th century from the Dutch *landschap*, making it a younger concept than 'wilderness' (in the English language) by at least three centuries. It 'signified a unit of occupation, indeed a jurisdiction ... that might be a pleasing object of depiction' (Schama 1995, 10). Landscape has become, perhaps, the quintessential appropriation of space by Western culture that stands in the way of knowing the particularities of local places. The American landscape scholar J. B. Jackson (1984) believes that we have come to use the word *landscape* carelessly. For Jackson, the old-fashioned definition of *landscape* as 'a portion of the earth's surface that can be understood at a glance' (1984, 8) has begun to change and evolve. The geographer D. W. Meinig (1979) presents a simple exercise worthy of consideration. He writes of getting together a group of people from a similar cultural background and standing with them upon a vantage point in the countryside. All are viewing the same scene. Independently they see, or construct, the same landscape differently as nature, habitat, artefact, system, problem, ideology, wealth, history, aesthetic, and place. Meinig argues that each may construct the same landscape in multiple combinations of these interpretations – often internalising complex and contradictory meanings.

This exercise is a useful starting point with students. It can be done for a place with which they are already familiar or a place that is relatively new to them. Attempting to see a landscape through each of Meinig's 'lenses' begins to bring to the surface their own preferences. It is possible for them to gain some insights into the contradictory sets of values and expectations that we often harbour for the same place. But it is a limited exercise. It is largely an intellectual task and does not have much of an experiential component.

From this perspective we are now more likely to accept Schama's (1995) suggestion that landscape has more to do with the intellect than it does with the body: 'Before it can ever be a repose for the senses, landscape is the work of the mind. Its scenery is built up as much from strata of memory as from layers of rock' (pp. 6–7). For Relph (1985), landscapes 'cannot be embraced, nor touched, nor walked around. As we move, so the landscape moves, always there, in sight but out of reach' (p. 23). Thus landscape is a dominant and pernicious idea in Western culture. We are fed a constant diet of landscape images through the media, each scene carefully captured and arranged in all its imagined perfection. We then carry this image-bank around with us, struggling to match the reality of what we find – the light not quite right, the crowd of (other) tourists getting in the way – with the scene we had already anticipated. We need to be wary of confusing the  assumptions entailed in the viewing of a landscape with the phenomenon of experiencing a place.

The Canadian James Raffan explains (1992) that 'although land exists, the *scape* is a projection of the human consciousness … [the] *land* – the thing you can walk on, measure, map, paint, buy, sell and assay – is transformed in the human mind into land*scape*, a much broader, far reaching, and illusive entity' (p. 6). Therefore, the landscape is always shaped and arranged by the viewer, and not by the land itself. The picturesque landscape is 'seen from a "station", a raised promontory in which the spectator stands above the earth, looking down over it in an attitude of Enlightenment mastery' (Bate 2000, 13). In colonial times in Australia forest trees were cleared from chosen vantage points, and platforms built in order that the artist could see the scene 'properly' and thus render it onto canvas (Bonyhardy 2000). The equivalent, in contemporary times, is the endless proliferation of viewing platforms built in National Parks and on the carefully selected sites of scenic drives. The landscape designer has already preceded the tourist and selected and arranged the scene before them.

There are several dangers in these definitions of landscape and their uses. Yes, a material Earth is acknowledged as existing, but it always seems to be valued as secondary to human socially constructed projections cast upon it. The problem is exacerbated when the viewing subject interprets the scene and confirms the cultural norm. This leads to the belief that 'nature', 'wilderness', 'landscape', 'place' are just more of a vast range of our intellectual inventions that can readily be re-invented, re-imagined and re-projected to fill or modify the space before us.

Experiencing places only as landscapes, as projections of our assumptions and desires, makes them more readily available for our expropriation and consumption. We do not need to look far to be reminded of how places are presented, packaged and consumed in such pervasive, everyday media as tourism marketing, land developers' billboards and the travel pages of the weekend newspapers. Natural places increasingly seem to be close and attainable but as we reach for them the shimmering image retreats or fades.

In such media and processes the sensing body has become sidelined. Our preference for particular historical-cultural ideas and interpretations seems to precede our experience. Authentic nature, or place, becomes unattainable. Is there a way through this impasse? To grapple with this question we need to turn our attention to the differences in how we relate to places as insider or outsider (Relph 1976).

## Insider or outsider

In *Place and Placelessness*, Edward Relph (1976) was clearly inspired by the writings of the German philosopher Martin Heidegger. Relph sought to understand not just the identity of a place, 'but also the identity that a person or group has with that place, in particular whether they are experiencing it as an insider or as an outsider' (p. 45). To be an insider is to belong to a place. To live in a place is to be safe and secure in the world, to have a centre of meaning and existence. To be an outsider is to be adrift, to be constantly homeless – an alien.

One of Relph's most pertinent contributions to the discourse of place remains his characterisations of what it means to be an insider or an outsider. When Tuan (1977) writes that modern humans rarely establish roots and that the 'experience of place is superficial' (p. 183) he is suggesting that lack of sufficient time in one place, as a result of mobility and lifestyle, ultimately makes it nearly impossible for a member of modern society to experience place authentically. What hope is there then for the outdoor education participant who may visit a place once, or even if they were to begin the process of developing familiarity with a place through repeated short visits?

The outsider is one who has a 'largely unselfconscious attitude in which places are experienced as little more than a background or setting for activities' (Relph 1976, 52). Much outdoor recreation and education that uses places as an arena for human development clearly risks this lack of identification with place and results in a short-term raid mentality, as the Australian academic Andrew Brookes (1993) has characterised it, where the experience of the activity is what matters and participants are considered to be self-sufficient, requiring no dependence upon the local community or setting for information or resources.

Imagine a piece of land set up as an orienteering course to teach navigation skills. The novice walkers are given a map marking the checkpoints. They then spend a few moments plotting an efficient cross-country course to collect the checkpoints. Compass bearings are taken and walked, or run, along and various navigation strategies are employed to minimise the possibility of missing a checkpoint and wasting time. Students learn to interpret subtle features on a topographic map, an implied knoll or re-entrant perhaps. They learn to use a ridgeline as a 'handrail' and a creek as a 'catching feature'. But really, the surrounding land and its rich history and ecology are completely ignored.

One defence of the above scenario could be that the experience was simply planned around developing some navigational skills so that students could go on a bushwalking or tramping journey in the future. Once there, they would have more time to learn about the place that they were in. However, the difficulty that arises with this approach is that the first experience has set the tone for the next. The student has already learnt how to *be* in the bush. The next journey becomes an exercise in applying that hard-won new set of ideas and skills, albeit in a more demanding situation. The students spend more time looking at their topographic maps and setting compass bearings than, say, following the remnants of an Aboriginal trade path or an explorer's trail. They may, for example, locate themselves by deploying technology and techniques rather than contour around a hill-face along a vegetation line. To the learner the place is experienced as devoid of history and ecology. It is simply a surface, with a few obstacles in the way, to move over. This cultural template of the existential outsider is persistent and pervasive. We may tend to replicate it as educators because we ourselves have been schooled in it and have succeeded, without ever realising that we were internalising a set of ideas and values that diminish the potential of local places.

In Relph's continuum, there are only two levels of insideness that depict a deeper attachment to local place. The first of these is the empathetic insider. According to Relph this requires a willingness to open oneself to the significances of a place. One needs to strive to respect and develop a feeling for local places.

> This involves not merely looking at a place, but seeing into and appreciating the essential elements of its identity. Such empathetic insideness is possible for anyone not constricted by rigid patterns of thought and who possesses some awareness of environment ... To be inside a place empathetically is to understand that place as rich in meaning, and hence to identity with it, for these meanings are not only linked to the experiences and symbols of those whose place it is, but also stem from one's own experiences. (Relph 1976, 54–55)

According to Relph (1976), empathetic insideness can be achieved through 'training ourselves to see and understand places in themselves' (p. 55). For Relph, the final and most advanced level of emplacement is the existential insider who equates with Heidegger's inhabitant who dwells and cares for their home-place, possibly without even thinking about it, through the nature of their everyday activity. For the existential insider, place is full of significance which is experienced without the need for conscious reflective effort. It is characterised by an implicit acceptance that you simply belong to, and identify with, this place. Only in these final two levels of identification with place, if we interpret Relph correctly, is an authentic response to place possible.

> An authentic attitude to place is thus understood to be a direct and genuine experience of the entire complex of the identity of places – not mediated and distorted through a series of quite arbitrary social and intellectual fashions about how that experience should be, nor following stereotyped conventions. (1976, 64)

The existential insider is an indigene, a long-time or lifetime inhabitant. It is depth or length of time that matters. There is a distinction to be drawn here between two different types of occupancy of a place. David Orr (1992) sees a significant difference between the 'temporary resident', who cares little about where they are, and has little desire to put down roots, and the inhabitant.

"For the existential insider, place is full of
significance which is experienced without the need
for conscious reflective effort."

The inhabitant, in contrast, 'dwells', as Illich puts it in an intimate,
organic, and mutually nurturing relationship with a place. Good
inhabitance is an art requiring detailed knowledge of a place, the
capacity for observation, and a sense of care. (p. 130)

But Relph also sees possibilities for the empathetic insider who strives to
recognise this form of deep attachment to place, even though they can never
experience it fully. Ultimately for Relph, it is in these final two categories of
insideness that people seek to be 'at-home', which becomes 'an irreplaceable
centre of significance' (p. 39). Such an 'at-homeness' represents a sense of
'absoluteness of place, of 'time immemorial' and of a mutual belonging
between a place and a people' (Massey 1995, 51).

Yet it is possible that the empathetic insider has an advantage over the
life-long inhabitant when it comes to recognising the unique ensemble of
qualities that make up a place. The empathetic visitor to a place is someone

who searches for local meanings and seeks to gain a sense of a local place's unique qualities. They may see and feel things that the inhabitant has become so used to that they are no longer consciously aware of them. They experience and interpret the phenomena of a place in contrast to where they have come from but also by actively opening themselves to possibility of a place.

Relph's structures of place, although not without problems, remain useful sensitisers. They alert us to likely differences between local and visitor, but do not discount the possibility that the attentive and responsive visitor may see and experience place in great richness and depth in a relatively short passage of time, and even experience some sense of attachment and commitment to that place. The lesson for outdoor educators, it would seem, is to stay alert to the possibility that place experiences for both locals and visitors alike are rich in educative potential, but may require different pedagogic strategies. Intensity of experience may produce its own manifestations of the place experience, particularly as they live on in the memory of participants. The journeys of participants through the outdoors may constitute their own subjectivities of place and time, not considered by Relph and Heidegger, who maintained a focus on residency, inhabitation and dwelling. A crucial aspect of understanding how humans develop levels of attachment to places has to do with identity.

## Place and identity

It has been suggested that place(s) can serve as a source of security and identity at both an individual and collective level (Gentry 2006; Nicol and Higgins 1998; Relph 1976). Gentry (2006, 13) has pointed out, 'We all come from some place, and we all live in some place. Our identity and our very sense of authenticity, it seems, are inextricably bound up with the places we claim as "ours"'.

Clearly the formation of identity does not occur in a social or cultural vacuum (Weigert and Gecas 2005), nor does it occur in an isolated space devoid of the meanings ascribed to, and taken from, lived experiences of the individual or broader social groups' interactions with their locales. Identity is constructed and reconstructed through interaction; the physical, social, and cultural contexts and discourses enable and constrain the possibilities for identity formation. For as Berzonsky reminds us, we cannot 'whimsically construct or make up anything we desire' (2005, 128). What place literature draws our attention to is the importance of the lived experience of place for individual and collective identity.

As discussed above, places are not simply locations or abstract concepts, rather they are sites of lived experience and meaning making. A number of New Zealand and Australian writers have focused attention on how places, both real and imagined, contribute to discourses of national identity.

George Seddon's books, *A Sense of Place* (1972), *Searching for the Snowy: An Environmental History* (1994), *Landprints: Reflections on Place and Landscape* (1997), and *The Old Country: Australian Landscapes, Plants and People* (2005), have made a lasting contribution to place scholarship both in Australia and internationally. Seddon was a polymath who would bring to the study of a place his knowledge of geology, geography, history, literature, and art, not to mention the wearing out of a lot of boot leather walking the land itself. The important point is that in questions relating to a place, Seddon started with the place itself. He believed that the concept 'sense of place' should be applied 'with caution, because it is a form of appropriation' (1997, 106). Its popularity has made the concept problematic, 'championed by outsiders' (Bonyhardy and Griffiths 2002, 9), a catch-all phrase just as likely to be deployed aggressively in tourism promotion and real estate development, and even conservation campaigns. When people become aware of their intense connection to particular places, it is possible that contradictions emerge to directly challenge the basis of those connections.

When the Australian historian Peter Read (2000) refers to 'proper country' in his book *Belonging: Australians, Place and Aboriginal Ownership*, he is referring to the Gai-mariagal country, the deep sandstone region just north of Sydney. 'Proper country' is formed out of his 'deep memory and experience' (p. 7), gathered through growth from childhood to adulthood, and in particular through fresh insights from his friend Dennis Foley, an indigenous (Gai-mariagal) custodian of the region. According to Read (2000), his memory-map of the area would 'take a day to draw' (p. 8). For Read there is a significant dilemma with his attachment to this country. The place he loves, and is tempted to call his 'soul country', has already been 'wrested from Indigenous people who loved them, lost them and grieve for them still' (p. 2). Read (2000, 9) asks: 'Do I have the right to belong to this soul-country?'. He personifies Seddon's question: Whose place is it to belong to in the first place? We may feel compelled to reflect and ask, especially when we adopt the perspective of the empathetic insider: Who am I to identify with this place? How can I become reconciled with this place's past, and the memories that it carries, as I develop my own attachment to it?

The question of how colonising peoples can belong or claim attachment to a place has been the topic for debate and discussion amongst both academics and social commentators. By way of example, the author Witi Ihimaera has suggested that in New Zealand people have a fixation on their identity (Ihimaera 1994). While Ihimaera's comments are located in a New Zealand context, it could be argued that these sentiments resonate in many countries where indigenous peoples have been affected by large-scale migration from other cultural groupings. For Māori, identity can be rooted in the claim to be *tangata whenua*, the first people of the land. While for Pākehā (loosely defined as the original settlers or the descendants of British colonisers), and other immigrant groups, it is based on being here as 'secondary' inhabitants. Questions about belonging and connection feature in public discourse as non-Māori New Zealanders attempt to make sense of who they are in relation to this place; a place that is their home and has been for their forebears. Park (1995, 320) re-iterates Seddon's sentiments about whose place it is, when he asks in the New Zealand context, 'What is this place about? How do we fit into it?' Again writing from a New Zealand perspective, but with a similarity to Australian settlers of European origin, Claudia Bell (1996) has suggested that for settlers the relationship with the land

> became a component of national identity constructs. Settlers did not have the kinship networks and family relationships, or long-term family associations with place, that they had in Britain, or that Māori has here. Identification with the environment gradually became defined not by one's connections or family location in Britain, but by owning land here. This early influence of the environment on 'national character' has been claimed by historians as having an enduring affect on national imagery for New Zealand. (p. 5)

Images of European settlers taming the wilds of the Australian bush, or bringing water to the inland desert, or clearing lowland forests in New Zealand for dairy farming, permeate both countries' settler stories and they continue to 'frame' images of national identity (e.g. Barry Crump's *A Good Keen Man*, 1960). Bell suggests that New Zealanders (and possibly Australians?) have adopted two different versions of the romanticised landscape in claiming a distinctiveness in their identity. The landscape is 'either beautiful but potentially dangerous: sanctified, visited, enjoyed, photographed, then left; a vision to inspire. Or it is beautiful and beautifully cultivated, a tribute to both nature itself and to the efforts of human labour' (C. Bell 1996, 29).

The following quotation illustrates the connection between place and the collective imagination which finds expression in national identity:

national identity based on physical geography, and on idealisation of lifestyles within nature, is persistently used as our claim to fame ... Most [of the population] live in cities, well away from the sublime landscape. We know these cities are much like those of everywhere else while our nature isn't. Nature persists in the imagery that shows our difference, and is a reality that can be affirmed by a short drive out of town, reinforcing the aptness of these representations over those of city life. Perhaps it is because we feel we have little else to offer that nature gets such high mileage.[2]

An Australian reader of Bell's quotation might have conjured images of white sandy beaches, the red sand and vast skies of the outback, the bulk of Uluru, kangaroos, or perhaps the Great Barrier Reef. For New Zealand readers, it might be the jagged Southern Alps, thermal mud pools, the tumbling glaciers on the West Coast, or the kiwi. For readers from other countries different images will have sprung to mind – the point worth emphasising here is that we often associate our 'uniqueness' with reference to the distinctiveness of our place (even at a national level). The appeal to the 'specialness of our place', as distinct from all others, as a source of identity, is mirrored not only at a national level but is used by local councils and shires to promote the uniqueness and character of their particular location or region.

However, modern society is fragmented by increasing mobility, transient work arrangements and changing family and kinship formations. It has been argued that these changes mean that 'places are no longer the clear supports of our identity' (Morley and Robins 1993, 5). As alluded to earlier this point has been extensively explored by the geographer Doreen Massey who has argued that places are open, porous and fluid rather than static and fixed. She argues that just as people have multiple identities so to do places.

Massey notes that in the post-modern society there is a line of thought which suggests that 'in the middle of all this flux, people desperately need a bit of peace and quiet – and that a strong sense of place, of locality, can form one kind of refuge from the hubbub' (Massey 1994, 151). However, she believes this may be little more than 'romanticized escapism from the real world' (p. 151). For Massey (2005) any sense of authentic place will remain elusive, for if modernity has taught us anything, it has taught us that there can be no rules for place. For people, place happens, but in that happening it is already changing into something else.

Massey argues that 'what gives a place its specificity is not some long internalized history but the fact that it is constructed out of a particular constellation of social relations, meeting and weaving together at a particular locus' (1994, 154). The passage through, and settlement of, places by different peoples with different purposes illustrates the fluidity of meanings ascribed to places. By way of example, the New Zealand government has recently tabled a discussion document concerning mining in land currently in National Parks. This has sparked strong debate as environmentalists, local residents, economists, miners, and politicians stake their claims as to what these places represent (economic opportunity or environmental disaster?). This provides a good example of Massey's assertion that places have no singular unique identity. Massey suggests that rather than viewing places as areas with specific boundaries

> they can be imagined as articulated moments in networks of social relations and understandings, but where a large proportion of those relations, experiences and understandings are constructed on a far larger scale than what we happen to define for that moment as the place itself, whether it be a street, or a region or even a continent. (pp. 154–155).

Viewing places and sites of contestation and change, within broader social relationships and interactions, problematises simplistic attributions of identity with place. Massey contends that the anti-essentialist concept of place undermines claims that there is an immutable 'authentic character of any particular place' (1994, 121).

However appealing it may be, it is difficult to argue, from the position outlined above, that it is possible to construct a coherent and essential sense of personal or social identity by a simple recourse to a place. What Massey draws our attention to is the interconnectedness of social relations and the changing, contested meanings attributed to places. Place, as 'open and porous networks of social relations' (Massey 1994, 121) recasts the role that places play in identity formation and creates space for individuals and groups to 'become' in a creative rather than prescriptive manner.

The role of place, as a source of identity, is overlooked or only acknowledged tangentially in outdoor education text books, the notable exception being *Outdoor and Experiential Learning: Views from the Top*. In that text, Brian Wattchow (2005) suggested that in discussing our relationship to place we need to move beyond the simplistic descriptor that outdoor education is about learning relationships in, about or for the environment/nature. He has suggested that, 'An Outdoor Education in *experiencing* relationships *in place* is better, as it signals the fundamental importance of experiencing and the crucial contribution of place in identity formation and sustenance' (Wattchow 2005, 14).

If, as mentioned earlier, 'a sense of place is a fundamental human need' (Park 1995, 320), then we could do well to understand our own and others' values in relation to places and its meanings for how we construct and understand our identities. To treat outdoor places as merely a venue or vacant space for learning impoverishes their potential for education. Important questions and themes for a more place-responsive outdoor education practice begin to emerge here. Outdoor places, like home places, have a vital role to play in the development and sustenance of identity. These places are always produced via a set of complex human-land interactions that is larger than the individual. Outdoor places need to be approached with a sense of humility: What has happened here? Who has lived here? How have they lived here? What seems to be happening to this place now – how is it changing? What is my role in that change? How we experience a place is shaped through our modes of travel, how long we are prepared to linger in a place, whether we put down roots or explore our origins in a place, and how much effort we are prepared to make to get to know and empathise with locals.

## The body in place

In his phenomenology of the place experience, Edward Casey (1993) is prepared to extend a notion of Heideggerian dwelling-as-residing with a dwelling-as-wandering in wild-places. A wild-place has different connotations to a wilderness. Indeed, for Casey, an *embodied implacement* as a wanderer in the wild is possible if we become attuned to the sensing body and its fundamental significance in the place experience. Such a belief leads us to the consideration of corporeality and the role it plays in the lived experience of outdoor places.

In the previous chapter we discussed how the role of the body in learning is potentially sidelined in outdoor adventure education in two ways. First, in an adventure paradigm the location utilised may be treated as an arena, where human action in a novel terrain is directed towards personal achievement at the expense of sensing where one actually is. Second, the preference given to cognition in experiential learning cycles may discount other more embodied ways of knowing as participants struggle to articulate how they felt about the experience. In this chapter we have already spent

Embodied ways of knowing

some time considering how place results from a complex amalgam of geophysical qualities in the environment, community interaction and cultural beliefs that develop for a place. Now, we must return to the role of the body in the experience of place.

We have suggested that places are, in part, a product of culture. But places, especially how learners begin to sense a place, need to be considered at another level to be a personal, intimate and embodied encounter. Outdoor educators, with their preference for learning about the outdoor world experientially, have a powerful pedagogic advantage over many other subject areas. We believe that the sensing body is a pathway to embodied knowing that is currently under-utilised in outdoor education practice. In addition, when we make ourselves aware of the sensing body in learning, we immediately become aware again of how crucial place is to the educational experience. For body and place are inextricably linked.

In their book *Places Through the Body* (1998) Nast and Pile argue that a consideration of place immediately implicates the body, and vice versa.

> Both bodies and places need to be freed from the logic that says that they are either universal or unique. Instead, it would be better to think of the ways in which bodies and places are understood, how they are made and how they are interrelated, one to the other – because this is how we live our lives – through places, through the body. (p. 1)

The Australian historian William Lines, (2001) recalling his childhood in Western Australia, wrote

> My body linked me to the material. I ached fiercely with attachment and love for the wild. I walked barefoot through the swamp and felt water and algae close on my legs and mud ooze through my toes; I walked barefoot through the sandy scrublands of the coastal plain and felt needles and barbs prick the soles of my meet and cut my shins; I walked barefoot through the rocky forest of the Darling Scarp and felt the pressure of the stone underfoot. (p. 14)

Lines (2001) has argued that we develop an everyday metaphysics for what we sense is real through our bodily interactions with the world. 'I learnt about Australia through my body' he writes, 'through what I could sit on, touch, taste, see, breath, smell, and move within. My surroundings gave me my reality. My corporeality incorporated the world's corporeality' (p. 65). Lines rejects the postmodern belief that our experiences of the world are only a matter of our enculturation. The corporeal experience of place is not something necessarily lost as the child matures. Rather it becomes suppressed in the adult world of the mind, a process we see promoted by current methods in experiential education.

Casey's (1993) notion of embodied implacement is a vital addition to Heidegger and Relph's theories of place. It gives a clearer notion of how we are always indebted to the experiential qualities of life. Together they provide a valuable insight into our potential work as educators in the outdoors. It is learners' bodies that remain the ultimate centre of their learning. Learning cannot be considered separate from their embodied interactions and connections with place. Thus there is the possibility of a mutualism of embodied and reflective/interpretive learning which establishes the pedagogical boundaries of an educational practice that occurs within a place. We might think of this as a pedagogical meeting ground between body, mind and place. It is important that, as educators, we develop a good understanding of this phenomenon.

The French philosopher Maurice Merleau-Ponty suggested that there is a rich vein of experience that may be tapped that exists beneath all of our social and cultural layers of interpretation. There can be no individualistic, disembodied, detachable consciousness from either the body or the world. This does not deny that we also exist in social and cultural worlds, and 'our perspective is determined not only by space and time, but by history and culture' (Matthews 2002, 21). The influence of society upon our perspective places a limitation on us, but this limitation does not extend to the world itself. Merleau-Ponty did not argue that we should dismiss science, geography, philosophy or any other knowledgeable system humans have developed in order to know about the world. Rather he asserted that we should consider the world of experience prior to our worlds of abstract meanings. Matthews (2002) summarised Merleau-Ponty's views on this point.

> Because we are active within the world, that world must present itself to us as meaningful; but because we are also finite and within the world, those meanings must always also be ambiguous and the world must transcend our capacity to know and understand it. Reality is 'inexhaustible', and there can be no possibility of the philosopher, or any other human being, arriving at a final 'system' that will make ultimate sense of it all. (pp. 20–21)

Outdoor education practice exits, then, in the fine balance between the pre-discursive and pre-conceptual sensual experience of the learner, the ability to reflect rationally upon their experiences, and in the acts of representation of those experiences and reflections. This sounds similar to the action-reflection divide that we critiqued in the last chapter. The difference is in stressing the interdependency of each.

Rather than promote a mind-body separation, a mutualism of body-mind is celebrated. And the learner's body-mind becomes deeply enmeshed with the place that is experienced. As outdoor educators it is at once both sobering and liberating to realise that we cannot teach embodied implacement. We can only shape the opportunity and guide learners towards the possibility of this kind of experiential encounter. How then should we consider the phenomenon of the body in a way that will assist in developing new approaches to practice in outdoor education?

More than any other of the phenomenological philosophers Merleau-Ponty (2002) established that the essence of our experiences in the world is one of an embodied-relatedness.

> We witness every minute the miracle of related experience, and yet nobody knows better than we do how this miracle is worked, for we are ourselves this network of relationships. (p. xxiii)

As Seamon (1979, 47) suggested, 'movements are learned when the body has understood them, and this understanding can be described as a set of invisible threads which run out between the body and the world with which the body is familiar'. In other words, an important aspect of embodied emplacement has to do with a person's ability to live and move in ways that are harmonious with their place. Without the ability of the body to learn to live and move in this way, we would not be able to function in day-to-day life. Merleau-Ponty's conceptualised this notion as the 'body-subject'. This raises concerns about outdoor education practice when participants are continually taken to novel terrains, or are given increasingly challenging tasks to complete. In this scenario learners never become comfortable with their situation. Instead, they feel like they are living, or rather clinging, to a risky edge. A sensation of being on the uncertain frontier is felt rather than being at ease. What are the consequences of taking learners to novel terrain, and how do they adapt? How do we sustain ourselves in familiar and unfamiliar places? These are important questions for outdoor educators.

What is most important here from an educational standpoint is a renewed belief in the value of embodied ways of knowing. This is an important element that could give outdoor education an alternative and distinctive pedagogical advantage. Rather than become increasingly like other subjects that strive to prescribe, abstract, objectify and evaluate learning (cognitive learning at least) within an inherently conservative education system, outdoor education could be renewed around a set of beliefs and practices immersed in the significance of outdoor places and how learners experience them. Rather than persist with an adherence to some rather time-worn ideas about adventure, novelty and risk, outdoor educators might actively seek collaborations with other educators who also resist the disembodiment and decontextualisation of knowledge from the learner's knowing and experience.

Outdoor educators may then find strong allies in the creative arts (such as dance, drama, art), which also rely very much upon the body as a medium of expression and learning. Strong similarities could also be drawn with the humanities where, as we have seen with cultural geography, historical fieldwork and creative writing for example, it is possible to commit to exploring and experiencing the richness and potential of a topic and/or place as much as is humanly possible.

## Conclusion

In this chapter we have discussed the foundations of place scholarship and attempted to consider them in relation to the challenges facing outdoor educators, guides and participants. At the most fundamental level we have made a case for place as a central and crucial component of living, including young people's experiences within education. People and places always exist in mutual bonds of interdependence. Both people and places have a physical reality, but it is the identities of both people and places that are continually emerging as an unfolding, interdependent phenomenon – always evolving, always becoming. As the future of places is inherently linked with how humans experience them, there is tremendous potential for outdoor education to make a significant contribution to the wellbeing of both people and places.

In the introductory chapter we mentioned the significance of educating for a changing world and how learners need to be able to critique, and contribute to, the community of which they are a part. We have not written about the forces, such as global climate change or political and economic instability, which will impact and perhaps even accelerate learners' experiences of their world changing. Regardless of whether the forces that bring change are global, national or regional, they will always be experienced by people locally. That is the central argument we are making in this chapter. People, local places and the experience of change are indivisible.

For this reason we turn in the next chapter to current accounts of place-based practices in education and to recent research conducted in outdoor education that has considered the significance of place in learners' experiences. This sharpens the focus considerably on the likely issues and challenges facing outdoor education as it moves from contemporary approaches towards an alternative philosophical foundation and renewed forms of practice.

*Chapter 4*

# The Emergence of Place in Outdoor Education

In this chapter we discuss the emergence of place as a pedagogical concept within both broader education and outdoor education discourses. Place-based pedagogies have been discussed in educational literature in North America for some time. As we have already argued, 'place' and 'sense of place' have become popular concepts, and a number of writers and practitioners have begun to explore connections between pedagogy and place. In the process of writing this book we came across several articles in teacher journals where 'place lessons' were presented as 'mapping your neighborhood' style lessons in geography, or 'recording local stories' approaches in history. While these initiatives are encouraging, we argue that they do not yet represent a view of curriculum, teaching and learning where place provides a significant philosophical and pedagogical foundation. Put another way, when an interest in place is 'retro-fitted' to current educational curricula as a theme or a lesson it is likely to be treated as just another topic to cover in geography, history, English or even outdoor education. This approach is unlikely to produce a new educational philosophy or significant reforms to pedagogic practices. It does not represent the kind of fundamentally different way of *doing* education, and of learners *experiencing* their learning in localised contexts that we are arguing for in this book. If place is fundamental to human identity and experience, then it needs to be thought about in ways outside of current, fragmented ways of learning through the disciplines. At the very least within the educational context place must be multi-disciplinary, or better, trans-disciplinary and experiential in character.

Place is not a thing, an object. It is, as we discussed in the previous chapter, an unfolding phenomenon. But it can, at different levels, be studied and reflected upon in terms of how it might influence practice. Therefore, in educational contexts, place is best understood as a meeting of learners' experiences, the ideas and ideals of their group and culture, and the geophysical reality of the site of learning itself. This view of place gives outdoor education practitioners a unique advantage. Arguably outdoor educators have fewer disciplinary constraints than educators in many other disciplines and perhaps greater exposure to experiential approaches to teaching, guiding and learning. Yet, as we have already discussed in chapter three, there are a number of barriers and likely resistances that will be encountered in any move towards a place-responsive curriculum and pedagogy in contemporary outdoor education. One of these resistances, perhaps the most significant, requires further elaboration here.

It may be all too easy to think of the concept of place as a kind of substitute for nature and/or community in the popular understanding of outdoor education as learning about self, others and nature. We have already discussed the existence of a preference for a romanticised view of wild nature and a Utopian sense of the small-scale community in outdoor education. However, we feel that it is necessary to start this chapter by extending the discussion of how educators' and learners' relationships with the natural world have been represented in outdoor education discourse in recent years, particularly by academics striving to develop and articulate new theoretical and practical approaches to outdoor education. There are elements of this professional discourse that is useful, yet there are also some important differences between these proposals and the case we are making for a place-responsive pedagogy. Therefore we begin this chapter with a discussion about how and why the concept of place-responsiveness provides a distinct pedagogical difference to outdoor education directed towards developing critical and sustainable relationships with nature.

We then discuss the contribution of broader educational discourses on place-based education. There is considerable potential for outdoor educators to both benefit from, and contribute to, the broader debate about the role of place-based and place-responsive learning experiences in education. The last topic we consider in the chapter is the emergence of a nascent body of research literature about place and sense of place in studies conducted into outdoor education practice in Australia, New Zealand and overseas. Several crucial concepts about the potentials and pitfalls of a pedagogy of place are developed which are carried forward as guiding questions into the case study chapters that follow.

## Outdoor education, nature relations and place

In a recent review of the aims and purposes represented in outdoor education textbooks, Andrew Brookes (2004) identified three 'absolutist tendencies'. First, authors of the textbooks focused almost exclusively on individual learning. Second, consideration of the local geography was either absent or regarded as being the same as 'the outdoors' (i.e. a taken-for-granted or considered a 'blank' space in which to perform). We have already discussed how problematic and pervasive the notions of individualism and a universal view of the outdoors as natural space can be in education. Finally, Brookes (2004) claims that the educational aims of outdoor education represented in the texts were largely abstract and based upon broad generalisations. He also noted the lack of any serious attempts to connect with wider educational discourses.

Thus there seems to be an insularity in much of the programming and educational literature of outdoor education (see M. Brown 2008a for a further example of this lack of engagement). Outdoor education is treated, both by practitioners and some of its advocates, as a discipline detached from the rest of the learner's educational journey. To the field's detriment it would appear that all too often outdoor education seems to occur in a bubble, insulated from broader educational debate and discussions about curricula and pedagogy.

Peter Higgins (2003), for example, believes that while there has been an increase in debate among academics about the impact of globalisation and modernity upon outdoor education practice, there has been little representation of this within practitioner-focused journals and associations. In Higgins' view, practitioners may be dangerously unaware of how their practices may be inadvertently subject to these wider forces. Humberstone, Brown and Richards (2003) point out that "'old" romanticised ideals of outdoor leisure are becoming reconstructed through the demands of "mass market" consumers for "authentic adventure"' (p. 7). Thus the modern outdoor adventure educator sees and seeks nature as 'an assault course, gymnasium or puzzle to be resolved and controlled. It is a resource to be commodified instead of a home to which to relate' (Loynes 2002, 114).

An outdoor education that appears to deny place through the Romantic desire for 'wild' nature, misunderstandings about the corporeal nature of embodied experience, and the erasure of local meanings to form novel adventure spaces, maintains universalist assumptions about knowledge, values and practices that are held throughout education and wider Western culture (Orr 1992, 1994; Bowers 1993). The education system, of which outdoor education is a part, has become crucial in the initiation of young people into modern views of knowledge, experience and forms of rationality. Teachers, leaders and guides, through their own education and training, may themselves have become authorities in this system and perpetuate its establishment, whether it be in the classroom or the outdoors. Such a system silences more basic questions about learners' experiences of particular outdoor places.

The rhetorical shift towards a critical orientation in outdoor education which focuses on the development of sustainable relationships with nature is evident within the professional outdoor education literature and can be traced through a series of academic papers. This discourse dates from the 1990s and we will be discussing the contribution of several of these influential papers in this chapter. Perhaps this critical interest in 'nature' is the latest iteration of the goals and purposes of outdoor education articulated in the Dartington conference and other forums since. Yet this discourse has developed amidst a growing awareness, outside of outdoor education, of the diversity of meanings that Western industrial cultures have for 'nature' (see, for example, Chambers 1984; Heller 1999; Marshall 1992; Schama 1995; Soper 1995; Soule and Lease 1995). This list of possible 'natures' is long and is seemingly inexhaustible: nature as unknowable universe, Magna Mater, wild kingdom, Gaia, pristine wilderness, picturesque landscape, gymnasium, temple, sunship, ecological process, habitat, environment, and so on. Soper (1995) considers that each of these social constructions tends to be representative of two basic views. On one hand there are those that promote a 'nature endorsing' discourse of ecological reality. On the other, are the postmodernists whose 'nature-scepticism' doubts that any such reality can exist beyond its cultural inscriptions. Both perspectives, Soper (1995) argues 'need to be more conscious of what their respective discourses on nature may be ignoring or politically repressing' (p. 8). Lease (1995) offers a slightly different, but equally illuminating perspective on our collective struggle to come to grips with the panoply of views about what nature is or might be.

> Western thought had culminated in an impasse regarding nature. Was it the material world of experience, experiences that could be shared, repeated, and tested; or was it the ineffable, invisible, and transcendent world of divine origins, available only to acts of faith … After wrestling with the notion of nature for well over two thousand years, Western tradition had come up dry: neither an identification of the human species with nature nor a strict dichotomy between the two proved ultimately successful. (pp. 8–9)

In broader terms this impasse has been described by Lakoff and Johnson (1980) as a standoff between two central myths of Western philosophy, the myths of objectivism and subjectivism. In the first myth humans believe that objective reality can be proven if the human errors of illusion, perception, judgment, emotion and personal and cultural bias can be avoided. It is believed that words and language, as the main medium through which we express our experience of reality, can have fixed meanings if metaphoric, poetic, fanciful, rhetorical and figurative language is avoided. Alternatively the myth of subjectivism, exemplified by the Romantic poets, proposes that in our everyday, practical activities 'we rely upon our senses to develop intuitions we can trust' (Lakoff and Johnson 1980, 188). Activities like poetry and art are seen to transcend rationality, taking us to a new level of awareness, a 'more important reality of imagination and feelings' (Lakoff and Johnson 1980, 188). Both myths are wrong, Lakoff and Johnson argue, but need each other. They are a binary pair where each position defines itself in opposition to the other. The impasse occurs when we cling to the belief system of one while rejecting the possibility of the other.

Within the space of this impasse nature has become a contested ground on which opposing ideological interests fight for the ascendancy of particular cultural and social meanings over others (Soule and Lease, 1995). Already we have seen that outdoor educators privilege certain interpretations of nature: nature as an *arena* where students experience personal development through challenging activity; or nature as a *venue* or *landscape* that can be appreciated and encountered aesthetically and for which we should develop some affinity, or nature as an *environment* in need of sustainable management practices by humans.

Brookes (1993) argues that outdoor education practices uncritically treat the 'bush' (a particularly Australian vernacular construction of nature) as a resource.

> Seen against an emerging backdrop of environmental degradation as the unintended outcome of subconscious attitudes, any outdoor education practice might appear to be just another form of assault on the bush. What hunting, grazing, mining, clearing, harvesting and the introduction of exotic plants and animals began, outdoor education and its cousin tourism will finish off. (p. 11)

We might assume from the above quotation that Brookes (1993) sees each outdoor education student as extracting his or her experiences from the 'bush', and he asks: 'What's in it for the bush? What's in it for the community?' (p. 11). Later Brookes (1994) characterises such approaches as 'short raids on the "bush" as strangers, rather than [as experiences that] develop a sense of place' (p. 31). That outdoors nature in Australia and New Zealand has been perceived as strange to European settlers and their descendants, and the negative consequences for both the environment and traditional cultures that followed as a result, has been well documented by environmental historians and anthropologists (Bolton 1981; King 2003; Lines 1991; McKenna 2002; Park 1995, 2006; Read 1996, 2000; Rose 1996, 2002, 2004; Seddon 1994; Sharp 2002; Sinclair 2001). David Tacey, a scholar of Jungian psychology, argues that the psychic estrangement from nature continues to be a major source of dislocation from place for settler Australians (1995, 2000, 2003).

### Searching for a metaphor: 'Nature as friend'

In searching for a way to encourage and reconnect outdoor educators and their students with nature, Brian Nettleton (1993) suggested that the relationship between humans and nature should be based on friendship. Nettleton highlights how friendship requires a reciprocal, diffuse and multifaceted relationship very different to a relationship of exploitation or distanced otherness.

> The natural world is seen as a friend and from the immediacy of daily interaction, and not seen by modernity as from afar, as an object or as an inanimate other; as a whole and not as a composite of clever fragmentary insights painstakingly gleaned from the measurable aspects of nature. (p. 19)

Nettleton's nature-as-friend metaphor should be admired for its sentiment. However, Seddon (1997) argues that while it is 'perhaps corrective for a society that has seen nature as the enemy to be told to see it as a friend … it is neither' (p. 20). Martin and Thomas (2000) attempted to further elaborate a model for human-nature relationships that extends Nettleton's nature-as-friend metaphor to one of interpersonal relationships. They develop their model based on the theoretical understandings of the constructs of human relationships (skills, concern, interaction, trust, knowing) and present it as a pedagogic tool to be considered by other educators who would like their students to move from a level of 'acquaintanceship' with nature to one of more 'intimate friendship'. Barriers to developing intimate friendship are seen to occur when participants experience fear and uncertainty. The authors conclude:

> For programs with a clear intent of initiating human-nature relationships, the activities and places selected need to be those which enable participants to easily develop a sense of safety, comfort and well

being – this may contrast with the high adventure goals and practices of more traditional outdoor programs. (Martin and Thomas 2000, 41)

Martin and Thomas' 'constructs of relationships' seem, like Nettleton's nature-as-friend, to be a little too anthropomorphic, a point the authors concede. When a person develops a relationship with another person they establish, as a result of experience, an intimate knowledge of the other's character, behaviour, idiosyncrasies and unique qualities. One of the difficulties inherent in a discussion of human-nature relationships within outdoor education is the tendency for 'nature' to remain an abstract and universalised concept. Any relationship between an individual person and nature is likely to be a one-sided affair. It is possible that we might feel a love for nature, but is unlikely that it will love us back. Instead, what we might experience is a reflection of our own desire where nature acts like a mirror (Cronon 1996). At its most extreme, the starry-eyed nature lover, like Narcissus in Greek mythology, is in danger of becoming stranded, unable to pull him or herself away from the beauty of his/her own reflection.

A second problem with the self/nature relations approach is that it potentially abrogates the responsibility to develop relationships with actual others in the outdoor places where the educational program is being enacted. Through placing an emphasis on 'developing an intimate relationship with nature there is the possibility that local people, their experiences and histories will be overlooked. An unintended outcome may be that it provides a cultural licence to pass local people by, not engaging with their often interesting and informative local stories and histories. In addition, we might ask, how might relationships with non-human others be conceptualised, explored and experienced? How do we relate to the chatter and song (two more anthropomorphisms) of birds in the forest as we lug our packs up the trail? Their song is, after all, probably a warning call easily interpreted by all in the forest but us, about the danger of a bunch of sweaty, noisy humans suddenly appearing in their home. People and other life forms do interact in significant and in potentially meaningful ways. The nature writer Barry Lopez (1986, 1988, 2003), for example, has explored this theme extensively.

Lopez has traced the complex interactions of people, animals and landscapes in specific North American locations for many decades. In doing so he draws upon scientific, historical, mythological, and anecdotal sources of information and blends these with his own experiences. Thus his accounts start by being grounded in a place as he draws upon experience and different knowledge systems to build up the complexity of the web of relations between people, animals and land. A potential criticism of Lopez, and other nature writers in the North American tradition, is that they tend to write about remote and seemingly intact wild places. There are, however, important exceptions. Aldo Leopold was writing over a half a century ago about experiences of land and nature as he attempted to rehabilitate a degraded piece of farmland in the sand counties of Wisconsin. Despite its limitations, the approach of the nature-writers would seem to be a more meaningful approach to the study of human/nature-relations than striving for something that is almost certainly unattainable – the individual on a quest to relate to the abstract and elusive concept of nature.

Several research studies in outdoor and environmental education seem to confirm the consequences of seeing outdoor education as engaging with the outdoors as a means to relate to nature (see, for example, Haluza-Delay 2001; Haskell 2000; Johnson 2004; Martin 2005), and its impact on participants. The ideal of wilderness continued to provide a potent cultural 'template' for teenage participants on a backcountry journey in North America (Haluza-Delay 2001). The result, suggests Randolph Haluza-Delay, is that the teenagers saw nature as being 'out there' and as a completely different kind of environment to that of their home in suburbia. David Johnson's (2004) study explored the activities and reflections of students from a Melbourne secondary school who visited the Gippsland Lakes region of Victoria for a ten-day program of sea kayak and sail training, environmental activities and an expedition. According to Johnson these adolescent students were already keenly aware of a perceived division between 'city' and 'nature'. The city was seen as frenetic, noisy, dirty, exciting, but also familiar. By way of contrast, students reflected that the outdoors was clean, quiet, relaxing and beautiful. Students reported that 'the Lakes' was a nice place to visit for a while, but they would not want to live there – it was too primitive. Peter Martin (2005) reported on research into university undergraduates' perceptions of nature, and how they changed during the years of their studies in outdoor education. These young adults were seen to be on a continuum from being alienated from nature, travelling through nature, caring for nature or becoming integrated with nature.

There remains in outdoor education, as Brookes (2004) has pointed out, a strong tendency to treat 'nature' or 'wilderness' as monolithic. In many ways this is the antithesis of what we mean by place. Where nature is experienced as universal, place is always encountered within the parameters of a particular location. Admittedly, humans inevitably experience both nature and place subjectively. But a focus upon place in learning keeps bringing our attention back to the local, to the specific meanings and experiences that are attached to our embodied experience. In doing so, learners will always be responding to both universal cultural ideas about 'nature' *and* the local, particular qualities of their encounter with a specific outdoor place.

Within a region we may be able to respond to many similarities. If, for example, we grew up and developed a depth of experience in one place on the southern coastline of Australia, we might find that we experience a sense of the familiar in many places that we visit from Cape Howe (the south eastern most point of mainland Australia) to Cape Leeuwin (the south western most point of mainland Australia). If we are walking on a southern beach we may accurately anticipate a change in weather as a cold front spins out of Antarctic waters and approaches us from the south-west. We take notice of the cloud progression and shifts in wind direction. We feel changes in temperature and humidity. We might put on our snorkelling gear and dive beneath the surface of the ocean and see a similar array of flora and fauna species stretching along thousands of kilometres of coastline. There will be changes of course but we know enough to accommodate them. We learn how to interpret this 5000km edge zone of the continent. But turn the corner at Cape Leeuwin and begin to travel north and the place suddenly feels unfamiliar to us. The southerly running Leeuwin Current brings warm water from the tropics and as a result there are many changes in both land and sea. What we know from our south coast experiences no longer seems enough. The geology, weather, climate, ecology all suddenly change dramatically. Human patterns of settlement also change. The very history of the place seems to be dramatically different. We have reached a boundary between places. If we choose to cross it we need to begin the process of relearning what it means to be a local again if we want to make much sense of the new places we experience.

So to research and talk about the universal qualities of nature and wilderness does provide us with some useful insights, but it is unlikely to be enough if we want to develop a stronger sense of the significance of the local and the particular. The temptation of universal and abstract notions such as 'nature' are that they seem precise and that it is possible to transport them from one location, or context, to another. But this is illusory. It is only part of the picture. Some ideas and understandings relocate, others do not. A strong debate being played out in farming in New Zealand at present illustrates this point. The desire to engineer ideal dairy farming conditions on the dry and windswept Canterbury Plains, through extensive irrigation and water

*[handwritten marginalia: these are the things that make me feel that I am connected to a place]*

management strategies, is a dramatic manifestation of this desire to replicate an idealised nature.

Outdoor educators would be better to shift their focus away from the abstraction of nature to the particulars of a place, and should understand why a particular place matters to their students. Some of these places may be places where the primeval qualities of nature seem more evident than the marks of culture. But, as we discussed in the last chapter, in almost all locations, even this is an illusion. As Geoff Park (1995, 2006) demonstrates so clearly in the remnant lowland forests of New Zealand, even in the most wild-like places, the evidence of human occupation and how it has impacted on and changed the landscape, is there for those who take the time to learn to look for it. Similarly, in the most cultured of landscapes, Park finds evidence of the primeval life force of wild nature, constantly trying to re-establish itself. A focus upon a particular place collapses the illusion of boundaries between culture and nature. Outdoor educators need to understand that increased competence in interpreting places requires specific pedagogic strategies. As outlined in the previous chapter, the empathetic insider draws upon all of their senses and disciplined study skills to get as close as possible to the insider's experience of a place.

## Critical outdoor education

Peter Martin (1994, 1995, 1998, 1999) has argued that outdoor education should promote critical reflection on human-nature relationships: 'I am a critical outdoor educator. For me, developing sustainable relationships with nature is the ultimate good' (Martin 1999, 14). It is a laudable aspiration, but is this a realistic goal for outdoor educators? There are several reasons why such proposals for a critical outdoor education for sustainable nature-relations should be approached with a degree of caution. Critical social theory is summarised by Macauley (1996) as being characterised by a 'critical perspective on technology, power, scientism, and instrumental reason along with an opposition to exploitative capitalist social relations' (p. 2). According to Carr and Kemmis (1986), the enacting of social critical theory into practice requires:

> a social process that combines collaboration in the process of critique with the political determination to act to overcome contradictions in the rationality and justice of social action and social institutions. A critical social science will be one that goes beyond critique to critical praxis; that is, a form of practice in which the 'enlightenment' of actors comes to bear directly in the transformed social action. (p. 144)

It is the everyday encounter with, and the transmission of social inequity in all its forms and the cultural mechanisms that make this process persistent, that critical theorists in education want to interrogate, challenge and change. Such an approach has been used effectively, for example, to highlight the hidden social curriculum in health and physical education (HPE). The example of how a critical theory has been applied in HPE is worth exploring in more detail. Tinning (2002) and Macdonald (2002) draw on a discourse spanning the last three decades (by Giroux, Bain, Kirk and Fernandez-Balboa, to name a few) in examining issues of power, privilege and oppression in the hidden curriculum of HPE. Interestingly the ascendancy of a critically-inspired social justice agenda in physical education, Tinning argues, 'now behoves university teacher education programs in Australia to actually set about teaching student teachers how to implement a HPE curriculum that is coherent with social justice principles that are inscribed in contemporary policy and curriculum documents' (2002, 229). Yet Tinning notes difficulties that should be of interest to critical outdoor educators. He describes the resistance of undergraduate physical education students to the critical agenda suggesting that their desire for technical competence and certainty rather than ambiguity, even if that sense of certainty is largely itself an illusion, were significant points of resistance. Tinning cites research where physical education undergraduate students, by and large, rejected the overtures of the socially-critical agenda in their teacher education training as they confronted the seemingly more immediate demands of developing the knowledge and technical and pedagogic competence they felt their profession required.

There is an important lesson here for those who would endorse a critical agenda (for sustaining nature) in outdoor education. The ability to critique is not enough if we want to change practice, and practice is always experienced locally. Viable alternative forms of practice have to be proposed, experienced by educators and learners, evaluated and reported on, if the critique of contemporary practice is not to ring hollow. Gaps between rhetoric and reality need to be closed. As we have seen, it is too simplistic to make a strong case for human/nature-relations in outdoor education as a guiding principle. Nature, as a concept is too complex, culture bound and disputed to provide a meaningful foundation for pedagogic decision-making. In addition, critical approaches in education have tended to focus on social rather than ecological injustices – perhaps for the very reason just mentioned.

While it is clear that social justice issues (gender, sexuality, race, equality of access, and so on) are gathering momentum in outdoor education discourses (see for example, Humberstone; Brown; Richards 2003, Warren 1999), it is not clear that a socially critical agenda can be readily extended to include a critical pedagogy for relating to nature. Gruenewald (2003b) warns that

> Critical pedagogy can work to reinforce cultural beliefs ... that underlie ecological problems and that are reproduced throughout conventional education: namely, individualism, the belief in the progressive nature of change, and anthropocentrism. (p. 4)

Such an approach avoids the more difficult task of negotiating practical solutions locally from a socio-ecological orientation (Mulligan and Hill 2001), or through a critical pedagogy of place (Gruenewald 2003b), which would appear to hold greater potential for a place-responsive pedagogy. What is required for outdoor education to be an effective form of cultural criticism, according to Payne (2002), is a more earnest '"reflexive turn" about its "own" activities and constructions of experience, learning, education and nature' (p. 17). Brookes (1994) also remains cautious about the limits of a critical approach.

> Ecologically responsive experience is negotiated with a particular place, using our bodies and all our senses, and is (necessarily) mediated by culture ... We can tell of the experience later (like a novelist), and interpret its cultural dimension (like a critic), but rational theory cannot wholly script, nor wholly explain, the experience. (p. 32)

In summary, then, we contend that the emergence of a discourse for relating to nature-as-friend or for a critical outdoor education that focuses on sustainable human-nature relations, while corrective to persistent interpretations of outdoor places (as arena or wilderness, for example), does not acknowledge how people actually live in and experience the world. The anthropologist Clifford Geertz (1996) reminds us that 'no one lives in the world in general' (p. 256). This emerging discourse in outdoor education has, no doubt, moved the profession in the right direction. But, we argue, another significant step is needed for it to provide a useful pedagogic strategy that changes practice and which will close the gap between rhetoric and reality. That step is, conceptually at least, a relatively simple one. We need to step back from the apparent grandeur of nature to embrace the mundane, everyday experience of particular outdoor places.

Very little outdoor education practice has been researched to assess the role of place and how it is encountered and experienced (or not) by outdoor education participants. Alistair Stewart (2004b) neatly articulates how problematic this may yet prove to be.

> While the idea [of relationships with nature] is commendable, without consideration or acknowledgment of the place, culture, context or situation of an experience it could be argued that this is another form of colonialism, or neo-colonialism perhaps. I am fearful that our colonial history has produced a blind-spot in how we seek to relate to 'nature,' for 'nature' is again subjected to our desire for 'mastery' in our attempt to connect to it. (p. 47)

Educators, and outdoor educators, have fallen into step with the other groups in society in promoting a nature-endorsing argument. Place, a more appropriate everyday human scale phenomenon, continues to be too close to be seen by most educators. Why? According to David Orr (1992), educators have failed to see much significance in understanding, or attempting to teach, place. He explains that 'place is nebulous to educators because to a great extent we are deplaced people for whom immediate places are no longer sources of food, water, livelihood, energy, materials, friends, recreation or sacred inspiration' (p. 126). The typical curriculum, according to Orr, is based upon abstraction, which disconnects people from 'tangible experience, real problems, and the places where we live and work' (p. 126). Outdoor education, in its difficult quest to forge sustainable relationships with nature, is in danger or becoming just another example of this typically placeless approach to curriculum and pedagogy – brimful of good intent, but exceedingly difficult to put into practice.

So we have reached a turning point. We must now begin the journey back to place. This becomes the focus for the remainder of the book. We begin with examining what has been written about place-based education and an analysis of recent research into outdoor education where place is acknowledged as having a role to play in participants' experiences. Together, these begin to shed some initial light on the challenges that must be overcome if outdoor educators are to develop an alternative, place-responsive form of practice.

## Place-based education

Much of the writing on place-based education has come out of the United States (see, for example, Gruenewald 2003a; Gruenewald and Smith 2008; Hutchinson 2004; Smith, 2002). Other writers have discussed similar ideas using terms such as 'ecological literacy' (Orr 1992) and 'ecological identity' (Thomashow 1996) which include elements of a place-responsive approach. Much of this discourse seems to feed off of the literary tradition of North American nature writing. In particular, writers such as Henry David

Thoreau, John Muir, Aldo Leopold, Rachel Carson, Annie Dillard, amongst others, are often cited as providing model examples of multidisciplinary and experiential inquiry into living simply in response to a place. Thoreau's *Walden*, for example, is a revered book in North American culture, 'a mosaic of philosophy, natural history, geology, folklore, archeology, economics, politics, education, and more' (Orr 1992, 125). Yet, as we have seen, nature writing is not without its limitations in terms of depicting and valorising the author's own narrative as an individual seeking contact with the wild. The author, like Thoreau in his year living beside Walden Pond, goes to the edge of the 'civilised' world, experiences the rawness and wildness of nature, and reports back.

David Orr (1992) and Mitchell Thomashow (1996) have begun the process of articulating an alternative argument for the aims, intents and practices in education that respond to a moral ecological imperative. The approach proposed by these authors is to examine and respond to those cultural forces that continue to cause damage to ecological systems on which communities depend. Orr (1992) refers to ecological literacy both in terms of what is required to become learned (ie to be literate) in how ecological systems function. But he also argues that it is about experiencing the world in a particular way – having the desire to develop the 'capacity to observe nature with insight, a merger of landscape and mindscape' (p. 86). In the effort to develop ecological literacy Orr (1992) suggests that we need to open up a dialogue with nature. Thomashow argues that this may lead to 'a reconstruction of personal identity, so that people begin to consider how their actions, values, and ideals are framed according to their perceptions of nature' (1996, xiii). The reconstructed identity is then assumed to operate from a renewed ethical standpoint in the world. This Leopoldian form of thinking supports the eco-philosopher's famous dictum, a thing (a human decision or action) is seen to be right when it 'tends to preserve the integrity, stability, and beauty of the biotic community. It is wrong when it tends otherwise' (Leopold 1987, 225).

Both Orr and Thomashow acknowledge the crucial importance of place and community as appropriate settings for the kinds of ecological work that they are proposing. Though they draw extensively from a particular literary tradition that includes Muir, Thoreau, Leopold and others, their work, perhaps, marks a significant departure rather than continuation of this literary tradition. Notions of individualism, rationality and a preference for wildness are challenged and the work of providing alternatives is begun. Both argue that mainstream education is part of the problem. They make an overwhelming case for the need for educational reform as a part of a larger paradigmatic shift in cultural awareness and beliefs about how humans live within communal and ecological systems and habitats. However, the scale of eco-revolution they appear to be advocating seems unlikely in the near term. Orr and Thomashow's arguments are compelling but place an enormous onus of responsibility on the shoulders of teachers and students to take on and overthrow doggedly persistent cultural beliefs and systemic educational and political structures. Perhaps a more practical and viable, albeit humble, alternative is to begin the process of reforming educational practice from within.

Gruenewald and Smith (2008) see place-based educational initiatives as part of 'a broader social movement reclaiming the significance of the local in the global age' (p. xiii). It is part of a 'new localism' that is a reaction to economic globalisation and corporate capitalism. Schooling and education can be seen as contributing to these globalising forces through centralised curricula, the promotion in schools of a national and international agenda at the expense of a regional and local one, and in the processes of preparing students to participate in the modern economy. Rather than getting muddy in a study of the local wetland, and perhaps even beginning the process of its ecological rehabilitation, students are more likely to be found online, gathering facts about the problems of deforestation in the Amazon. The hidden curriculum here favours students developing info-tech literacy, the notion that the global crisis is far away and the experiencing body as irrelevant in education.

Gregory Smith (2002) reviewed a number of place-based educational programs and initiatives in North American schools. He noted five distinct types of programs. First, cultural studies programs that involved students and teachers investigating local and historical phenomena that impacted on their lives. As a result they have produced oral histories, journalism, dramatic plays and so on. Such outcomes resonate with the traditions of oral culture and local storytelling. Second, Smith highlights local nature studies where students engage with and learn about nature in their local environment. Most outdoor and environmental educators will already be familiar with these style of programs. Third, both of the first two types of programs may be extended into 'real-world problem-solving'. Students identify a local issue or problem and develop strategies to solve it through taking action. The teacher works as facilitator with the students and possibly as a broker with outside groups. There is a strong sense of Dewey inspired democracy at work here, although there may be an assumption inherent in the belief that humans can practice a form of mastery over their situation by evaluating, solving and managing complex social and ecological phenomena that are simplified as environmental problems.

Smith also considers internships and work experience opportunities within schooling to have the potential to be run as placed-based learning experiences. What becomes important here is the realisation that local employment opportunities exist for students, particularly in rural and inner city locations, when they may have assumed that they would have to move away from home to pursue work or further study. Such experiences are seen to provide an alternative to the common belief in modern industrial and post-industrial societies that the population (especially young adults) will need to move, perhaps many times, to establish themselves. This capitalist assumption, as we noted earlier, may be manifest in outdoor adventure education where risky expeditions in search of opportunities far away from home are endorsed. Finally, Smith (2002) claims that opportunities for learners to be inducted into the community process of local decision-making can also be seen as examples of place-based education. This brings notions of place politics to the fore. As argued in the previous chapter, place is not simply a question of personal identification. Rather place emerges as a phenomenon that is manifest between person, location and community interactions.

These types of educational programs, and Smith cites many examples from across the United States, might be seen as grassroots resistance movements against both national agendas and globalising forces. They germinate and grow when they are nurtured locally. Like the slow food movement, perhaps, they are action based but suggestive of deeper philosophical roots.

> The attention to experience in place-based education locates its pedagogy in the broader traditions of experiential and contextual education and in the philosophical tradition of phenomenology. Places, and our relationship with them, are worthy of our attention because places are powerfully pedagogical. (Gruenewald and Smith 2008, 143)

What seems attractive about these initiatives from an educational perspective is that they engage with the learner's lived experience of their immediate world. They occur on an appropriate scale for the learner. They begin with the view of the learner as an inhabitant of a place. There is a home-grown feel about them: 'Let's consider our situation and make some realistic decisions together about what seems like an appropriate course of action.' 'Let's give it a go, be aware of what happens and modify things along the way if necessary.' 'When we finish it, we'll evaluate how we think we went and tell our local community about it.' 'We'll keep some records and stories about what we've done for ourselves and for others in the future.' 'We'll then be in a good position to think about what to do next.' Of course this somewhat simplifies the complex thinking and educational negotiations that go into many of these types of initiatives.

David Gruenewald (2003b) has previously argued that for these kind of educational experiences to have a deeper and longer lasting impact upon both the individual learner and society, they need to function as an education in decolonisation and re-inhabitation. David Orr (1992) contrasts the inhabitant of a locale with that of the resident. The resident, he argues, puts down few roots and establishes few real connections with his or her local environment. Although they may live part of their life there for a time, they do not *dwell* there. The inhabitant, on the other hand, lives in a reciprocated union with a place. Inhabitants live within an intricate web of associations (work, family, family history, leisure, belief systems and so on) with the place they call home. Gruenewald (2003b, 9) continues:

> Decolonization describes the underside of reinhabitation; it may not be possible without decolonization. If reinhabitation involves learning to live well socially and ecologically in places that have been disrupted and injured, decolonisation involves learning to recognize disruption and injury and to address their causes. From an educational perspective, it means unlearning much of what dominant culture and schooling teaches, and learning more socially just and ecologically sustainable ways of being in the world.

There are several possibilities here for outdoor educators. Clearly, outdoor educators who are sympathetic to the cause of educating for ecological sustainability (and, by association, with community sustainability) would see the potential to form alliances with other place-based or place-inspired educators and programs. Indeed, these educators have found a way to draw upon the *mutuality* of communal and ecological systems. Outdoor educators might also see themselves as bringing particular skills in experiential pedagogies and understandings of how to introduce students to, and teach in, outdoor settings. Smith (2002) notes that one of the hallmarks of place-based education is that 'the wall between school and community becomes much more permeable' (p. 593). Outdoor educators might position themselves as educators well-versed in assisting with learners making frequent transitions between schools (or other institutional settings), their larger communities and the ecologies within which they are located.

## Nascent research into place in outdoor education

As we mentioned at the outset of the book, John Cameron (2001) challenged outdoor educators to move beyond the dualistic separation of wilderness and everyday places. Yet there are only a handful of examples in Australian and New Zealand outdoor education literature which raise questions about outdoor pedagogy and look beyond outdoor educators' own discourses to those of 'place' for inspiration (M. Brown 2008b; Hill 2010a; Irwin 2010; Mullins 2007; Preston and Griffiths 2004; Stewart 2003a, 2003b, 2003c, 2004a, 2004b; Wattchow 2001a, 2004, 2005, 2007, 2008). This is not to say that place-based and place-responsive outdoor education programs do not exist. They almost certainly do. But little evidence of them has been published in the outdoor education literature (although the *New Zealand Journal of Outdoor Education* has recently published a special edition on this theme in 2010). This may be because peer-reviewed academic journals and conference proceedings tend to publish the writings of academics and postgraduate research students and much of this is theoretical in nature. Anecdotal accounts of programs written by practitioners are few and far between.

However, there are a small number of research studies that shed some light on the place dimension of outdoor education experiences (Cuthbertson 1999; Henderson 1995; Mullins 2007; Preston and Griffiths 2004; Raffan 1992; Stewart 2003a; Wattchow 2006, 2007, 2008). These studies stand to offer important directions and insights for outdoor education practice. Collectively, perhaps, they represent the first steps towards a deeper understanding of the role of local places in outdoor education experience. Wattchow's (2006) study of undergraduate student responses to river places in south-eastern Australia is reported on in one of the case study chapters to follow. The other studies are discussed in the following section of this chapter.

### Stepping back into place

Lou Preston and Amma Griffiths (2004) used a similar approach to Cameron (2003a) when they constructed a collaborative action research project with postgraduate outdoor and environmental education students that involved a minimum of four visits of two hours' duration to a 'natural place' selected by each participant. On each visit students explored the place using a different 'frame' – either the experiential, historical, scientific, or aesthetic. In between visits they attended classes and completed readings and tasks associated with these seemingly different ways of knowing their chosen place. Evidence from the study seemed to demonstrate how the experiential frame often provided a foundation in getting to know a new place. As one of the participants in the study noted:

> For me the biggest thing that helped me to connect was when we used the experiential frame and I went there and just observed and touched things. Using all my senses and looking from every angle is what worked best for me to get to know my place. (Preston and Griffiths 2004, 39)

Over repeated visits a layering effect resulted where the participants were surprised by feeling increasingly connected to 'their' place as they learnt about it through historical, scientific and aesthetic forms of inquiry. The authors of the study noted that the multi-pronged teaching approach which included discussion groups and journal keeping between visits were important components of overall learning. Yet, ultimately, Preston and Griffiths comment that 'we remain ambivalent about the durability of the connection once the influence of this intense experience recedes' (p. 43). Once again, it seems that students in the study have responded to the cultural idea of the separateness of nature from their everyday life. This student's honest summary should give cause for deep refection on the part of all outdoor educators.

> In many ways I have kept my experience and connection with place separate from my daily life. While I was there I was intrigued. I wanted to see everything, experience everything and understand everything. But I found that after returning from a visit I was quickly reconsumed with the events of my daily life … quickly slipped back into my societal role and continue to live as I do. (Preston and Griffiths 2004, 42)

Perhaps, like Cameron, who used similar student–place projects with social ecology students, regaining a child-like sense of wonder located in the sensual saturation of getting to know a place became an end in itself for the participants.

> I have observed a tendency amongst some students to take refuge in their chosen places, to derive personal comfort and significance from these visits, to revel in the newfound place attachment, and not to relate to the larger questions of sustainability, or cultural change, or control of economic power. It is a risk for educators that experiential learning can lead students so deeply into their internal experience that they are reluctant to emerge from it. (Cameron 2003a, 188)

## The land as teacher

James Raffan's (1992) doctoral thesis 'Frontier, homeland and sacred space: A collaborative investigation into cross-cultural perceptions of place in the Thelon Game Sanctuary, Northwest Territories', explored how the land may act as teacher in shaping people's perceptions of a place. While his study did not directly involve the collection or interpretation of data from an outdoor education program, Raffan made deliberate links to experiential outdoor pedagogy. Raffan's goal was to better understand the range of human responses to a specific place, the Thelon Game Sanctuary, in Canada's Northwest Territories, and how people learnt from the land. He collected data through an extensive range of interviews with indigenous and Euro-Canadians and also used his own poetic and artistic responses to the land on a six-week-long canoe journey to build insights into the person–place connection. It is this grounding of research activity in place, its local terrain and its people, that makes Raffan's work so instructive. While commenting on the work of phenomenological investigations into people's experiences of places by scholars such as Tuan, Buttimer, Relph and Seamon he observed:

> There is, however, a problem with the bulk of sense of place research, namely that it is rarely based on primary field work. Tuan, for example, writes lyrically about sense of place, drawing from the mythology and traditions of a wide diversity of cultures, but in the end, one cannot ground his work in any one place. As such, the concepts are strong, but the work is almost too clean, not concerning itself with politics or the interactions within and between people. (Raffan 1992, 23)

At the time of writing Raffan described the Thelon Game Reserve as a 'contentious piece of land' (1992, ii) in the central Northwest Territories of Canada. A number of indigenous groups were in the process of making territorial claims for the land and it had a complex history of European exploration. Indigenous peoples continue to live and hunt in the area and canoe companies guide expeditions with Euro-Canadian visitors. Raffan's dissertation was an exploration of how the land did, or did not, act as a teacher in terms of shaping perceptions about the Reserve as a place for these various groups of people. As a result of the study Raffan (1992, 1993) identified in the data four guiding concepts that constituted how the land acted as teacher. He advocates them for consideration by educators, as a means of exploring connections to outdoor places.

The first component that Raffan (1992, 382) refers to is the experiential component of a sense of place as the personal link to the land itself through experience, although he notes that not 'every experience leads to a deepening sense of place'. Raffan concluded that dependence on the land for survival necessitated a much deeper attention to land, 'an exponential jump in magnitude' (p. 384), and thus a deeper sense of place than resulted, for example, from a self-contained canoe journey. Raffan calls the second component the toponymic sense of place. This refers to the origin and significance of place names and the process of naming places. The third component relates a narrative sense of place and how stories about the land came to be, and the cultural significance of oral traditions, and tales of travelling the land: 'What sets apart [indigenous] from most Euro-Canadian narrative is that native narrative is set into the land-knowledge triangle, and integrated into the mix of place names and personal experience that has for many years been used by elders to teach young people about land and survival' (1992, 381–382). Raffan (1992) describes the land knowledge triangle as an embodiment of three ways of knowing: 'place names, land related stories, and personal experience living, hunting and trapping on the land' (p. 370). The final component Raffan describes is the numinous, a sense of divine presence in spiritual encounters with the land. Such a response by the author seems to result from the indigenous participants in the study who still retained mytho-poetic relations with their lands. A numinous response was far less evident among Euro-Canadian participants.

For Raffan, each of these concepts differentiated ways that people were potentially linked to, and learnt from, place within the holistic concept of 'the land as teacher'. Even though much of Raffan's study was based on an ethnographical inquiry into indigenous peoples, he found that these dimensions of the place experience held for some, but not all, Euro-Canadians who visited the region. The influence of Raffan's canoe journey and his poetic and artistic responses to the land and the participants in his study cannot be underestimated. Like Geoff Park's descriptions of his explorations of the remnant lowland forests of New Zealand, the reader becomes aware that the sensing body of the author/researcher plays an important role in the production of the final text. The writer is not a disembodied and invisible authority. Instead, the reader encounters a storyteller drawing upon all of their faculties to try to work their way inside a place and take us, the reader, with them.

People's experiences of places, their spiritual or numinous encounters, the names and naming of outdoor places, and the stories that people both tell and listen to in a place, provide outdoor educators with important clues in thinking about what a place-responsive form of practice might look like. However, Raffan (1992) also sounds a note of caution when he concludes:

"People's experiences of places, their spiritual or numinous encounters, the names and naming of outdoor places, and the stories that people both tell and listen to in a place, provide outdoor educators with important clues in thinking about what a place-responsive form of practice might look like."

It is possible, or so it would seem from the Euro-Canadian accounts, for a person to visit the place with an outfitter on a guided trip, or even on their own trip with perspective narrowed to the river corridor exclusively and/or with sight shortened to map references only, and to return with no appreciable new insights or observation of what the land was like or what the land had to offer. (p. 382)

## Researching the outdoor education journey from a place perspective

The studies by Henderson (1995) into outdoor travel and guiding, Cuthbertson (1999) into expeditionary encounters with place, and Stewart (2003a) into environment specific learning while on a three-week outdoor journey, were all concerned with the experiences of undergraduate university students on extended outdoor field trips. There are several overlapping qualities in these three studies. Henderson and Cuthbertson both completed studies using an inductive, qualitative methodological approach and both adopted a socially critical orientation. Cuthbertson and Stewart's inquiries were both case studies of specific field programs, whereas Henderson's was a retrospective account based on data collected from multiple programs. All utilised participant-written accounts of experiences and the researcher's (as leader/guide) observations, reflections and interpretations. Cuthbertson was the only researcher to also utilise interviews as a means of gathering data, whilst Henderson was the only researcher to conduct a 'member check' with participants of his research findings and interpretations. Collectively, their findings and interpretations add further to the framework provided by Raffan (1992, 1993).

'What does it mean to be "OF" a place?' asks Henderson (1995, 33).

> It is certainly a far cry from let's 'overcome' this route, 'challenge this whitewater,' 'beat this mountain,' 'study the particulars of this setting or phenomena.' Perhaps it is a greater traveller's challenge to be 'still' and come to see really where you are. (p. 33)

Henderson collected and interpreted student journal entries written over ten years, based on two long-standing field programs – an eight-day canoe tour and a five-day snow shoe trip, both in eastern Canada. The journeys seemed to encourage heritage values of travel and exploration in the Canadian outdoors. Stewart's (2003a) study of Australian participants on a three-week long bushwalk was designed to gain insight into the experiences and learning gained from travelling through three different, but neighbouring environments: 'It is not an inquiry into 'people' alone, or of a certain environment, but rather of a particular people encountering particular landscapes' (Stewart 2003a, 26). Participants in Stewart's study traversed alpine country between Mount Jagungal and the Main Range of the Australian Alps, the sub-alpine country around The Pilot and Chimneys, and then an area around a section of the Snowy River, as they walked between food drops. The participants on this walk maintained a field journal to capture their own reflections but also to respond to a series of guiding questions (about outdoor leadership, community/social interactions and the natural environment). The participants in Cuthbertson's (1999) study faced possibly the most arduous physical challenges in their outdoor expeditions; a month long back country skiing trip and, a few months later, a six week sea kayaking journey. Both of these expeditions were conducted in western Canada. Cuthbertson's research began with a simple and humble goal.

> I wish merely to add to the concept of place so that those of us who live primarily in urbanized areas, but who still seek a profound relationship

with nature may do so without feeling it to be somehow inferior. (Cuthbertson 1999, 6)

According to Henderson (1995) 'deep' connections with community and ecology can lead to a transformation of self for the participant – the ability to 'realise' oneself and one's connection to the world differently. In addition Cutherbertson and Stewart felt that the undergraduate participants that they researched were able to develop a critical awareness of their outdoor journeys and their significance. Collectively, this research suggests that such responses are possible as a result of relatively short, but intense, outdoor journeys (six weeks). But does this constitute responsiveness to the places where these journeys were conducted?

Two of the researchers commented that participants struggled to feel connected to the land they were travelling in when their personal comfort (physical and emotional) was challenged (Cuthbertson 1999; Stewart 2003a). All three researchers noted the significance of solo-time and the observation that participants responded to travelling through a 'storied landscape'. Interestingly, Cuthbertson's study, perhaps due to the expedition's duration and arduous nature, revealed how participants' personal experiences were 'fickle,' in so far as participants encountered phases of the expedition experience when they definitely wanted to go home, and other times when there was no other place that they would rather be. As may well be expected in studies that inquire into the 'lived experience' of outdoor education participants, people are revealed as being complex and capable of holding contradictory emotional responses to their experiences.

All three researchers noted the importance of community relationships – that is, for the small group community of the expedition. Places encountered were often recalled in relation to social events that occurred there. Cuthbertson noted this social layering of the experience of place as the dominant theme of his findings. Interestingly, and perhaps as a result of the duration and arduous qualities of the expedition experience in his group, Cuthbertson was alone in commenting in any depth on social influences that did not seem conducive to experiencing the place, such as gender-based conflict and the formation of cliques within the larger group.

There was little evidence that encounters with wildlife played a significant role in the participants' experiences in these studies (at least in how the participants' experiences are represented), and this is perhaps surprising. Instead, outdoor nature was largely referred to in more encompassing and possibly universal terms, such as mountain, forest, river. Cuthbertson noted that the romanticisation of outdoor nature at the expense of the city was a regular feature in his group, while Stewart concluded that expectation often resulted in a mismatch where the encounter with places (for example, an ecologically damaged river like the Snowy) resulted in unexpected emotional responses such as sadness, disappointment and even a sense of rejection of place amongst some participants.

Henderson found that the simple means of outdoor travel and living, such as using fires and tarpaulins instead of stoves and tents, maintained a sense of openness to nature. Yet both Cuthbertson and Stewart found that the structures of the experience (for example, carrying heavy packs over demanding terrain and extended periods of single file travel whilst ski touring), could impact negatively on participants' ability or desire to relate to where they were. Cutherbertson, in particular, devotes considerable textual space to discussing the influence of technology, and its cousin technique, and how they result from various social and cultural imperatives in relation to outdoor experiences.

A particular strength of the three research studies is that they were place-based. Yet, apart from some introductory commentary about the locations of the programs, detailed descriptions of the places encountered by participants are not particularly evident. This contrasts for example, with nature writers and some recent environmental historians (see, for example, Park 1995; Seddon 1994; Sinclair 2001) who dedicate long passages of their text to providing careful descriptions of place locations, meetings with local people, and environmental contexts (such as landscape, light, temperature, time of day and so on). Such descriptions, if well crafted, give the text a resonance that allows the reader a greater level of insight into the representations of participants' experiences and the researcher's own journey of discovery. It highlights that the place matters.

The final research study we discuss involves the experience of river guides working as outdoor educators on the Snowy River in south-eastern Australia (Mullins 2007). Marc Mullins describes how outdoor education programs often hire leaders who are also credentialed guides for a range of reasons: to manage safe passage of the group downriver, to provide technical training, and to meet the educational objectives of the organisation that the program participants are drawn from. However, the river guide-as-educator is often provided with little advice or assistance about how to navigate through this set of demands.

In his study, Mullins collected the reflections and views of three river guides who each had a long history (more than ten years) leading educational expeditions on the Snowy. The study included a series of three interviews (life history, river guiding and sense of place, follow up on emerging themes) with each guide. Mullins revealed how the guides balanced their own sense of attachment to the Snowy with the needs and desires of the program participants and their host organisations. At a personal level it was found that the guides had a sense of belonging and care for the Snowy River accrued through a layering of many experiences over an extended period of time. As one of the guides commented:

> I'd love to go down the Snowy every year until I couldn't walk again … I just want to be able to keep my connection … if I can keep the personal connection that, that's really important. (Mullins 2007, p. 77)

Mullins himself has worked as a river guide on the Snowy and has similar feelings of connection with the river as his co-participants in the research. In the presentation of his findings he couples representation of the participants' views, with discussion and quotations from his own journal kept on a descent of the Snowy, which he completed during the analysis phase of the data he collected in the interviews.

River Journal,

Day 2, Friday September 20th 2006 – Campsite at McKillop's Bridge.

Sleeping under a simple tarpaulin shelter I feel the bush start to come alive at first light. A bronze glint reflects off waters that have their source a long way from here, flowing from upstream tributaries like the Delegate, Jacobs and Pinch Rivers. The annual snowmelt, and the waters that steadily seep through Sphagnum Moss beds for months afterwards, no longer make the 500km journey from headwaters in the Snowy Mountains. Instead they are captured to spin turbines before being channelled west of The Great Dividing Range for irrigators and other downstream users.

Even from a silent campsite it is hard to hear the slow moving river as it flows over a sandy bottom that does little to disturb the current. Only when you listen carefully might you hear the river song chortling softly like a magpie as it surges over river rocks. Yet these are mostly invisible things for those that arrive here to begin a rafting expedition on the river. I have stood here many times as a guide amongst a clatter of equipment, food and people knowing that my job is to get it all on the river. Normally there is distance to be covered meaning that all this must be done in a very short time. But more difficult than this is the sizeable weight of expectation that people bring with them to a wild river. This part of the river seems to be a difficult place for people to connect with, not fitting the beauty expected of wilderness and without the 'grandeur' of the gorge country. It seems to fit better as a remote and unlovely necessity, a staging ground for the expedition.

For those who are new here, and keen to take on the challenges that have been constructed well beforehand, early glimpses of the river raise the question 'Where are the rapids?' I have often read the story in their faces, as they think 'The 'real' river must be down there somewhere in the gorges'. It will be a couple of days at least before most will even begin to listen to the unique song of the Snowy River ... (Mullins 2007, p. 72)

For the outdoor educators whose narratives are told in Mullins' (2007) study, including his own, it is clear that they have developed a strong sense of attachment to the remote country of the Snowy River. Despite this deep sense of connection and a multilayered knowledge of the Snowy (including its history, geology, ecology and so on) the guides often had to work to the agenda of the host organisation that the students or clients came from. As one of the guides stated:

It doesn't matter which context you're working in, the ultimate responsibility is to keep people physically and emotionally safe. And then under that, is just to provide a really good experience that meets whatever criteria the groups happening, whether that be adventure, or personal development, or environmental education, or whatever it may be. (p. 70)

The guides represented a strong sense of service culture, delivering their skills and technical knowledge of rafting and river travel. The guides reported that host organisations were almost always interested in fairly typical outdoor education learning objectives (such as learners' personal development, team building, opportunities to experience leadership and develop technical skills). Servicing these aims was found to work counter to the unique local knowledge of the Snowy. In other words, the singular focus on the learners' development or the expressed program criteria of the host organisation worked against an experience of the Snowy as a place, to which each of the guides had a deep sense of attachment. How did the guides cope with this professional dilemma?

The three river guides in this study were all exceptionally experienced on the Snowy and as outdoor educators. They found ways and times to become storytellers, when they would introduce historical and ecological knowledge to the clients and students in their care. In some ways they were subverting the host organisation's stated educational aims. The research concluded by recommending that the outdoor education host organisations (most often secondary schools and TAFEs) needed to provide a 'cultural license' for river guides to draw deeply on their sense of place knowledge. In addition, Mullins makes a case for the accreditation of river guides to acknowledge the importance of guides' place-based knowledge of the rivers where they work. This would mark an shift in the outdoor education community away from generalised models of outdoor education to more nuanced and place-specific approaches that was more responsive to Australian and local conditions.

Collectively, these research studies provide considerable food for thought. How do contemporary pedagogic structures such as outdoor expeditions and journeys compare to repeated visits to one location in terms of place responsiveness on the part of educators and students? Is one of these forms of practice better than the other? Are they both defensible but require different pedagogic strategies? How do outdoor educators develop a deep sense of attachment to particular outdoor places and how do they use this with students? The only way to begin to answer these kind of questions is to continue the work started by these researchers, building on their insights into outdoor education philosophy and practice. Research into the subjective responses of outdoor educators and students, specifically into their lived experiences of particular outdoor places, is the most likely form of inquiry to yield rewarding insights.

## Conclusion

As we have seen, outdoor educators have often privileged the role of experience in the way that learners learn. Yet the structures and qualities of human experience are elusive by nature and they cannot be fully captured and articulated. Cuthbertson (1999), for example, comments on agonising over the issue of representation of participants' experiences in his study. There will be aspects of learners' experiences, particularly their embodied learning, which continues to elude representation. How then should outdoor research into participants' experiences of outdoor places be researched and evaluated?

This becomes a crucial question for outdoor researchers and practitioners alike as, surely, gaining greater insight into the quality of the lived outdoor education experiences of both educators and learners will enable us to make better choices about pedagogic approaches in future programs. This is the overarching intent of the four case studies that follow.

Through this process we hope to provide the reader with material for deep reflection about the qualities and structures of the outdoor education experience from the perspective of one inside the experience. We hope that this will reanimate the reader to both empathise with the narratives in the case studies and to reconsider the character and nature of their own work as outdoor educators – either accepting, confirming, adapting or rejecting what we present in terms of their own situation and context. On a larger professional scale we hope to reinvigorate an interest in the importance of outdoor educators as researchers and writers, whether their starting point is as a theorist or a practitioner, in telling each other about the philosophical and pedagogical dimensions of our work.

# Chapter 5

# Expeditionary Learning and a Sense of Place

## ~ Brian ~

As we have seen in the previous chapter, the journey or expedition has long been part of the staple diet of pedagogic approaches to outdoor education. We have suggested earlier in the book that notions of adventure as a form of cultural practice and assumptions about the ability to generalise learning from novel experiences are problematic. Even so, we also acknowledge that outdoor travel is likely to continue to be an important element of outdoor education programming. So what are the pitfalls and possibilities of outdoor travel in terms of participants developing a deeper understanding of, and sense of attachment to, an outdoor place that is remote from their homes? Is an expeditionary pedagogy that is responsive to a remote place possible, and what would be its educational value? These are important questions for outdoor educators and guides. As we previously argued, humans pay a price for modern levels of hyper-mobility. Yet, to an extent, this mobility is inevitable. Humans are, by their very nature, travellers as well as home-makers. Can a sensitive and place-responsive pedagogy of outdoor travel be developed?

This chapter discusses a research study into outdoor education participants' responses to expeditionary style travel on a section of the River Murray in south-eastern Australia. I wrote about working with place-responsive pedagogies in outdoor education practice over the last ten to 15 years in my earlier narrative in chapter two. My doctoral studies gathered data from undergraduates from that time and inquired into what aspects of their river experiences seemed to deny place and which seemed to develop the potential of place attachment. Accounts of that research have already been published (Wattchow 2007, 2008), but I think it is worth revisiting some aspects of it and developing them further here. In the original study I contacted many of the students I had guided on those river journeys and gained permission to use the reflective writings they completed about their experiences at the time (of which I had the original copies). I also used these writings to select a number of the past students to interview. The time span between the participants' writing about their river travel experiences and the interviews varied between one and nine years.

It is worth briefly mentioning several salient points here. I noted that on fast-moving water the students' attention was often highly focused on developing competency in their kayaks, canoes and rafts. They strove to develop their skills to the point of being comfortable in the demanding environment of the white water rapid, though few achieved this in the time available. Interpreting their written and spoken words I concluded that, in the main, they saw these places as having wild, awesome and enduring qualities. These are classic images drawn from a Romantic disposition towards the land, as discussed earlier, and I concluded that this was largely problematic for experiencing the more nuanced and local particularities of the rivers we were journeying along. The students' experiences of slower flowing rivers, such as the Murray on its floodplain, were much more relaxed and none expressed any fears about being on the river or in the outdoors. As one of them recalled in an interview:

> It wasn't a threatening environment to me … the adrenaline levels weren't huge … it was achievable … stress wasn't there and the risk was low … Quite enjoyable and not out of your comfort zone. Comfortable trip.

But their language continued to suggest that they were still encountering the river through the Romantic constructions of the outdoors as a sublime, vast and eternal entity: 'The tranquil movement of the canoe on the water, the dripping sounds of the paddle blade, the alternative view of the surrounding environment, and the romanticism of being in a Frederick McCubbin painting' (female participant). But within the written and spoken data for these 'slow river' experiences there were many notable passages that suggested more responsiveness to place was also going on.

In this chapter I want to re-visit the data from that study, to look more closely at those canoe journeys along the Murray, where certain elements of the experience seemed to allow the participants to open themselves to the place. I have been quite selective when returning to the data to search for such indications. I also want to write about how I am continuing to try to develop an approach to expedition travel that encourages what Relph (1976) calls an 'empathetic insideness' – a sensitised traveller rather than a touristic consumer. There were some common elements to these canoes journeys which are worth briefly noting.

- Students first encountered the River by arriving at night and camping on its banks.
- There was a slowness to the travel. Much of the first day was devoted to drifting at the pace of the river.
- There was minimal technical instruction about canoeing on the trip.
- Students experienced canoe travel solo, with a partner, with boats tied together in rafts of two, three or even all boats tied together.
- The 'rafts' became a site for travel, games, reading, storytelling, even cooking.
- Campsites were not preselected, they were chosen en route. Camping involved sleeping under tarpaulins, or under the stars, or under simple shelters built from the canoes. No tents were taken on the trips.
- Unprocessed food was taken that required a lot of communal preparation (such as baking bread). Students were set a food budget and much of the fresh produce sourced by students was organic and bought from local markets. All cooking was on campfires. No stoves were taken. All food scraps were brought home and composted.
- Students were encouraged to wear natural fibre clothing rather than high-tech outdoor gear.
- Solo time and predawn paddles were timed around the most favourable conditions.
- All students were encouraged to carry and use journals (blank cartridge paper style journals for sketching and writing).

There was no set formula for the journeys. Each one would 'emerge' out of the ingredients above. Before writing further about the participants' responses to these programs I must first introduce you to the River Murray's story.

## Carting cultural baggage to the River

Let us start with the general and work towards the specific. Rivers in a land as flat and vast as Australia are a very curly proposition. Their cultural meanings, and hence travellers' experiences of them, are far from straight forward. It is little wonder that European settlers and visitors in Australia could not fathom the rivers that they encountered as they travelled inland, away from the verdant fringe along the east coast. These rivers simply did not behave like the rivers that they were familiar with in Europe. They didn't seem to be real rivers at all. Instead, they often encountered dry watercourses with no flow at all, and when it did rain 'the tendency was for flood water to spread out, to disperse through a lacework of temporary channels, which, far from concentrating the water, fanned it out to cover huge areas of normally waterless desert' (Carter 1988, 55). Carter concluded that it became near impossible for the explorer to 'invest the space of his journey with meaning' (p. 56) as a result of his experience with these 'unimaginable' rivers.

Put simply, the inland rivers of Australia did not fit the 'fluvial mythology' (Schama, 1995) of the Old World that stretched back beyond Classical Antiquity to the times of ancient Egyptian settlements along the Nile. This long history, built up through centuries of river travel and trade, irrigation and river-based industry, has left a lasting legacy of expectations about how rivers should look, behave, and about their function and sacredness. The inevitable mismatch between European expectations and Australian reality has had dire consequences for rivers in Australia.

For the new settler Australians rivers 'refused' to maintain regular flows during dry periods or stay within their banks when the rains came. Stories of drought and flood became legend, none more so than on the major waterways of the Murray and the Darling. It was not long before systems of locks, weirs and dams were surveyed and built to force rivers to conform to settler expectations. The story of environmental degradation that has resulted from both inappropriate early settler farming practices (particularly sheep grazing), the damming and regulation of river flows, and inappropriate irrigation-based agriculture, is too extensive to tell here. Fullerton (2001) does a particularly good job of summarising this history and representing current debates about the competing demands for water from Australia's river systems. Interestingly, it is a view of water as a placeless commodity that dominates these current debates, and the pre-regulation stories of the River have largely been forgotten in the modern discourses of water and river management (Sinclair 2001).

The Murray River, known simply as the River to locals, provides a compelling example. The Murray's headwaters collect in Australia's highest mountain range in southern NSW. The River falls rapidly and leaves the mountains to commence its long journey of 2500km across the inland flood plain. In pre-European times the indigenous peoples who lived along the River had a number of names for it – Indi, Millewa, Dhungulla, Kalara,

Tongala, Milloo and Murrundi (O'Neill, 2005) – each representative of Aboriginal nations. The River was first sighted by the European explorers Hume and Hovell near the current day township of Albury on 16 November 1824 on their journey from Sydney to Port Phillip Bay. A few years later, Captain Charles Sturt led his inland expedition overland from Sydney and then down the narrow Murrumbidgee River to where it entered the Murray. Sturt and his crew arrived at the confluence just after 3.00 pm on 14 January 1830. The captain noted in his journal that evening:

> It is impossible to describe the effect of so instantaneous a change of circumstances upon us. The boats were allowed to drift along at pleasure ... whilst we continued to gaze in silent astonishment on the capacious channel we had entered ... We had got on the high road, as it were, either to the south coast, or to some important outlet; and the appearance of the river itself was such as to justify our most sanguine expectations. (Sturt 1833)

Sturt's expedition had begun to fill in the blank spaces of the colonisers' maps and ignite the imagination for the possibilities of European settlement and trade along the River. The following 180 years would bring profound changes to the Murray. The Aboriginal population was decimated by diseases such as smallpox, measles and influenza as a result of contact with Europeans. The River became an important overland stock route and squatters soon followed, establishing sheep and cattle properties along the River's banks. By the mid-1850s steam-driven paddle wheelers were beginning to ply their trade, taking supplies upriver that aided in establishing new settlements, and bringing loads of wool downriver on their run to the Port of Goolwa near the River's mouth. Wire fencing, the cutting of large volumes of timber along the banks to both build and fuel the steamboats and radical changes in human population, were rapidly impacting upon an ecology and culture along the River that had changed very little in the preceding 5000 to 15,000 years.

Large-scale irrigation commenced in 1887, led largely by the Chaffey brothers in the irrigation colonies of Renmark and Mildura. 1912 saw the launch of the scheme to build a series of locks along the River in order to make its navigability by the paddle wheelers more predictable. Construction of the Hume Weir, above Albury, commenced in 1919 and was completed in 1936. This allowed for the storage of winter snowmelt and spring rains, which then could be released to downstream towns and irrigators during the summer months. This reversal of the River's flow regime has fundamentally changed the nature of the River's ecology. The final significant change to the River involved the post-World War II construction of the Snowy Mountains Hydro Scheme. This nation-building project was intended to drought-proof the important inland agricultural districts along the Murray by redirecting flows from the Snowy River into the Murrumbidgee and Swampy Plains rivers (and hence into the Murray). Yet even this additional water has not been enough to satisfy the combined needs of agriculture and settlement downstream. The extended dry of the last decade sees the River and its communities at crisis point, struggling to find a way to live within the new reality of diminished river flows and agricultural systems built upon grossly excessive water allocations. The consequences may be dire as the Murray-Darling basin is Australia's most productive agricultural region.

The section of the River that we journeyed through is referred to as 'The Barmah'. Just in this week of writing it has been declared a National Park and the traditional peoples of the area, the Yorta Yorta, will have a significant role in its management. This decision does not please everyone. Cattle graziers and timber cutters will no longer be able to use the area for these purposes.

The Barmah Forest is 28,900 hectares in size, of which 4500 hectares is swamps and lagoons. The River in the Barmah owes much of its current character to two colossal damming events – one deep in geologic time, the other in recent settler history. The Cadell Tilt block was formed by a geologic uplift 25,000 years ago, which crosses the River near the site of the Barmah township. This dammed the River, splitting it into two streams (the Murray flowing south and the Edwards anabranch flowing west). As a result the uplift forming a natural dam, the River regularly flooded an immense area, creating the distinctive forest and wetlands. The second damming occurred when the River's waters were impounded behind the Hume Weir, completed in 1936 (260 kilometres upstream from Barmah). This human regulation of the River made it possible to control winter and spring floods, and thus allowed extensive European settlement along the Murray Valley. It also made it possible to reverse the flood regime of the river, storing water in winter and releasing it for summer irrigation downstream. The River's water thus became an economic commodity that could be traded, between governments and water users. As a result the forest no longer experienced regular flooding and its ecology must now be managed by controlled floods.

The Barmah region was originally populated by the Bangerang Tribe, which was decimated by two smallpox epidemics in 1788–89 and 1830 (the current indigenous peoples of the region call themselves Yorta-Yorta).

Dispossession was followed by pastoralists in the 1940s when Edward Curr established the Currs' Lower Moira run to graze sheep, cattle and horses in the forest in the driest months of the year, after the spring and winter floodwaters receded. Firestick farming by the Bangerang created the open forest pastures so attractive to those who would displace them. Cattle grazing, timber harvesting, bee keeping, camping, fishing and tourism became the main ways that people interacted with the River and forest. Now the cattle are gone and the chainsaws are going. As we have written earlier, places never stay the same, they are always evolving.

This briefest of introductions the River reveals it as a complex place – one that has changed so quickly in the last two centuries that it is hard to keep pace. As the River historian Paul Sinclair (2001, 21) states:

> These stories, memories and histories need to become the tools that Australians use to reimagine a future for the Murray and the communities who rely upon it. Without stories of what the river once was, it will be impossible to identify the qualities Australians wish to protect and restore in the new regulated river. Australians need to recognise how the decline of the Murray has not only eroded biodiversity, but also diminished our culture. (Sinclair 2001, 21)

Along the River tourism promoters hail the achievements of the river regulators who brought the River under human control, while simultaneously championing the natural and wild river as a splendid landscape for visitors (Sinclair 2001; Stone and Stone 1996). Thus when outdoor education participants make their way to the River they are already carting with them a series of contradictory images and expectations – a curious mix of European river mythology, a view of the River as a nationalistic icon (both for its wild and tamed connotations), and perhaps some knowledge of more local ecological and cultural conditions.

### Sensory reciprocity with the River

David Abram (1996a, 41–42), paraphrasing Edmund Husserl (1859–1938), the founder of modern phenomenology, suggests that beneath the layers of diverse cultural lifeworlds we have for a place like the Murray, there exists 'a deeper, more unitary lifeworld, always there beneath all our cultural acquisitions, a vast overlooked dimension of experience that supports and sustains all our diverse and discontinuous worldviews.' We wrote in chapter four about the significance of human body in 'sensing place'. Perhaps place-responsiveness requires both a well-developed sensory awareness *and* a knowledge of ecology, history, politics, and so on. Perhaps an experience of place is to be found in the tensions that exist between cultural lifeworlds and bodily sensations.

Within the written and oral data from several participants in the study there was the suggestion of awareness that there were subtle aspects of their experiences that seemed just beyond articulation, and that they felt may even be endangered by words. As one participant put it in relation to her River experiences: 'I am afraid I might destroy them by analysing them and reducing them to words'. It seems reasonable to suggest that these type of responses indicated ways that participants responded to their situation at a sensory level and began to develop feelings of connection to the River. Perhaps, like Abram (1996b, 85), they had found that by 'examining the contours of this world not as an immaterial mind but as a sentient body, I come to recognize my thorough inclusion within this world in a far more profound manner than our current language usually allows'.

Recognition of these types of experiences could be crucial for a place-responsive outdoor education. They could so easily be missed precisely because they are difficult to express. They are there in the seemingly simple utterances. For example, one male participant who, in recalling a predawn paddle on the Murray, said that he was 'simply keeping the River going', or for another for whom the 'the River has a voice … it speaks to me in its own way', or for the participant who stated that she might 'explode with the enormity of my feelings'.

These expressions are crucial for the possibility of a place-responsive form of outdoor travel. Because without this acknowledgment of the deep significance of our sentient engagement with the world, 'place' would become nothing more than another addition to the already diverse and sometimes contradictory cultural lifeworlds that govern the interpretation of our experiences. A crucial component of place-responsiveness must be how we attend to 'sensing a place'. As John Cameron (2003a, 173) puts it; 'The word "sense" does not refer simply to the physical senses, but to the felt sense of a place and the intuitive and imaginative sensing that is active when one is attuned to, and receptive towards, one's surroundings'. Although it will, and indeed must, escape complete representation in language, I believe that some of the data collected in this study begins to reveal the experiential structures that encouraged these travellers on the River to become open to, and to connect with, the River.

Revealing these aspects of participants' experiences seemed to confirm the French philosopher Merleau-Ponty's (2002) conclusion that we are not finished at the skin. Participants' bodies and the River were constantly overlapping and transgressing each other. Of course, this must be equally true for all the river places encountered in the original study which included other fast-flowing rivers – from crashing rapid, to sandy beach, to quiet meander. But it was in response to the calm, less forbidding encounters with the River on its floodplain that some participants stated that they felt this most acutely. Interpreting their words it is possible to suggest that there were times when they felt that their own fleshy margins had become osmotic with the River.

For participants in this study there seemed to be three overlapping phenomena. First, a releasing and opening of both the participant's mind and body to the experience. Second, a sensing and filling, where the body's fleshy perimeter seems to be breached, and what was outside floods in while what was in drifts out. Finally, there is a powerful sense of connection.

While it is clear that this is not a fully indigenous experiencing or knowing of a place, nor even a holistic cultural experience (which must include the interpretive lifeworlds of the individual), it may be the crucial first step towards connection with outdoor places that it seems has been so hard for settler Australians to take. As such, this overlapping phenomenon is worthy of examination in greater detail.

## Releasing and opening

The initial phase of connecting to place for many of the participants in the study involved a release from analysis of their situation and action. I do not think that this signals an abandonment of the human qualities of rationality, but it does re-position them as secondary to our ongoing embodied relationship within our surroundings. One student related a story in his written reflection, completed not long after the journey. I think the story is compelling.

> I just want to tell you a story that sums up one of the reasons I paddle. It was on the third evening of the Philosophy [the Murray River canoe journey] trip last year. This is why I paddle and why I think others should too.

> We pull the canoe up onto the bank and [canoe partner] takes out her thermarest, sleeping bag and clothes to make a comfortable bed. We rearrange the gear, move the camp oven and shove the packs into places they shouldn't fit. The sun slowly sets as we push the boat back onto

the lazy, swirling waters of the Murray. The rustling, wobbling and shuffling slowly dies down as [she] makes herself comfortable in the front of the canoe and drifts into sleep or something almost as restful.

I paddle the canoe as smoothly and quietly as possible, breathing out with each 'j' and in with each recovery. I listen to the sounds of the encroaching evening as I watch the concentric circles formed from water dripping from the blade and the small whirlpools meander away after each stroke. My mind is comfortably blank, no assessing, no philosophising – the canoe, the surrounds and the river. A kingfisher swoops past, some wallabies hop casually along the bank, I feel as though I'm a silent, invisible observer.

The first star shows itself and others follow, each slowly, steadily brightening. Every time I look at a section of sky that is starless another one appears. The sounds of evening fade into the comfortable silence of night, the only sounds being the gurgle of water sliding past the banks and the drops falling from the blade of my paddle. Soon my sight is no longer necessary, I feel my way down the river, keeping the canoe between the two whispering banks, looking up to see the stars between the crowns of the red gums that form a haphazard queue along the banks.

I know when I am approaching a corner because the avenue of stars above me seems to end until I draw near enough to find is swings either left of right. I round a corner and see a small red glow in the distance, I have no idea how far away it is but I know [another student] and [another student] have built a fire and the glow I see means camp. [She] stirs for the first time in hours and I remember that I am not alone. We talk about the universe and other things that are best discussed under a blanket of stars. [She] tells me that she has been breathing with the roll of the canoe caused by each stroke. It is an amazing feeling to know that I have been breathing in time with [her] for several hours although my mind cannot summon the energy to analyse the meaning of it. I am glad for not having a hyperactive mind.

The glow has become a dancing conglomeration of reds, oranges and yellows. We hear the crackle and smell the smoke. [She] asks me to stop paddling so that we don't have to leave the river and the stars too soon.

With a 'blank mind' the body 'feels' its way along. The body-subject, as Merleau-Ponty would say, knows how to find its way. There is little feeling of intent in the experience. It simply unfolds. As I mentioned earlier, as a guide I was quite consciously encouraging students to engage with the River in quite different ways – such as just drifting along in the canoe rather than paddling. Another male participant in the study expressed in an interview his memory of what it felt like to try to let go of one way of being that he brought to the River, and to find another.

> Pushing off in a canoe is … a release, and it's … like a plunge, like a drift into loveliness, drift into peacefulness … it's a bit of a journey to get there … so I'll do a lot of sighing initially and just releasing crap that I've got in me, and then … I'll gradually evolve into getting into river pace, and then once I'm there I could be there for two days, ten days, 20 days, six months, three years I reckon. Once you are in that sort of zone, you're just existing. So, it's really a feeling of peace and connection, like I'm part of the river. I feel like I am the river.

These outdoor canoe journeys that the participants are responding to here were deliberately crafted to be slow, simplified, communal and open to possibilities. The following comments by one of the female students capture a sense of the slowness and simplicity of the journey:

> sitting in a boat, just drifting along, like that's the times I enjoy the most on the river are the times when I'm sitting and just moving with the river not, not trying to go upstream or across the river or faster than the river. Just moving with the river … I felt that we hadn't journeyed on the river as, as with it … just move with the river, the pace of the river, and go where the river takes you.

Because of the nature of the River, we could travel at night or predawn. The canoes themselves could be tied together in catamarans or even a giant raft and drift along at the speed of the River while we told stories about the place, or played games, or simply relaxed to soak it all in. Campsites were established on the bank where good food was cooked from basic ingredients on wood fires. Participants slept under tarps, the night breezes of the River bringing subtle sounds and aromas with them. I think it is reasonable to suggest that this form of travel may remind us, or even allow us, to experience that 'the world is not what I think, but what I live through. I am open to the world' (Merleau-Ponty cited in Matthews 2002, 61).

## Filling with place

The River, and its floodplain, is a sacred place. It may be wounded by reduced flows, salinity, increased water turbidity, cattle grazing, and so on, but it is hard to ignore the remnant earthen mounds and canoe trees indicating that Yorta Yorta and their ancestors have lived here for millennia. It is also hard to not recognise the sleeper cutter's camps, the small weirs along the anabranches, or take note of the names of specific campsites such as Stewart's Kitchen, Punt Paddock, Green Engine Lagoon. On a slow journey such as these where it would be hard to not notice that the place had been 'made' through a long history of human-river-forest interactions. Travellers on the River are still awakened each morning by a cacophony of galahs and corellas in the red gums and are accompanied downriver by waterbirds, snakes, and turtles – all living in the ribbon of life that the River provides.

As one participant commented:

> My attention to nature's detail also increased with each stroke of the paddle; the sounds, the colours, the smells, all flooded my senses. This made me slow down my thinking and my movements to suit the environment that surrounded me and I was alerted to the importance of the forest to so many people.

Almost every participant who experienced the predawn paddle on the Murray River trips commented upon the sense of heightened perceptual acuity to their surrounds. At its deepest level this was manifest as an experience of the limits of the body becoming porous, and a feeling that the place entered the participant:

> But I never felt that connectedness [before] … it didn't sort of feel as though that entered me at that [other] environment. Whereas I did feel [it enter me] that morning.

As a result of such as experience it becomes possible to feel and believe that 'intelligence is no longer ours alone but is a property of the earth; we are in it, of it, immersed in its depths' (Abram 1996a, 262) As another participant noted; 'it's very hard to describe. Just awestruck by being part of the environment … I just felt like I was blending in with it.' Such a realisation shakes our foundations, as no amount of effort on our part can make or re-make place. Nor can we imagine or re-imagine place. Neither ourselves nor places exist 'out there', or even 'in here'. We fill with our surroundings when we let go of the illusion that we are finished at the skin. As Abram astutely concluded:

> A genuinely ecological approach does not work to attain a mentally envisioned future, but strives to enter, ever more deeply, into the sensorial present. It strives to become ever more awake to the other lives, the other forms of sentience and sensibility that surround us in the open field of the present moment. (1996a, 272)

Abram's sentiment was well captured by one of the student's on their canoe journey, who penned the following poem.

I think of and feel
Gravity, Slope, Time and Energy,
Life around.
Moon shadow
Moon reflection,
On the boat,
On the water,
On the forest,
On the bow wave
Stars pass behind treetops
I feel the speed of the river
I travel at the river's pace.
…
The bow gurgles, a frog sings
Gently, the bow nudges the shore,
All I hear now is the forest, river and me
The life I surround and am.

## Connecting

I think that the experiences portrayed by these participants suggest that a personal connection to a place that is visited, where we have limited or no ability to put down roots and build a home, is possible and even educationally valuable. It is not equivalent to the holistic and seamless lifeworld of place that belongs to the indigene, the person that Relph (1976) calls the existential insider. However, I think this is an important element of what Relph refers to as 'empathetic insideness'. It goes beyond a cognitive appraisal of place and includes an embodied response, a feeling for place. It occurs beneath language and is pre-discursive. It is perhaps the first step, for those of us steeped in an outsider's heritage, towards an indigenous experience of place. It brings sensation and reflection into correct relation with each other. This may be crucial to the future of the River which has national, regional and local significance as an ecological and agricultural region. It is possible that there are vitally important lessons to learn in these outdoor places and they should be visited and experienced by all students whose lives are interconnected with them.

On several of the canoe journeys down the River we were fortunate to be in the company of a Yorta Yorta man. For many students, this was the first time that they had met, let alone been in the outdoors for five days with, an Aboriginal person. As the journey neared its end, we would camp at the point where a small anabranch called Cutting Creek, leaves the main channel of the Murray. On that last evening, stories were told of the spiritual significance of this particular place to the Yorta Yorta. Early the next morning we paddled down the narrow creek. Eventually the trees lining the banks gave way to tall bulrushes. The channel tightened until it was little wider than the boat, creating a feeling of enclosure. Then, quite suddenly, the bulrushes gave way and the travellers found themselves in the open space of Barmah Lake. Having been on the 'corridor' of the main channel for several days it was a stunning transformation to open water, huge skies, the reflections of clouds, and the distant sounds of swans and ducks slapping their feet on the water as they tried to take off. Let's follow the story of one of the students.

> On the last day when I left early to watch the bush come alive as the sun rose on Barmah Lake. [The Yorta Yorta man] told us the night before how this was a special place, the centre of his 'mat'. It has now become a special place for me. As the sun slowly rose above the trees and I felt its warmth, the birds began flying about. This was the only sound, even though there were a few of us there on our own. I can't remember feeling more relaxed and closer to nature.

> There was a mist rising off the water and there was not a single sound and there was not a ripple on the water at all. And it just sort of drifted for about a quarter of a kilometre along into the lake and it almost seemed a sin to put your paddle into the water and to disturb it and when you did you made sure that you didn't make any noise doing it because there was, I was also conscious of the rest of the group being there. But everyone was absolutely dead silent … just taking this almost spiritual moment I think it was – and it was really powerful.

As a result of his endeavours to develop place-responsiveness with his students, Cameron (2003a, 194) noted; 'As many of my students discover, a felt response to place without ecological understanding is as one sided as scientific or historical knowledge of a place without any emotional engagement with it'.

## Conclusion

The ability to let go of self and to become open to place requires a certain amount of vulnerability. It requires the absence of fear and a heightened sense of comfort in one's surroundings. It is the near opposite of the popular 'out of their comfort zone' model in outdoor education. To return to the story of the student drifting on Barmah Lake:

> It was some sort of journey that I'd been through to get to that moment … It was one of the most inspirational, deeply impacting experiences I've ever had. (male participant)

The journey is, of course, physical, emotional and intellectual. But perhaps the most significant journey is across the boundary we imagine lies between ourselves and the place that sustains us at that moment. Such an experience of place, though fleeting, may ripple through a lifetime. However, such a pedagogic approach, to encourage an ever-deepening sensory exploration of one's place, is not without risks. You may recall that we drew on the work of John Cameron in chapter five, who cautioned against the tendency to leave students adrift in this state of sensual saturation. Experiential educators, he argues, can be guilty of not bringing students back to the harsh demands of politics, ecology, economy that may imperil a place's future. Educators and learners have to engage with these realities as well.

Part of the lesson here, I think, is the simplicity and everyday quality of the experience. One participant reflected in her interview about the clear differences she saw between this kind of journey in relation to other, perhaps more conventional types of practice, that she had experienced as part of her outdoor education training.

> that was something I learnt about the Murray … the whole way the State Park was … managed compared to National [Park]. You'd see people fishing in their tinnies … lots of snags and lots of evidence that there'd been big groups or big base camps, campers or caravans or four wheel drives. I didn't mind that. It felt like, 'Hey, I can do this, this is really ordinary. Anyone can do this.' And it doesn't feel so elite and exclusive. It's like, 'I'll just come in there and I can hang out with … old Joe and his fishing boat and me and my dog'. It was nice and ordinary for

"Perhaps the most significant journey is across the boundary we imagine
lies between ourselves and the place that sustains us at that moment.
Such an experience of place, though fleeting, may ripple through a lifetime."

a change. Oh, just sometimes the trips that we did were so specialised.
You had to have everything and you were so remote and you had to be
so highly skilled to be able to get to those areas. Whereas you just go to
the Murray and you've got your boat, got your dog, got your cup of tea,
paddle down, maybe fish. I just found that really humble.

I mentioned earlier about how much the student letters, and subsequently the
research study which included the interviews, revealed to me about my own
practice as an outdoor educator. One of the failings perhaps, of these canoe
journeys, was the 'risk that place immersion could remain an individualised
phenomenon' (Cameron 2003a, 189). I feel that this style of program was
very good at providing opportunities for students to have a personal and
sensory engagement with the River, but less effective at providing a systematic
knowledge about the region's politics and economics. It is encouraging that
several of the participants in the study, but by no means all, had returned to
the River many times and now run their own educational programs there.

As we have seen, places such as the Murray River and the Barmah Forest
continue to change. A decade has passed since these paddling programs and the
whole management system that governs the area has evolved. The Australian
historian Peter Read (2000, 20) writes: 'It's the connecting sensibility; and

that's what Aborigines are doing talking about the dreaming and the land ...
Connect Connect Connect'. A traveller begins the process of becoming an
empathetic insider the moment that he or she commits to making the effort
to both open their sensing body to the possibilities of a place *and* to learn
what a place 'is' to the local community and to the broader region for whom
the place has significance. Students are not likely to discover a pleasing story
in a place's troubled history and politics. All ground is contested ground.
But they will get closer to the unique character of a place, and its profound
significance, than they would if it were to be encountered as an arena void of
meaning or as an adversary that must be overcome.

In addition, outdoor educators might see that an important aspect of their
work involves teaching learners *how* to travel. It is unimaginable that high levels
of mobility are likely to change in the near future. When I write *how* to travel I
mean how to adapt and become comfortable in a place, how to work your way
inside it both bodily and intellectually. Indeed we have argued that experiencing
travel from one place to another is a natural part of the human condition. As
Tuan (1974, 102) suggests, '"home" is a meaningless word without "journey"',
for humans are not trees, destined into immobility through 'rootedness' in
one place. Learners are destined to be travellers – better that they learn to be
responsive to the places that they travel to and in.

*Chapter 6*

# 'That Feeling of Familiarity': Developing Place-Responsiveness

## ~ Mike ~

As a researcher (and teacher) I am very conscious that it is relatively easy to critique and a lot harder to offer a realistic and viable alternative. Merely identifying an issue or problem with current theory and practice too often feels like unfinished business. I will sometimes read an academic article and come to the last paragraph and think 'so what'? What difference will this make to how a program might be delivered or how students' learning will be enhanced? In an attempt to 'walk the talk' and offer an alternative I have rewritten a paper (a unit of undergraduate study) that I teach and have modified the field work component to better support the theoretical aspects that have been introduced. My hope is that students who take the paper will come away better informed about the potential for outdoor education to enrich the lives of their students and their communities when they teach or lead in the future. This chapter details some of these changes made in the paper, both theoretical and practical, and several students' perspectives on the field work component.

This case study draws on interview data from students who participated in a short journey as part of a compulsory component in the paper entitled Learning in Outdoor and Adventure Environments in 2009. This is an optional paper offered at second year level in the Sport and Leisure Studies department; the only requirement for entry is successful completion of first year level papers. Thus students can come from a variety of backgrounds and outdoor experiences. It is a popular paper with Sport and Leisure Studies students, Tourism students, and overseas students on exchange programs.

In 2008 I taught this paper for the first time and based the field work component on the model that had been used for several years by previous staff. This journey program began in 2009 and marked a shift from previous outdoor experiences offered to students at the University of Waikato.

## Outdoor experiences pre-2009

Prior to my appointment the outdoor experience component was contracted to an outside provider that operated from a residential centre some hours' drive from the university campus. The format for the program had largely been negotiated by my predecessor(s) and senior staff at the centre. The program consisted of what I would term 'traditional' outdoor education activities: goal setting, group initiatives; a series of half-day activities (e.g. abseiling, ropes course); a 36-hour journey including an overnight stay; and a final debriefing session. From an organisational perspective this was an easy way to conduct the program. Transport was booked via a local bus company and the outdoor centre provided consent forms, equipment lists and looked after risk management and all onsite logistics. As the lecturer I was free to 'roam' and observe various groups and participate as and when I wished. The program was run professionally and students had an enjoyable experience. However, several aspects of the experience troubled me:

- We spent most of a whole day travelling to and from the centre which reduced time for participation.
- I was conscious of the 'hidden' messages that were being conveyed to students (e.g. outdoor education requires specialist equipment and personnel).
- The environmental impact of travelling to the centre was never questioned.
- Promotion of the belief that outdoor education requires a wilderness environment to be effective.
- The role of the 'normal teacher' (in this case me) was marginalised. The instructor was the expert and it was they who developed relationships with their group rather than the person who would have an ongoing involvement with the student.
- There seemed to be an implied message that outdoor education is expensive – or certainly not cheap.
- Outdoor education consists of a series of novel or exciting activities, (e.g. the flying fox across a gorge, or caving).

- The difference between the location of the centre and the day-to-day lives of the students accentuated the separation of the outdoor experience from 'real-life'.

- The 'consumerist' approach inherent in this style of outdoor provision. For example, meals were cooked for students (except on their night out) and students could select activities from a list. It felt as if we were on a package tour – you're met off the bus, exposed to a variety of experiences and then waved goodbye.

While the students generally came back enthused about their experiences many found the field trip to have been a repeat of their school outdoor education program and thus not particularly valuable in the context of this university paper. Some students were clearly 'over' this type of outdoor education. They appreciated the opportunity to get to know their classmates better but the activities were similar to, or a repeat of, what they had done as part of secondary school outdoor education or leadership camps.

Listening to the students' responses, combined with my own experiences, reading around place-based education, and my recent arrival in the Waikato region spurred me to think about exploring the possibilities for a small journey in the local area as a viable field work option.

## The development of the journey concept

In the semester that followed I spent some time exploring the local area and developing plans for a three-day journey which would begin and finish at the university campus. The Waikato region was an area I had passed through on many occasions but prior to moving here, it was not an area that I knew particularly well. The activities of kayaking on the river and long cycle rides in the countryside opened up possibilities for a modest, yet potentially interesting journey.

It is interesting settling in a new area. A 'newcomer' may look at features of the landscape in a different way to those brought up in the local area. The ordinary or mundane gives rise to questions such as what function did those stone foundations serve, or when was that bridge built and how did they build it? I think that many antipodeans experience a sense of awe when travelling to Europe for the first time – one gets intoxicated by the age and history of buildings when the locals look on in bemused wonder at what all the fuss is about.

The Waikato region is the hub of the dairy industry in New Zealand. Much of the land has been drained from its swampy past. Rural roads crisscross the predominantly flat landscape and serve as a conduit for the passage of milk tankers that make daily pilgrimages from farms to the processing plants. Intensive dairy farming has sculptured the landscape and the paddocks have largely been cleared of trees to facilitate ease of irrigation and stock movement. Small stands of native trees are now noticeable for their uniqueness – a vast change from a century or more ago when these lowland areas would have been covered in Kahikatea (a podocarp). It is through this large fertile basin that the Waikato River cuts its path; a path that has changed dramatically over time. The river itself has been 'harnessed' for hydroelectric power generation, the last dam being at Lake Karapiro, about 8kms upstream from where we begin paddling.

On the edges of this large basin lie a number of notable 'mountains'. They are named mountains, and do stand out in an otherwise flat landscape, but it is a somewhat grandiose title given what are classified as mountains in the South Island. Several of these peaks are hilly and rugged enough to have either not have been cleared in the first place, or have proven uneconomic as farms and have been allowed to regenerate. One of the 'mountains' Maungatautari has become the centre of a much lauded and successful project to provide native flora and fauna with a chance to regenerate. It is interesting that one of the earliest and most intensely farmed areas in colonial times is also the site of one of the country's most ambitious restoration programs. It is the contrast between the polluted streams and lakes in the lowlands and the efforts to restore the damage caused by pests (e.g. cats, mice, possums) and deforestation that captures many students' attention and provides a powerful example of the effects of optimism in the face of adversity. It is a region of contrasts, both physically and culturally with the Crown recently (in 1995) making amends to the Tainui people for the injustices of illegal land confiscations and dispersion of communities.

Interestingly all of these features (the river, Maungatautari, dairy farms, and of course suburbia) are within a 30km radius of the university campus. The need to travel hundreds of kilometres to gain an outdoor education experience seemed, from my perspective, unnecessary.

I was conscious of a number of factors when designing the program. These included:

- being 'self-propelled'
- utilising the resources in the area
- using simple low-technology equipment that was readily available and inexpensive

- taking time to pause and understand the local history and ecology of the places through which they travelled
- providing a model of outdoor education provision that could be replicated by students in the future, and
- avoiding an overt focus on risk as a means of learning yet retaining an element of challenge.

The journey has now been run for the last two years and consists of the following elements:

## Day 1

The first day is a bicycle ride from the university, along country roads and through several townships, to a small village called Pukeatua. The distance is approximately 65kms and is a mixture of flat and undulating bitumen roads. The ride encompasses the outer edges of suburban Hamilton, country roads passing through dairy farms, horse studs and several small rural service towns, some no larger than a school to serve the local farming community. We camp in the Pukeatua Primary School's playing fields. We arrive after school has finished and depart at about the start of the school day.

## Day 2

This day consists of an approximately 18km walk from Pukeatua over Maungatautari (a local 'mountain' with a height of 797m) and then a 7km ride to a council-owned campsite on the shores of Lake Karapiro. Maungatautari is volcanic in origin and was once home to an estimated 5,000 people in pre-European times. Its abundant wildlife was supported by extensive forests on both the mountain and the surrounding lowland areas.

From the school we walk about a kilometre and enter the Maungatautari Ecological Island Trust's enclosure.[1] The MEIT have placed a 47km pest-proof fence around the mountain and have completed a pest eradication program. The scale of the project is astonishing (e.g. 850,000 staples, 100,000m$^2$ of fine steel mesh, 8,500 three-metre posts) and encloses 3,400 hectares. The removal of pests (rats, feral cats, possums) has allowed the forest to rejuvenate and the reintroduction of native birds such as the kiwi, takahē and hihi. Students are introduced to the aims of the trust, and we visit the aviary where recently arrived birds (e.g. kākā) are contained prior to release and climb the lookout tower which takes us up into the foliage and forest canopy. In addition to the birds the trust has also been successful in assisting in the preservation of geckos, skinks and the rare Hochstetter's frog. We then traverse the mountain (inside the fence) and cross farmland to pick up our bikes and ride the final leg to the campsite.

### Day 3

This day begins with a 9km ride into Cambridge from where we kayak down the Waikato River finishing at the Hamilton City Gardens (a paddle of about 25km). From there we walk the two kilometres back to the university campus. The trip down the river is in double sea kayaks and the river meanders through farmland, a short gorge, exclusive riverside properties and industrial areas. There are several public access points to the river via reserves and boat ramps. At various points on the river storm water discharge outlets are a common site as are pumps drawing water out of the river for irrigation and local town water supplies (after passing through treatment stations). The river is wide and follows a clear channel with no obstacles, apart from some willows near our point of entry. In many ways the 'architecture' of our experience mirrors European societies' utilitarian approach to the river, which is in contrast to that of the local *iwi* (tribe), for whom it is alive and a source of spiritual significance. For example, an older established town such as Cambridge is built away from the river as in early times it served as their means of transport. Industrial subdivisions of the 1960s and 1970s were built with the rear of the properties facing the river and you can see discarded machinery placed away from public view. In other parts of the river you sense an awakening awareness of the scenic value of the river, with large houses built to take in the view and manicured gardens stretching down to the river's edge.

In total we travel about 125kms over the three days and the three modes of travel provided different challenges and experiences.

## Pedagogical impulse

As Brian mentioned in the previous chapter, journeys or expeditions have featured in many outdoor education programs. However, it would appear that for many New Zealand school students, if my undergraduates are a representative sample, the most common form of outdoor education experience was at a residential centre. Thus for most of these students the notion of going on a journey was novel. Each year two trips are run about a week or two apart. Given the number of students in the class it is necessary to contract a small outdoor education company who help to provide appropriate staff:student ratios. In addition we use a local kayak hire company and guide for the river section. However, none of the activities involves highly technical expertise and the students are only required to bring a bike and 'sensible' clothing for a three-day trip. Day packs and sneakers are suitable for the walk and most students have or can borrow a bike and tent – in fact students in the two groups often share resources.

The outdoor provider supplies a vehicle and trailer to transport food and bikes (for the shuttle around the mountain) and their instructors lead small groups over Maungatautari. The students are required to cook in small groups (first night) and communally (second night). The journey is both an opportunity for them to be a participant but also to ask questions of the staff. Often opportunities are taken at suitable 'teachable moments' to explain reasons for doing things in particular ways and to use stories of successful strategies when working with school groups.

As part of the journey, students are paired up prior to the trip and they can choose a topic relating to the history, ecology or cultural significance of the area through which we travel. At the appropriate times we stop and students share their knowledge of the local area (e.g. a particular plant, site of a battle between colonial troops and local Māori, or the environmental impact of power generation on the river). Not only do contributions come from these pre-prepared talks but often students who live nearby, or, in the case of some Māori students, whose families are linked to the area through many generations, add depth or different insights to the discussion. Thus the role of teacher – student (expert–novice) is disrupted as new insights are gained and contributions come from unexpected quarters.

This shared experience forms the basis of ongoing discussions in class and a means to connect theory with practice. For many students it serves as a stimulus to rethink outdoor education and question their beliefs about the taken-for-granted assumptions that they had based on school camps that consisted of a series of 'fun' activities. The sense of satisfaction (or maybe it was relief) on arriving back at university is palpable. In post-journey class discussions many students express surprise that they could have an 'adventure' so close to town. Many are amazed at the sense of 'wilderness' they felt on sections of the river (which may have only been 500m from the main state highway), while few knew of the Maungatautari Ecological Island Trust, which is the largest such project on the New Zealand mainland.

## Student perceptions: A small case study of a developing place-responsive outdoor education program

The following interviews were conducted with five[2] ex-students about 15 months after they completed their journey. At the time of the interviews I was not teaching any of the students. Each student was interviewed individually and the recordings were transcribed. The interviews were of a 'conversational nature' based around a loose framework of questions. For example, I had an opening question, 'what do you recall from last years' journey?' I might then have asked the student to expand on a point that they had made. This semi-structured format worked well with students with whom I had already shared the journey experience.

I read through the transcripts a number of times and consulted with a colleague, Crispian Hills, to confirm that my reading of the transcripts and the emergent themes were consistent with interviewees' accounts. The interviewees were provided with a draft of this chapter for comments and feedback. Given the small number of interviewees I am hesitant to make any claims beyond the bounds of this program. What I have done is highlight some of the themes that have emerged from the discussions that I had with the students. The process has been useful in helping me to make sense of what the students, or at least some of them, might take from an embryonic place-responsive program. As part of the standard quality assurance mechanisms within the university, evaluations are conducted that provide some student feedback about the paper. However, the opportunity to speak with ex-students about their experiences has provided further valuable and insightful feedback in the ongoing development of both theoretical and practical aspects of the paper.

### Journey: Generation of different meanings of outdoor education

Many of the students had some experience of outdoor education through school trips to one of the numerous outdoor education centres in the Waikato/Bay of Plenty region. These experiences of 'traditional' outdoor education meant that initially the journey approach was treated with some hesitation or mild confusion. As Dave stated;

> Initially when I knew we would be doing the three-day field trip as opposed to the outdoor pursuits thing, I was, in a somewhat selfish way, a bit disappointed because I wanted to go and experience the high ropes and all the things that it has to offer; but in hindsight and even during the process and learning about the process of a place-based approach

and the journey aspect, I'm rapt that I've done it because I just think it's got a lot more meaning than going and jumping in a kayak or doing ropes as far as my use of it in future education of students.

Jan had studied outdoor education as part of the senior Health and Physical Education curriculum that had a heavy emphasis on the assessment of skills (e.g. rolling a kayak, tramping, etc.). The nature of the journey, with a lack of focus on technical skill development, instructor-driven lessons and assessment, meant that for Jan this was a new way of experiencing outdoor education.

> I really enjoyed it and it was completely different to how I had … like, compared to my seventh form. Each night we went over what we enjoyed and things like that and that was completely different, I hadn't experienced that before … at school it was kind of like, well, you do this you pass, if you don't, you don't pass, basically, so that was a big difference probably – was that you got to choose whether you wanted to do it or you didn't want to do it.

There is no doubt that part of this difference observed by Jan relates to structural issues concerning assessment that differ between the secondary and university sectors. However, it also reflects an approach to learning that recognises the value of experiences as being of value in and of themselves, rather than as a largely unproblematic 'resource' that can be broken down into discrete parts against which a student can be assessed as competent (or not).

Sarah also contrasted the journey to her experiences as a school student where outdoor education was conducted at a residential centre.

> I remember my time there: you got up at a certain time and you went and had breakfast. It was cooked for you, you just did the dishes afterwards and they said, right, today we'll do this and we're going to do this and followed by this, here's your lunch, see you later, come back, lights out at a certain time, ready for the next day when we're going to get on the bus and we're going to go here and there, there, there and, like, we just went with the flow, we didn't have to think about anything, we were just clowning around the whole time. So … yeah, it was a great, as a kid it was awesome, but there was no – it was just an experience, there was no sort of learning outcome or anything; it was just a really cool experience.

Despite Dave's initial feelings, he described how for him the journey format had 'more meaning'. In response to a request to clarify what he meant by the term 'more meaning', Dave replied:

> More meaning in that it addressed issues such as environmental impact, getting to know your own area – like, one part of it we had to do a little … what do you call it, a little prepared sort of presentation on the local area and that in itself I found really interesting, just to learn about what's happened in our local area and stuff; and I guess more spiritually fulfilling. Yeah.

Andy used the term 'more special' to describe his experience of being on the journey in places with which he already had a level of familiarity:

> I feel that it was more special in the way that we're very close to where we are rather than just up and leaving when we've already got it here …

Dave and Andy's assertions that the journey provided an opportunity to connect with *their* local area, as something special or more meaningful, was also re-iterated by other interviewees.

## Increased or differing awareness of place(s)

The opportunity to be 'immersed' in the environment, as compared to being cocooned in a vehicle, provided different ways of experiencing the taken-for-granted aspects of the local environment. The students expressed this different appreciation for the places they encountered on the journey, which they frequently pass through in their day-to-day lives, by reference to direct experience and the opportunity to research and share their knowledge of the cultural significance of places.

One of the defining features of this area is the Waikato River (hence the name of the region and the university) that wends its way through the city of Hamilton. It is not possible to live in Hamilton without encountering the river on a daily basis, albeit most likely from a car crossing one of the many bridges. However, this view from 'on high' looking down at the river conveyed a very different impression than that gained from being on (and partially in) the river. As Dave explained:

> The kayak back down the river was awesome and it was also somewhat eye opening to me because I wasn't expecting the level of pollution that there was or the level of development; I mean, I knew that we were going through a predominantly farming area but I expected there to

be some pockets of bush or something along the way as opposed to just fringes on the side around towns and that. Yeah, it opened to my eyes to the level of pollution in the river.

Andy spoke about the different way of seeing the countryside as compared to passing through it at high speed in a car:

it was taking you on a different sort of journey … as you were biking you were actually really taking in what you were biking past… when you're on your bike you're sort of actually really looking around at where you are and what you are doing so it's something quite different and you really actually take it in. So what you're doing is quite special, I guess.

Sarah commented that the slow pace of the journey and the frequent stops on the cycling leg forced her

to look at the environment and smell the horses and see everything. Yeah. So that had a big part in it …

Slow(er) paced travel enabled an appreciation and interaction with place(s) that resulted in the formation of different perspectives. The smell of the water or horses, the snaking ribbon of bitumen through farmland and the body's response to hills or the rise and fall of the kayak contributed a richness to the students' experiences.

## Greater awareness of the local

Most of the students interviewed came from the Waikato area or surrounding districts and several of them made mention of the impact of travelling in areas that were familiar, or of seeing aspects of the local environment in a different light.

Sarah expressed satisfaction that she was able to complete a journey in her 'own area'. She stated, 'it was nice for me because it was familiar'.

It was great doing it in the Waikato, and because I know the area, I know Pukeatua, I've got people, friends that live there and stuff so it was … yeah … nice, for me nice to do things in an environment that I knew.

Andy expressed a similar sentiment:

we could have actually gone somewhere else and done a very different thing and it probably wouldn't have meant as much to a lot of the people but since we did it here there was such a great experience, like, real close proximity to us where we actually already live and I think that was really wicked, I think that that's a real cool part … It was so different and new yet it was only just over there so there was that feeling of familiarity with the place, yeah.

On one of the trips we did a small (3–4 hour) project cleaning lichen off the predator proof fence at Maungatautari. The fence is constructed of fine mesh atop which is a metal panel which prevents cats or mice climbing up and over the fence. If too much lichen builds up it might be possible for the animals to gain a grip on this smooth surface. Andy described his reaction to this experience as follows:

> Learning all that stuff at Maungatautari was really quite interesting … just about all the, I don't know, just the wildlife and how they preserve it and even the fencing and stuff was quite enjoyable. And it was really interesting because of how much people all knew about that mountain and then when we went to clean the railings, everyone just got into it because they actually felt like they were a part of what they were trying to achieve with that place; it wasn't like, 'oh shit we've got to do some cleaning', it was a bigger picture, you know, we were trying to keep predators from going in there and wrecking that environment.

The enthusiasm from the students, working with volunteers from the trust, was most surprising. The realisation that a whole mountain could be fenced off, and noticeable advances in the regeneration of flora and fauna could occur in a short timeframe, seemed to capture their imagination. We were lucky that while in the enclosure we had seen kākā fly right up to us and the students' eyes would light up as they realised the privilege of such an encounter. I also think that as this project was 'in their backyard', was funded entirely from donations and volunteer workers, and was something that they could contribute to in a visible and immediate manner, it was highly appealing and meaningful to the students.

Simon stated that one of the high points of the trip was the peer presentation where he was able to share information about the area with his classmates. He and his partner told of the pre-European settlement at a site and the effect of colonisation and the resultant displacement of the local tribe. In a simple, but effective manner, they were able to point out where the present town boundary, which today is a wire fence, marked the limits of the land designated to be under the control of colonial troops.

That was good because it sort of, like, brought out my Māori side I suppose, and what happened around that area. I'm not from around that area but what we researched at that time was quite fascinating.

He went on to state that for him it was important that his classmates were made aware of the pre-European history of the area and the impact that conflicts over land ownership had on local Māori. Simon was interested in not only the cultural and historical relationship that people have had with the land but also the impact of changes in geology, wrought over a longer period.

I think it's good because you get to understand what had happened there: have there been any changes since then? Like, you know, the river might have dried up by now or something but before it was a river and you could see the deltas or something like that and that's interesting, and that to me is what ... that interests me.

I was able to tell Simon how on the most recent trip I had stopped at the spot where he and his partner had made their presentation and retold the story that they had shared the previous year. Simon's response was interesting;

Exactly and it's good that ... see, so you've told somebody else then they might remember it now then they'll, you know, and if ever they ever go over there with family they can pass on that knowledge as well so that's why I think it's good to make sure that everyone sort of knows what used to be in certain areas.

For Simon, as *Tāngata Whenua* (a person of the land), connection to the land and sense of identity is not restricted to present ownership rights or usage, but is a matter of connection through multiple generations of occupancy and migration.

## Developing creativity and possibilities

Part of my rationale for conducting this small journey was to disrupt existing models of outdoor education provision, or at least provide an alternative approach for students to draw on should they, in future, be in a position to organise or have input into a school-based outdoor education program. While not overtly promoting a place-responsive journey as *the* way to do outdoor education, I had hoped that students would see this as a viable alternative, rather than reverting by default to the belief that outdoor education could only be provided by specialists in a wilderness location. It was interesting to hear that several of the students would consider implementing such a program. Sarah, for example thought that she might be able to use the principles of this type of journey in a primary school context.

> Even if you just started off small like half-day things, like say, yup we're going to bike to this nature reserve or whatever, we're going to do a little study and we'll come back to school to carry on and then step up to like a day thing and then perhaps an overnight thing.

Dave found the whole experience more satisfying than he had initially imagined. The slower pace, the lack of rushing from activity to activity and the space to engage in lengthy conversations with fellow students while walking, riding or paddling changed the dynamics in the class. As Dave indicated:

> I felt more … I don't know, more satisfied, more … just yeah, more satisfied … and it sort of opened up to the possibilities of Outdoor Education rather than just think go camping, go high ropes or whatever; that there were other things we could do, yeah.

Jan picked up on the points made earlier about the value of the local and the realisation that travelling is not always necessary. If the option to travel elsewhere is set aside, then new possibilities for creativity may arise. As Jan suggested:

> You don't have to drive somewhere all the time. Yeah, like I never thought we'd be able to do so much in that three-day trip from university … I definitely think we can be creative and think of things to do and places to go and what you could do and stuff like that.

### Sense of satisfaction – being self-propelled and returning to the point of departure

The financial cost and environmental impact of travelling several hundred kilometres by coach was one of the factors considered in developing the journey program. However, I was also keen to see if it was possible, within reason, to design a program that allowed the students to complete a trip 'under their own steam'. In previous positions I'd both participated in and observed students journeying from one point to another or departing and returning to their home base or port. I had always sensed that departing and returning provided a sense of accomplishment for students and I was keen to encourage this if possible.[3] This aspect of the journey was commented on by several of the students.

The whole idea that we went to a place and came back on our own steam, I thought was really good. And, you know, from an environmental perspective, an achievement perspective, all of that was just a good idea and a way of doing things, I thought. (Dave)

It seemed so just basic and I think that was quite a wicked way to do it – just that everyone, you know, you packed a bag, there wasn't all these extras, you were kind of just doing it the long hard way but in the end it was just so much more rewarding. (Andy)

I liked the concept of we powered ourselves the whole way. (Sarah)

I think it's great starting here and finishing here; like, not having to get in a bus to travel somewhere to do an activity and then travel all the way back. Like, when we finished our three-day trip last year it was quite good because it was a sense of accomplishment – like, whenever I see Maungatautari I always say, well I walked over that, I rode all the way. Like, it was quite a big thing to start somewhere and then go right round kind of thing and come all the way back, I thought that was pretty neat. I really enjoyed that. (Jan)

Sarah also spoke of the difference in emphasis that she experienced as a result of the journey format. Sarah expressed a new appreciation for the environment that is 'passed through' and ignored in much day-to-day life. She made reference to her experiences of outdoor education in the past where the focus was very much on the destination rather than the journey – the bus trip was a necessary and tedious ordeal to get to the OE centre.

If you're driving in a vehicle or something you're not thinking about where you are or you're not consciously looking at your environment, you're just waiting for the destination ... (Sarah)

Andy also picked up on the importance of 'how you got there' as part of the experience:

I found a lot of the experience to me was the enjoyment of where you actually went and how you got there, so the things that you did on the way and the things that you saw. I thought that was the more important part of it.

It is encouraging to see students reflect on place and how it is experienced as inherently pedagogical rather than as merely a site for activities. Andy went on to explain:

> we could have done that whole three-day thing simply in an afternoon really if we had taken a bus there, gone to Maungatautari, came down, gone to the river, paddled a bit and then hopped back in a car and driven back, you know, and that would have taken away the whole special part of the experience, you know; and I think that's what's quite unique about it [the journey] you feel as though you've accomplished something so you can actually tell the story about from however long the cycle was, you know …

Simon commented on the bike ride as being difficult for him due to his self-admitted lack of fitness. Along with some of the other students he found riding for most of the day (albeit slowly with lots of stops) and sitting on a bike seat a challenge. Thus developing a place-responsive program does not necessarily indicate that physical challenges will not be present nor does it negate the claims of bonding and team cohesion associated with more traditional programs. For example, Simon's statement about the ride:

> we sort of bonded a bit more because we were going through it all together; you know, we could feel each other's pain I suppose.

Jan also commented on her desire to push her boundaries and find physical challenges:

> my goal was for the biking not to get off my bike and walk uphill and I completed that so I was pretty happy with that. I don't know, I just recall trying to do … like, not regret anything so for the tramp I made sure I went on the harder one more than the easier walk, I just – I didn't want to miss out on anything, I wanted to do, you know, everything the hard – you know, if it was possible, the harder way kind of thing.

## Affordability/accessibility

As a compulsory component of this paper the cost of providing the practical activity comes out of student course fees rather than being an add-on cost charged to the student. Thus there are financial constraints and budgetary considerations. As all providers will acknowledge, there is a price point which meets with increasing consumer resistance. While not being the sole driver, costs are important. Like school principals, outdoor education co-ordinators and parents, I am not immune from having to deal with the reality of justifying costs associated with the provision of outdoor education. Although planning a journey of this nature is more time consuming than using an outside provider, the costs are substantially less.

The need for students to buy or hire specialist outdoor equipment is also reduced. Dave (a parent himself) saw a place-responsive program as:

> A viable alternative and an enriching experience, and for me in particular – I'm referring to that 'future use' thing – I want to work with kids from a lower socio-economic group and I think it just opens pathways into getting activities that are more affordable for them.

Jan contrasted this experience to her exposure to more skills-based programs. Implicit in this comment is an appreciation of the potentially restrictive aspect of outdoor education that focuses on the acquisition of technical skills.

> [Getting] skills is one thing but just the enjoyment of students to be able to get out there and do it without costing them an arm and a leg and I think that's really good.

Andy referred to one of the highlights of the trip being the (apparent) simplicity of the activities and the fact that it would be possible to repeat the trip, or aspects of it, with friends. He also repeated the appeal of the relatively inexpensive approach to outdoor education:

> since then I've wanted to take a few people back there, you know, and show them what I did because it's not an expensive way to do it or anything like that.

As students on limited budgets with competing demands, several made comments about their perceptions of the affordability of such a program:

> I thought that was pretty good actually because it was just using what we had and we didn't have to go anywhere to get – or get any special stuff; like, you could use any bike and could do any decent kind of shoes, I thought it was very good actually. (Jan)

Linked with affordability are issues of ease of access and the opportunity to repeat or revisit places of meaning and interest. As Jane mentions in chapter eight, attending a residential centre for a series of activities may be fun and stimulating but students' ability to repeat these experiences or share them with family members may be limited due to specialist knowledge/ equipment, the need to be part of a larger group booking, and the remote location on private land. One of the attractions for Sarah was the ability to either repeat aspects of this trip or to find other activities of a similar nature in the area.

> Like, anyone in the weekend could go, 'oh yup I'm just going to do something' … there's always opportunities and it opened my eyes to see that you can just go out and find things to do that are relatively cheap and don't take that much [money] … It was good, it just opened my eyes to what's out there in the Waikato.

Sarah felt that her previous outdoor education experiences, based at residential centres had led her to believe that:

> you could only do outdoor activity things if you were going somewhere. Whereas this one it was – yeah, like just made everything so accessible and you could see that you can do it anywhere and anytime.

> Like all through school … it doesn't seem anything's run in that area – you're always on a bus somewhere for a couple of hours, do something, and then you're back on the bus to school for a couple of hours … like, at school and stuff you sort of were given the impression you're going somewhere exotic and fun and you could only do these fun and cool things if you were away and … yeah, but it's not the case at all, you just get outside and do something.

Several of the students have been back to Maungatautari with family members and Simon described how his son went there as part of a school trip. Simon expressed pleasure at being able to talk to his son about his experiences, and the pictures that his son drew encouraged dialogue about what both had seen and enjoyed about the reserve.

I have now completed this journey a number of times, as well as doing various sections of it with friends and family. Each time I return, my understanding and connection is enriched, be it through observing a change in the developments at Maungatautari, hearing new stories about the places we visit (e.g. on a recent trip one of the students who grew up on a farm at Pukeatua told of how the post office was blown up by would-be burglars), or sharing stories and experiences with a new group of students. What was once unfamiliar and new is becoming more familiar, more rewarding, and more enriching as an educational experience.

"Each time I return, my understanding and connection is enriched, be it through observing a change in the developments at Maungatautari, hearing new stories about the places we visit ... or sharing stories and experiences with a new group of students."

## Conclusion

This three-day journey in the local environment is not inherently risky, in the sense associated with much outdoor education practice. It is does not contain any startling educational innovations, but hopefully it will have planted a small seed in the minds of some of the participants about alternatives and possibilities. Students conveyed a sense of satisfaction at completing a self-propelled journey that contrasts with the fast-paced life they normally live; juggling part-time jobs, study, family, social and sporting commitments. The 'immersion' in place(s) provided the opportunity for students to engage at multiple levels, at a sensory and visceral level (e.g. the smells of animals or the ache in the legs as they rode) as well as encouraging them to think, imagine and reflect on their impact on the places that they inhabit (e.g. the positive effect of fencing a mountain or the consequences of particular farming practices on water quality). The issues raised are not 'out of sight, out of mind'; they must engage with the river everyday as they travel around town, nor are their memories consigned to a 'mythical wilderness' because they walk past the departure and return point of the journey each day they come to university. It also illustrated the potential for a more egalitarian form of outdoor education or personal recreation that does not require high tech clothing or skills honed over many years.

This form of outdoor education might not be seen as adventurous or character-building by advocates of adventure education but it is rooted in sound pedagogical principles. Perhaps of equal importance is that this form of outdoor education is potentially more sustainable, both environmentally and financially, thus making it possibly less likely to be removed from an already crowded school curriculum. As detailed at the beginning of the chapter this is not a finished project nor is it held up as an exemplary approach to place-responsive programming. It is, however, an example of how a place-responsive program has been designed and implemented. What I have tried to do is provide an opportunity for students to learn, not only about place-based education as an approach to outdoor education pedagogy, but an experience of a program that moves *towards* a responsiveness to place (Cameron 2003a).

At the time of writing the journey has been running for two years, it may well change subtly in the future based on student feedback and changing understandings of best practice. What I hope I have illustrated is that it is possible to introduce a place-responsive program in an urban setting, albeit bordering large tracts of rural land. In one sense this journey differs markedly from those described by Brian (in chapters six and nine). Yet in another it also strives for simplicity and valuing the quality of 'everyday' experiences that was a feature of the River Murray journeys. Students were encouraged to engage in places that were familiar, places that they had frequently driven past or seen in the distance.

There is no magic formula to follow, the fact that we cycle, walk, and paddle is largely determined by where we are. The stories that are told of the peoples of this area and the particular issues that we face (due to intensive agriculture) are of this place at this time. They will not necessarily resonate with you or your students. The challenge for educators is to be aware of and responsive to the place(s) in which we find ourselves.

The development of this small place-responsive journey signals my attempts as an educator to address some of the shortcomings identified earlier in this book. It is not a universal remedy or the best example of a place-responsive pedagogy. It is in its infancy and we, both my students and I, have some way to go on this path; for instance we still use a vehicle for logistical support and our food is sourced from the supermarket rather than local markets. It is not a finished product and at present it lacks the nuanced and subtle pedagogical expertise evidenced in the case study of Arthur Curl, a place-responsive educator (chapter nine). Hopefully this will come with time as my experience in the local landscape here, and with the students, deepens. But what I hope it does is provide you with some ideas for working with your own students in your place(s).

Raising awareness of the importance of place(s) is a modest and defensible claim, as evidenced in the comments of these students. While place-responsiveness may not match some of the grand narratives associated with traditional outdoor education programming I would hope that in some small way John Cameron's (2003a, 195) suggestion that paying 'closer attention to place relationships helps to sustain the individual, as well as the society and its environment' holds true.

## Chapter 7

# Transitions: A Changing Sense of Place

## ~ Mike ~

The case study in this chapter draws on two interviews with staff involved in a research project[1] investigating the development of a place-based approach in two secondary schools in New Zealand. One of the requirements of Teaching and Learning Research Initiatives (TLRI) is to collaboratively work with teachers, as co-researchers, to develop programs that meet the needs of their school community.

The interviews were conducted at the beginning of the project in an effort to ascertain the teachers' understandings of outdoor education and the nature and scope of their current programs. Understanding teachers' beliefs about outdoor education is a valuable means of gaining an insight into their practice. As Allen Hill (2007) notes, there has been a shift away from trying to correlate student achievement with teacher behaviour towards understanding teacher beliefs as the key to effective practice. Thus at this early stage of the project efforts were made to explicate teachers' understandings, as this is seen as a key in any potential change process.

Neither of these teachers was a disinterested party; both were keen to explore different ways to conduct outdoor education in a secondary school context. Both the teachers and the school principal had agreed to participate in the project from the early stages of the research funding application. These interviews were conducted prior to discussion forums and the joint development of new program initiatives.

The intention in this chapter is to elucidate the teachers' current understandings of outdoor education and to discuss whether these beliefs and practices reveal an appreciation of the role of place in the learning experiences of students.

## The setting for the case study[2]

Mount Maunganui College is a co-educational decile five state secondary school.[3] The school is located in the western Bay of Plenty in a beachside township. It is a well-known holiday location and due to its favourable climate, excellent beaches, thriving port and agricultural hinterland, is a growing area popular with families and retirees. The school roll is about 1320, with 60% of students identifying as NZ European/Pākehā; 29% as NZ Māori; 6% 'Other' European; and 5% other ethnic groups.

Outdoor education, including whole year level camping experiences, is offered in the junior years (years 9–10) and can be elected in the senior years (years 11–13).

School camps are very much a part of the year 9 program (first year of secondary school) and these camps are staffed by teachers and senior school (year 13) leaders who have received specific training in the delivery of adventure-based learning (ABL).

At present whole year level outdoor education camps are offered at year 9 and year 13. The focus of the year 9 camps is to get students to know each other, as they come from five contributing schools, and their new form teacher. The year 13 leadership camp is conducted in the week before school starts and has a focus on leadership.

The Education Review Office (ERO) report contains a letter to parents and the following are extracts from this document. This is included to provide the reader with a brief insight into the school.

> Students have access to a wide range of educational opportunities both within and beyond the school environment. There is a planned approach to assisting students to make informed choices about career pathways, further education and employment opportunities. Performing arts is a strength, the school having achieved regional and national recognition in this area over a number of years. In addition students are able to participate and achieve in a wide range of sports at both a recreational and competitive levels. These programmes and opportunities enable students to pursue their strengths and interests, experience success and become involved in the wider life of the school.

> School-wide initiatives … are becoming well embedded and are contributing to positive and respectful relationships between staff and students, and increasingly amongst students … Senior students willingly assume responsibility and undertake leadership roles in

supporting other students, and in sporting, cultural, social activities and events within the school community.

Teachers demonstrate a commitment to the learning and wellbeing of students, and many involve themselves in extra-curricular activities with students. School-wide professional learning and development initiatives are having a positive influence on teaching practice to engage students as responsible learners.
(http://www.ero.govt.nz/ero/reppub.nsf/0/D467F41950D91E99CC25 7491000A8F5A/$File/118.htm?Open accessed 29 June 2010)

The Perry Outdoor Education Trust, a local charitable organisation supports the provision of outdoor education at Mount Maunganui College. The trust facilitates professional development opportunities for school staff and directly funds several local schools to enable students to access outdoor education experiences. The trust explicitly aims to empower and equip teachers to run these camps rather than contracting services to outside providers. Thus camps tend to be run in local areas and do not typically involve technically difficult activities. The trust recognises the benefits to be gained by teachers and students in developing relationships outside the confines of the school classroom. The trust also encourages senior students to take on leadership roles on junior year level camps, thus creating a 'spiral' of involvement across year levels.

## The teachers

Jane is the head of the Physical Education Department. She has been at the school for a decade and has been actively involved in outdoor education for much of this period of time. Erin has been teaching in the school for six years and teaches Health and Physical Education and oversees many of the outdoor education camps. One of Erin's roles is to liaise with the Perry Outdoor Education Trust to prepare programmes and funding applications. Thus both Erin and Jane have been involved in 'localised' outdoor education provision for several years.

## The interviews and analysis

Jane and Erin were interviewed separately. The recordings were transcribed, returned to the interviewees for comments/amendments and then read through many times by myself with Brian providing a second opinion in regards to the representation of the salient points which I believed emerged from the interviews.

Because it is a small case study no claims are being made in regards to the generalisation of the findings beyond this school's context. Transcripts were analysed inductively with several pertinent themes emerging. My attention is focused on issues of relevance to understandings of outdoor education and possible intersections or points of commonality with a place-responsive pedagogy. As with any interpretive research, my 'reading' of the transcripts will invariably omit and favour particular aspects of the interviewee's accounts. There is no attempt to feign objectivity or a detached perspective. All parties involved are placed within a collaborative research project that has a stated aim of exploring place-based approaches in outdoor education programming.

## Outdoor education: The quest for connection

In the sections that follow I present several themes that arose from my discussions with Erin and Jane. The order in which they are presented does not indicate a hierarchy of importance. I have tried to present the relevant points in a manner which provides some sense of flow, which may of course not be reflective of the order in which the issues were raised by the interviewees in the recorded discussions. The heading to this section gives a sense of the dominant theme to emerge from my analysis of the transcripts. I assure the reader that this heading was arrived at after reading the transcripts rather than the concept of connection being pre-determined and the material selected to fit with it. You are of course invited to arrive at your own conclusions.

### The importance of relationships

Both Jane and Erin stated that a valuable outcome for students who participated in outdoor education over multiple year levels was the acquisition of skills to be able to participate in outdoor recreation on an ongoing basis. While valuing the acquisition of skills, Jane also placed emphasis on the context or process involved in learning in the outdoors:

> It's learning in an outdoors environment, it's learning different skills and appreciation of the environment, it's learning relationship and leadership skills. All those skills are important, but it's more the context of learning in an outdoor environment away from the classroom where students are very different in the way they relate to each other and relate to the teacher. (J)

> As a teacher, it's been such a good experience to see students being able
> to experience the outdoors, and just their relationships, and to really see
> them grow and getting to see them in a different environment rather
> than a classroom environment has been really good (J)

Thus the context of learning was deemed to be important in developing a
new appreciation of relationships to peers and teachers. Erin provided an
example of this change in peer relationships in her comment:

> I think they can see it more clearly when they are in the outdoors
> and they become more tolerant because they have got weaknesses as
> well as strengths and that it is pretty clear when you get the written
> evaluations that they are able to see that in that environment, whereas
> in a classroom if someone is doing something wrong, they are like 'you
> dick'; in the outdoors they help them, and that's something we need to
> embrace really (E)

Given the importance of the outdoors as an opportunity for exploring
relationships that might differ from those experienced in a 'formal' school
setting; both Erin and Jane expressed a strong desire for teachers to
remain as the main providers of outdoor education experiences rather than
contracting external experts. Although contract instructors are required for
certain activities their role is to support the teaching staff rather than to be
the expert who replaces the teacher. Erin spoke of how she saw the teacher–
expert instructor relationship working:

> I still want to be the leader; I still want to make decisions with them.
> Like if it was really wet or the conditions were really bad I would not
> expect them to have turned up, and say they have made the call, 'we are
> not doing this', I would expect, I would make it clear that I am part of
> that decision-making process together (E)

In a further discussion, about the use of residential outdoor centres with
specialist staff, Erin commented that for her, a key aspect of outdoor
education is about students developing relationships with their teachers and
their peers. With specialist outdoor providers she expressed the following:

> the instructors are the ones forming the relationship and that relationship
> finishes in two days and it's all over. So I would personally rather have
> our staff taking the activities, unfortunately sometimes badly, but they
> are still there building the relationships and getting to know the kids in
> a completely different place than they would. (E)

Jane expressed a similar sentiment:

> You can go along (to an outdoor centre) and they have all these enthusiastic young instructors and that's fantastic and they can build a good relationship with the students and then you leave. They haven't got that connection with the school and a lot of it, in outdoor education, I feel like you have a real team atmosphere. I think that it is really important that the teacher is there, that you lose a lot if you don't have those, the people from your school environment with you if at all possible. Yeah I like it to be the class's experience, not provided from the outside if possible. (J)

Both Jane and Erin expressed a strong desire for outdoor education programs to be delivered, wherever possible, by teaching staff. Both were clearly able to articulate the importance of the student–teacher relationship in the teaching and learning process. The desire for teachers to be the primary deliverers of programs has some obvious implications for the type of program that the school can offer. Rather than narrowing the range of opportunities, the ability to draw on staff expertise in 'non-traditional' outdoor education activities has the potential to enrich the school's program. The Western Bay of Plenty has a strong beach/marine culture, and one of New Zealand's premier white water paddling rivers. Many of the staff at Mount Maunganui College reflect this 'outdoorsy lifestyle' (e.g. they are surfers and are active in the surf lifesaving clubs) and provide a resource to both assist in the running of activities and also a conduit into local clubs and recreational organisations.

The school is clearly responding to the environment in which they are situated. The activities that are being incorporated into the program reflect both the natural resources and aspects of the local culture that have been shaped by the environment. For example, Jane explained

> [the school] bought a set of boogie boards[4] last year and so they are learning the skills and it is so relevant and meaningful for them. They all go to the beach, so having surf-survival skills and surf-lifesaving skills is really important. And I have just brought some soft top surf boards as well for outdoor education … (J)

The desire to use teaching staff has obvious implications in regards to the necessary competence and qualifications needed to run 'risky activities' that often feature in media portrayals of the outdoors and in some residential centres' promotional material (e.g. abseiling or canyoning). While acknowledging the importance of appropriate risk management strategies and the need to comply with legislative requirements, both teachers emphasised the educational considerations in program planning over the provision of mere activities. When questioned about the role of risk in the provision of outdoor education experiences, Erin cited an example of an activity that encapsulated many of the aims of an effective teaching and learning experience:

> ... one of the biggest things is not abseiling, not the flying-fox, its *waka* ^open canoe^
> *ama*.[5] You know what's the perceived risk there? There is teamwork going on, there's communication going on, there is a challenge going on ... So yeah, I like the idea of them challenging themselves through thinking rather than shitting themselves, which is what a lot of them end up doing. (E)

Similarly, Jane did not see that activities needed to be of a high risk nature (perceived or real) to foster learning:

> I would rather that students learn the skills and have an opportunity to practice them and then they consolidate them in the outdoors. It is not about hardship or fear so much. I would rather them be in a situation where they have gained the skills that they can be in the situation that they are confident, that they know that they can do something and so it is the opportunity to put those skills into practice, but not be in a situation where they are scared. Yeah I like it when it is sequential ... if they are ready and they have the skills and they love it then that's what you want not for them to be pissing their pants. (J)

Jane and Erin's understanding of the role of experiences in outdoor settings as a means to foster improved peer and teacher–student relationships extends beyond the provision of simple get-to-know-you games and team-building activities. The desire to centre teachers and students at the core of teaching and learning process has important implications for what is offered in the school's outdoor education program and where these programs are offered. Clearly connections to, and between people, are important. It is to the emerging issue of connections to places that I now turn.

## Outdoor education as an exploration of local areas and a means to foster positive memories

Erin was overt in her desire for students to experience activities within the school's geographical area rather than travelling long distances to 'wilderness' areas.

I'm saying this is our direct area let's try to use it. I think that is huge, because our kids will go back there. We all do just disappear from this town and from this country, but we all come back and those are things that I will go 'yeah I remember doing that', that kind of thing. (E)

Erin has touched on several issues that will no doubt resonate with many antipodeans – the belief that the 'real world' exists beyond our small communities. The movement of young people from provincial towns to large cities or overseas destinations is a feature of many modern societies. We embark on odysseys for education, employment, adventure and perhaps sheer desperation in an effort to escape the overly familiar and mundane. Yet, in time many of us are drawn back to places, the places of our childhoods, holidays, or places with familial ties. Here Erin draws on her own experience of leaving and returning and her endeavours to engender in her students a connection with place through positive experiences. There is a recognition that many of her students may leave for the 'bright lights' but there is also the hope that the creation of positive memories will provide a touchstone in later life.

Erin also spoke of an early version of the year 9 camp that was based at the school. This account is linked to a formative experience from her own childhood and provides an excellent example of how personal narratives are interwoven with professional practice.

We based them at the school *Marae*[6] and they did all these activities around the Mount and on the last day climbed the Mount and learnt the history. We took a scientist from here and one of the *iwi* ladies I knew, so we had two perspectives. We got this mythology and we got this geography and the science of the, you know, the geography and history and things like that. And I was just blown away at how many kids had not been on the Mount. I was just shocked … over two weeks we had taken 300 kids up the Mount, and that was what they remembered. They didn't care about all the rest, they cared because they had gone up that hill. They had looked at it for 13 years and never gone on it. And that kind of made me think, why do people go away when we have so much here? It just clicked …

When I was 12 or 13 my parents took me overseas, took us all overseas for a year, and we went travelling and did not go to school, and we came back and we were home for about a week and Dad goes 'you have seen the world, now you need to see our own place'. He put us back in the car and took us for six or seven weeks around New Zealand. I hated

*[handwritten margin note: sometimes you have to have an "outside" experience to make you appreciate what you have @ home]*

him at the time, but afterwards I thought 'he is right, I haven't even seen my own place' … yeah, it's probably all come from that. But, yeah I like this, I like this sustainability thing. You know we take students on a tramp down in Lake Waikaremoana. They will have an amazing experience and probably get a taste for tramping and a love for it, but will they go back there? Probably not. You take them up the Mount and they go 'oh I can walk up the Mount now' you know and they will do that, yeah that's what I like. (E)

It is clear from Erin's story that her early experiences of travel in New Zealand, in her 'own place' has been influential in her desire to connect her students to their 'own place' in a way that will foster a positive connection. The role of personal experience and beliefs has been identified as a contributing factor in informing teachers' practice (Fang 1996; Macdonald and Kirk 1999).

Jane also expressed a desire for students to be able to connect with places in an ongoing manner.

Well I like the idea of a journey in your own environment and making the most of your local environment so that you can take your family and friends. It can be part of who you are and your connection to the land. And for me, for my interest in Māori education as well, those links to your whenua[7] I think are key and are really important. A lot of people have missed out on feeling they are part of a place … if you feel a connection with where you live and your environment and in turn you have more respect and you have got increased transference and take it on as part of your own identity. (J)

Both Erin and Jane have alluded to the difficulty of connection to places that are distant from the school (e.g. Lake Waikaremoana is several hours' drive away). Jane has made explicit the link between places and one's sense of identity. The program's emphasis on sequential skill development, and utilising local environs that are easily accessible, provides the potential for students to revisit and engage with these places beyond the confines of the school curriculum. This ability for connection contrasts with the difficulty, or inability, to reconnect when programs are conducted in difficult to access areas; at residential centres that require group bookings; or require technical equipment and/or an expert guide.

Jane also mentions what is often seen as the 'crux' for advocates of outdoor education: transference from the outdoors to other aspects of life. One of the issues with 'traditional' outdoor education programs has been need to show how unique, and frequently contrived activities conducted in remote or wilderness settings, have relevance beyond that setting. As I have discussed elsewhere (M. Brown, 2010), transfer is a highly problematic metaphor that reflects particular ways of understanding learning and what counts as knowledge. This is not the place to enter into a protracted debate, suffice to say that Jane has, perhaps unwittingly, found an elegant and highly practical way of circumventing the issue of proving transfer in her setting. By locating learning in the practices of the day-to-day activities of the community there is little need to prove transfer occurs. Schooling becomes an extension, or complement to, the life of the broader community.

Despite Jane's assertion that 'you have increased transference' both she and Erin highlighted the frustration that outdoor education was still not seen as an integral, and potentially integrative, means to connect disparate aspects of the school curriculum. As Erin commented:

> One of the things that disappoints me year after year and I really, really want to work on it, is bringing the learning that we do out there into here and having it flow through the class and the school and into their lives. I just don't think we do it well.

> [There's an attitude of] ok, so that was camp, let's move on and do English and maths, and that's the hugest part of it for me, I want to figure out how to do that (foster) … a cross curriculum approach … I have suggested it to them [other staff] and it just gets kind of washed away, so I think that's the big point for me, transfer of learning. (E)

This stand-alone nature of camps was also commented on by Jane where she expressed a desire to connect with other curriculum areas:

> If we had a more cross-curricula focus and if we have more of the departments on board, we could improve how we follow up after camps as well, so we need to set up an environment where transference is going to happen. (J)

One of the possible contributing factors for this lack of cross-curricula focus may be that the responsibility for camps falls to the PE department. As Erin stated:

> it looks like a PE camp, but it's not, it's an outdoor ed camp or an EOTC[8] camp, because that's what happening, everyone is like 'that's a PE camp', another 'Erin project' they call it … (E)

**"By locating learning in the practices of the day-to-day activities of the community there is little need to prove transfer occurs. Schooling becomes an extension, or complement to, the life of the broader community."**

Jane made a similar comment in regards to the perception that outdoor education camps are only relevant to PE staff and students within the school curriculum. She stated:

> we feel like we are on our own a little bit and the camps are for the whole school and not just the PE department. (J)

These comments reflect tensions in many professional workplaces. It is clear that the understandings and practices espoused by Jane and Erin represent a desire to move beyond existing ways of conducting outdoor education (outsourcing provision, the use of specialised activities requiring technical expertise, and one-off discrete experiences) with attempts to locate teaching and learning within the local context.

As Erin and Jane acknowledged, efforts to locate outdoor education experiences in the local community have not always been successful and this has created inconsistencies between what is an ideal and what can be achieved within the practicalities of funding, staffing and timetabling.

## Discussion

These semi-structured interviews provided an opportunity to hear from two outdoor educators who are called on to plan and deliver outdoor education and school camping experiences across a number of year levels. Attempts to tease out these teachers' beliefs about outdoor education is important in regards to the practices that they are likely to encourage or implement. Hill's (2010b) case study of four New Zealand secondary school teachers found that 'what teachers believe significantly impacts on how they teach' (p. 38). Thus the foundational beliefs about the value of connections to people and places, expressed by both Erin and Jane, support the school's exploration of a move towards a more place-responsive pedagogy in outdoor education. Their beliefs about the value of encouraging students' connections to others, and to the region in which they live, find support in place-based educational literature (Smith 2002). The selection of sections of transcript highlight the quest of these educators to provide students with experiences which will encourage them to get to know their peers and teachers in a different context, develop skills, and an appreciation and desire to engage with the environment in which they live. Jane's and Erin's concern with advancing the cross-curricula potential of outdoor learning is supported by Zink and Boyes' (2006) research that ranked New Zealand teachers' beliefs and values in outdoor education. In their study the belief that outdoor education could enrich all curriculum areas attained the highest ranking from teachers.

This is not an idealised account of an exemplary school. Rather it is an attempt to reveal how teachers in an urban, mid-decile secondary school setting, have sought to understand their situation and implement a program that is contextualised to their setting. There is evidence that Jane and Erin are attuned to the particularities of their place. It is clear that they are responding to their locality and their students' 'outside-the-school-world'. Bringing the 'outside' into the school outdoor education program will provide challenges, and may lead to questioning by other outdoor professionals who view outdoor education as consisting of more traditional activities. A seemingly humble or 'leisure-time' activity like boogie boarding or surfing is more than a simple and fun outdoor activity. It would appear to provide an opportunity to teach about important aspects of the local environment and simultaneously have the potential to develop strong links to local community via the surf club(s). These community-based organisations often do a lot of work beyond simply patrolling (e.g. youth groups, charity work, first aid training, even employment opportunities) and this connects to some of the points about place-based education made in chapter five. Additionally both teachers are responding to the multi-cultural character of their school. Acknowledging and incorporating Māori concepts, activities and stories into the program provides opportunities for many students 'outside-the-school-world' knowledge to be valued and shared in a meaningful context.

Jane's and Erin's efforts to empower teachers (and year 13 students at times) to deliver outdoor programs which are enjoyable and encourage ongoing engagement with friends and family in places that are accessible is illustrative of a program in transition. As Jane explained, outdoor education has not always been practised in this manner at Mount Maunganui College.

> Before I got there, [outdoor education] was like boot camp, almost army style and students felt happy that they had got through it, but they did not want to go back into the outdoors again, but I do really like how they learn the skills and they build on those skills and they feel confident that they can do activities safely and a lot have got their family into things as well and a lot of them have got into multi-sport and carried on with it, so yeah that is the biggest kick … (J)

It is clear that there has been a change in how outdoor education has been offered at this school. What is also clear is that these two teachers are keen to continue this process to investigate ways in which cross-curricula links can be forged and new ideas in regards to place-based approaches to outdoor education can be incorporated into their school's program.

As discussed in earlier chapters the notion that outdoor education consists of a series of generic activities, that if followed would constitute 'good outdoor education', is highly problematic. As we have indicated previously there is also no simple or generic recipe for implementing a place-based approach. Erin's desire – to 'see a school that has it sorted out' – is a reasonable enough request:

> a school that takes their subjects on camp and then brings their camps back into their subjects, I would love to see that. If someone has got it sorted then I would go 'tell me' I would really, really like to see how simple it can be. (E)

However, there is no prescription that will meet the needs of different schools in different communities in different places. The challenge for Erin and Jane (and their colleagues) is to continue to develop a program that responds to their place; a place that is constantly changing, both physically and culturally. There is little doubt that urban development, migration and the changing educational policies and priorities of government will require constant attention to the changing landscape in which the school, and the surrounding community, functions.

It is worth remembering that while there might be an imagined ideal outdoor education program; there is no perfect program. Just as place is unfolding and emerging so too will programs that are designed around the principles of a place-responsive outdoor education pedagogy. In many ways both Jane and Erin are well on the pathway to implementing a place-responsive approach in their practice; both recognise the importance of connection, the centrality of place to program design and the oft overlooked, in outdoor education, role of place in identity formation. Several years ago Robyn Zink and Mike Boyes (2006) questioned how teachers understood the outdoors and 'how clearly they are able to articulate the role the outdoors has in student learning' (p. 20). What is clear from these teachers is that they are highly conscious of the role that the outdoors, or the place(s) where outdoor activities are conducted, has in student learning.

The issues and challenges that Jane and Erin face are those that we all face as we attempt to make teaching and learning relevant in changing times. This case study documents the start of a process, an ongoing process that we are all required to tread as we respond to the place(s) where we live and/or conduct our programs. Yet as Hill (2010b) found, when there is consistency between teachers' beliefs and pedagogical practices, teachers considered it more likely that they would be able to make a positive contribution to the lives of their students. It would appear that the development of a place-responsive pedagogy may sit well with the espoused beliefs of these two inquiring teachers.

*Chapter 8*

## Knowable Places:
## The Story of a Place-Responsive
## Educator

### ~ Brian ~

This case study profiles the work of a place-responsive outdoor educator. Arthur Curl has coordinated, and taught in, an outdoor education program for nearly twenty years at the same independent primary to year 12 school in Victoria. I have known Arthur for all of that time. Initially we met when Arthur was an outdoor education student in the final two years of his undergraduate degree and I commenced working at Latrobe University in 1990. Upon graduation Arthur began his teaching career and we subsequently kept in touch. We completed several canoe-building projects together, one of which culminated in a long river journey with students. I wrote about this experience in a journal paper titled 'River ... I follow river' (Wattchow 1998). We also coordinated our programs so that my third year undergraduate paddling students could experience running an aquatic-based camp with Arthur's year eight students. Catching up gave us the opportunity to discuss and debate ideas about outdoor education philosophy and programming. Both of us were in the early years in our new work places, Arthur in his school and myself at my first university appointment.

Over the years I noted that Arthur developed a very thoughtful and distinctive approach to outdoor programming. It was quite different to other trends taking place in school-based outdoor education at the time, such as increasingly demanding adventure activities being delivered to younger and younger students, international trekking programs, and the outsourcing of camping programs to commercial providers. Outdoor education at Arthur's school seemed to be based around a strong set of ideals that had to do with how children experience a sense of emergent meaning in outdoor places. At one level the camps seemed low-tech, uncomplicated affairs. At another level they appeared to be built on an evolving set of complex values and ideas. In Arthur's fifth year at the school I wrote another journal paper exploring how choices made about outdoor equipment fundamentally shape educational possibilities. As part of that paper, 'A pedagogy of production' (Wattchow 2001b), I wrote about crafting outdoor equipment and drew on an example from Arthur's practice where students make rustic timber furniture as part of a camp in East Gippsland. In this paper I quoted a section of a letter (with permission) that Arthur had written to me about the camp. The letter, along with our conversations, confirmed that this school's outdoor education program was developing a unique pedagogic strategy for working with young people in outdoor places.

There are several reasons why telling the story of a teacher dedicated to an alternative ethos and practice may benefit other outdoor educators interested in place. Narratives about how professional outdoor educators work, their histories, beliefs and practices, are few and far between. Beyond the iconic figures of people like Kurt Hahn, John Dewey and a few others, there is largely silence about what it is actually like as an educator to work with children in the outdoors. While not abandoning the best of the legacy of Dewey and others, we need to step out of the long shadows cast by these historic figures and craft our own stories about local educators working in local outdoor places. We have made a case in this book for the power of narrative to inform in ways that reach beyond the limitations of textual description. Stories do this when they resonate with the reader. The reader shifts between interrogating the words for meaning and listening to the story unfold for its own sake. As a result of developing empathy for the characters in the story the reader may be moved to reflect upon their own past, values and practices. Possibilities may begin to emerge as the listener sees their own story in a fresh light. So Arthur's story as an outdoor educator is not presented as an instruction or 'how to' guide for place-responsive outdoor education. In fact, the intent of this case study is quite the opposite. The reader of the story must draw his or her own conclusions about implications for their practice with the learners and outdoor places with which they are familiar.

## Methodological considerations

Writing Arthur's story posed a series of interesting methodological challenges. A series of interviews were conducted to collect descriptions and reflections about his practices and values as a teacher. The interviewing approach employed in this study was based on what Seidman (1998) refers to as in-depth, phenomenologically-based interviewing. The goal is to have the interviewee reconstruct his or her experience within the topic of interest, in this case place-responsive outdoor education. The most distinguishing feature of this is the structuring of a series of three separate and distinct interviews. The first interview focuses on the person's 'life history'. As the interviewer, my aim here was to ask questions and gather meaningful background material that might help make sense of Arthur's values and practices as an outdoor educator. This included questions about formative experiences as a child in the outdoors and also his experiences in outdoor programs at school and university. The second interview relates to 'the details of experience'. The purpose of this interview was to focus on Arthur's experience of working in the outdoors with students in the way that he does. This includes how he works, where he conducts outdoor programs, how he makes decisions about aspects of programming; in essence, his pedagogic practices. There was an emphasis here on seeking detailed descriptions of events rather than reflecting on their broader meaning and consequences. What I was seeking were rich descriptions of practice. These first two interviews were conducted on consecutive days while camping on Arthur's 'rural block' in South Gippsland. Both interviews were audio recorded and then fully transcribed and the transcripts sent to Arthur for checking. As a researcher, I was already interpreting and attaching significance to Arthur's statements during the interview and transcription process. While listening intently, I was also making decisions about what follow-up questions to ask to elicit further responses and what to delay until the third interview.

The third and final interview is constructed as a 'reflection on meaning' where Arthur was asked to reflect on the meaning of the experiences he had described in the first two interviews. 'Meaning' strives to address the intellectual and emotional connections between the participant and the topic. Both interviewer and interviewee came prepared, having read the earlier transcripts highlighting topics, themes to explore in more depth, while also being aware of any significant gaps or relevant topics not covered that might be important to explore. The time gap between the first two interviews and the third was just over two weeks. The final transcript and then, later, a draft version of this chapter were also sent to Arthur for checking.

Part of the challenge as a researcher and a writer, as Anne Bell (2003) elaborates, is to

> attend to ways that the more-than-human world spoke through participants' stories. There is a danger … when focussing on the metaphors and storylines that structure human experience, to forget that our words, as David Abram (1996) puts it, emerge 'from our ongoing reciprocity with the world'. (p. 101)

Hence, in reconstructing Arthur's story as an outdoor educator, I have made choices about relaying some stories in considerable depth, and in that way invited the reader to interpret the character of a place as well as the human stories that are unfolding there. Devoting significant word space to this means that some topics and examples discussed in the interviews are not presented here. The story told is partial, but hopefully satisfying, in terms of inviting a reflective response in the reader. An understanding of how an outdoor educator like Arthur first became attuned to the significance of outdoor activities and outdoor places in his life makes a good starting point.

## 'An emergent feeling'

Arthur seems to have a predisposition for learning in a way that is well suited to a place-responsive educator. He combines an ongoing child-like inquisitiveness about the world with an active and considered pursuit of a range of ways of knowing something, whether it be a place, a person, a skill, an idea, or a story. Arthur traced this capacity, in part at least, back to early family camping experiences.

> In terms of the starting point there, of the connectedness between those childhood experiences and my practice now which, when I read the transcript [of the first interview] was even more clear to me than it had been before, and that was the idea that … a good deal of the planning was about just going to a place. And that was definitely what we did as children. We would just go, and sometimes we were going to somewhere like Lake Eyre because it was in flood and to see the birds, but essentially we were just going there. That's very much a part of what we do know. That's very much a part of how I do things. (Interview 3)

Where did this disposition come from and how was it cultivated? We explored this topic at length in the first interview.

> There's a combination of wonderful family camping trips, unhurried. We didn't go on extraordinary tours. We always went and propped. We'd drive somewhere, to the Flinders Ranges, a lot of them inland up to the Murray. We'd always just go and set up somewhere. A lot less spectacular than the current camps of today with the umpteen bits of equipment. Pretty simple camping and we just took the Valiant and we'd set up and stay in a place, and potter. We just pottered around. I've got two brothers and a sister who is much younger … so we kind of had an exploration group, which was great. We were busy in a way that we generated ourselves. Often it was just the kids and often Dad would come with us if we were going somewhere that he thought might be dangerous. He would just come along and it was fantastic, it was an incredible offering to our freedom. (Interview 1)

The interview transcripts suggest that Arthur is able to recall and reconstruct aspects of these experiences in fine detail. The story of one camping experience, when he was about ten years old, to Brachina Gorge in the Flinders Ranges, was described at length. The Flinders Ranges, in South Australia, are made up of a series of dry quartzite bluffs and ridgelines in the semi-arid mid-north of the state. Over five hundred million years of uplift, folding and weathering have produced a particularly visually striking landscape.

> Dad's instruction to go to the Flinders Rangers was to take us to the National Gallery and stand us in front of the Hans Heysen paintings. He said, 'that's where we are going', and we said, 'Cool, that looks good then'. Also I remember seeing three Namatjiras [the famous Aboriginal artist of central Australia], the three river gum Namatjiras that are in the National Gallery. We looked at those and Dad identified those as being characteristic of this place. It wasn't so much that we had a sense of the aesthetic as I remember, I remember being immediately struck that this was a place of entirely different colours and I knew, in me, that it was going to feel different. I remember having this kind of visceral sense that when I got there this was going to be a place [where] the air would be different and the ground would be different. (Interview 1)

I remember it emerging on the horizon … out of that vast plain to the east of it, and just seeing this kind of incredibly purpley-blue haze, and immediately going, 'That's like the painting! That's what it looks like!' Getting in there was hard. I think we got bogged a couple of times to get in to where we were going to camp, which was next to this exquisite water hole. And I remember the texture of the air. It was that incredibly cold, still air of the gorge and just those luffing warm breezes and going, 'Oh, this is different'. Then looking up to the very red rock and the amazing grass trees. We'd seen grass trees before but not like that. It was a very different aesthetic. That sandstone, I love it. That Upper Devonian, really rich reddish kind of sandstone. I've encountered that lots at Mutawintji and the Barrier Ranges and even up in Kakadu, but not in the same way. (Interview 1)

We had a wonderful rickety brown camping table and I remember sitting and having lunch and dinner by the table, and the smell of hurricane lamps. We only ever had hurricanes, and the smell of kero hurricane lamps was pretty much ubiquitous around our camping gear (laughs). Dad loved his hurricanes and so I remember that incredible smell. But the first night I had unbelievably strong and vivid dreams. And I'm not quite sure why, but I remember in the middle of the night getting up and I remember going outside and having this slice of just extraordinary dark sky and stars. Really, really vivid. And going 'Oh'. When I think of that place there are images … that are just burned into my psyche, I can still see now. I know exactly what colour it was, and I know exactly the feel. There was a spot that we stopped under a couple of trees and I am convinced that it was where Heysen painted that famous painting. I remember sitting there and I can see the contour of the land and the rise that we were sitting on and the arch of those trees and everything – it's just absolutely in my mind as a place. And I remember, I can remember what it smelt like, that light dry dust, the silky dust in the gorge, and the feel of the warm sand on top and the cold, as soon as your feet sink in it's cold, really cold and still. (Interview 1)

Arthur's stories of this family camping trip to Brachina Gorge in the Flinders Ranges in South Australia resonate with the sensual saturation of the child. We smell the quirky odours of the campsite. We see the gorge looming overhead and the shining waterhole, reconstructed as if through a child's eyes once again. We feel the ground through a child's small and sensitive feet. But other important elements of the experience emerge as well. The locations for the camping trips were often chosen by Arthur's father for the intrinsic interest of what was anticipated to reside there. It is also evident that Arthur was simultaneously developing a cultural literacy about the Australian landscape; its art, history, geology, botany and so on, through his family upbringing. At another point in the first interview Arthur described his fascination as a child with the expansive collection of natural history books in his father's library and he could recall the visits of a particular friend of his father who was a botanical artist. We might speculate that, as a child, Arthur experienced a reciprocal loop between learning about ways of knowing outdoor places culturally and encountering them through deeply immersive experiences. Cultural knowing can then be tested and validated, or not, by the child in the outdoors. There are two important threads being drawn together here. The embodied sense of knowing outdoor places combines with a more rational way of learning about them. Experience itself is neither one nor the other, but both of these working in tandem. Arthur describes what it meant to him as a child to blend these two different ways of learning to *be* in the outdoors in quite an interesting way.

> We never had what I see now in the lives of the kids that I teach, the idea of the bush as this kind of vast unknowable. There was never any of those notions of wilderness or remoteness. And often we were in incredibly remote places, but that was never a part of it. For us our experience was always that these were knowable places. (Interview 1)

## 'Just to be in the bush'

A similar story unfolds in relation to Arthur's outdoor experiences through his secondary schooling. One teacher in particular, who also ran the school bushwalking club, emerges as another important role model.

> I had some exquisite teachers … some absolutely extraordinary teachers who were unquestioningly teaching from a depth of passion and dedication. They weren't – there was no going through the process, and not the least Chris Howell. He was my biology teacher. He was just fantastic. Heaps and heaps of narrative teaching. Lots and lots of stories told about something happening … (Interview 1)

In addition, the extracurricular bushwalking club provided Arthur with valuable opportunities that he felt could not be fulfilled within the more formal structures inside the school.

The walks were just fantastic. We just went bushwalking. There was no fluffing around. They weren't doing great long distances. They weren't about kind of linking extraordinary places I don't think. We just went to places. And sometimes we went to quite mundane places. It wasn't a highly organised, managed affair. There was an element of uncertainty and excitement that anything could happen, and that was a big part of the anticipation. It was a pretty organised culture at the school generally … There was an urge for freedom. It was just to be in the bush, and all of the things that that brought with it. I loved learning the names of birds … some part of it was that I wanted that. I really loved that aspect of going to all of these different places and recognising familiar things in different places. And I loved the process of camping. Having everything on your back and loved the process of packing. Getting all of your stuff out and thinking of whether I've got everything and putting it all in there and then the assuredness that you have when you put your pack on and you think, 'I've got it all.' I really like that. I loved – I think the uncertainty, I think that was a big part of it. It was a place where things could happen. (Interview 1)

The first interview revealed a childhood and adolescence where Arthur had regular opportunities to engage with nature through family camping and extracurricular school bushwalks. There was never a sense that these were organised as deliberate educational programs with sets of learning objectives and outcomes. But significant learning occurred within the 'space of opportunities' that these experiences provided.

They [the bushwalking club] were right into sunsets and sunrises and being on top of hills in storms and things like that. They were into the kind of acquisition of experiences. But not at all in terms of there being things to know about a country in a kind of natural history sense. Actually, there was quite a strong kind of cultural history aspect to it. The track notes always had things about a place name, and why it was called that, and what the story was that went with that. That was fantastic. And there was a huge tradition of storytelling. You know storytelling about previous bushwalks or about happenings or about great adventures. (Interview 1)

Arthur's recollections reveal layer upon layer of experiences. In almost every case there was a parallel, but slightly unpredictable, cognitive learning going on that related to the place. It might be learning about the history of the long abandoned tramways in the Ada Valley forests, east of Melbourne. Or it might be about a particular bird or tree species and how it fitted within a particular environment. This learning was almost always encountered both in the physical world and via a story passed down from someone who had something important to tell. When asked, at the conclusion of the first interview, about how he feels now about those encounters, Arthur replied with the following:

> Still a whole lot of it is about what it was for me as a child, was that places are knowable. And they are knowable in an outward and an inward sense. That you can know them in a naming sense, and you can know them in a cultural, storied kind of sense, but you can also know them in a kind of embodied, visceral, felt sense. And that knowing resides in you in an inalienable way. It is a kind of infection in a way. It answers a kind of relationship that we have with ourselves and with the world, with the land that we live on, with the world that we live in, which is really, really important. That it is definitely about searching for – experiencing belonging. Not as a notion to be explored so much as an emergent feeling. (Interview 1)

## 'Inquisitive wanderings'

As mentioned in the introduction, Arthur completed an undergraduate degree in outdoor education at Latrobe University, Bendigo Campus. He also took a year off during his teaching career to complete a Masters in Social Ecology, where he met and studied with John Cameron, Stuart Hill and Martin Mulligan at The University of Western Sydney. Arthur had attended the 12th National Outdoor Education Conference held at La Trobe University in Bendigo, Australia. This is the conference that we wrote about in the introductory chapter to this book, where John Cameron articulated his quiet challenge to outdoor educators to overcome the dualistic divide between wilderness and everyday places. Cameron had provided an important vision for an alternative from of outdoor education practice for Arthur.

> But then that, it was an epiphany to hear John Cameron, I mean Stuart Hill was just as inspiring, but to hear John Cameron talking, and going, 'Yes, yes, that's it, that's what I want'. (Interview 2)

Arthur commented upon the value of both his undergraduate and postgraduate studies in introducing him to significant ideas and philosophies about the outdoors, ecology and education. He also mentioned that these were important opportunities to connect with others who seemed to be questioning how society valued and interacted with nature and, importantly, with those who were developing local community and education programs in response to these 'big' ideas. The descriptions that follow now focus on his pedagogical practices and are not chronological in terms of Arthur's development as a teacher. They are largely drawn from the second interview, which was structured as an inquiry into his contemporary practices and which sought rich descriptions of teaching programs. So we pick up Arthur's story again with the first camping experience that students at his school undertake. School staff and year three students first go camping together in a local coastal park not far from the school. The campsite chosen varies, but is typically on the south eastern shore of the Mornington Peninsula, on the fringes of suburban Melbourne. It is a popular summer time camping and swimming area, and is already well known to many of the children.

> The first trip is incredibly simple. We usually go to a beach, 'cause that's a very culturally familiar environment for them. We just camp. And the exercise of just camping and establishing a routine and a rhythm is a really big part of that. It's really just about being in that place and we can probably draw a radius of 400m around the entire trip. There is a real episode about putting up the big tarp for the kitchen and getting the kids to help with that. They all strain the rope up. And there is a real process to establishing our place there. That really helps them to establish a sense of belonging right there. [The big tarp] is somewhere that we go from and come back to, 'cause we have kind of made it in a way. We are really deliberate in assembling the tents like a little village, so that it is a lived place, quite quickly. (Interview 2)

Once the little village of tents and kitchen-meeting tarp has been constructed, a home away from home perhaps, the experience unfolds around a number of opportunities. For example, the group of staff and students might head down to the beach and reef nearby.

> I'd always make sure that they are bare foot and that they are really deeply tactile, engaged in a tactile way. Some of the kids will stop short, they won't get to the reef, they'll stop on the sand and start digging in the sand, or collecting shells or whatever and that's fantastic. So it really is about following their inquisitive wonderings. But kind of drawing the kids around a focus in that. And not so that they are all doing the same

thing, but they'll start walking out onto the reef and the kids who were doing something else will take a little while to catch up. And you just time it so that they are all just there when you start telling stories. Lots of ecological storytelling. Stories about dog welks and urchins and the lives of things lived on the reef, but very much in a story. (Interview 2)

The camp unfolds around the possibilities inherent in the place and the children, and in the capacity for the staff to know what is appropriate to do at any given point in time.

[It is a] beautiful little foreshore camping reserve and immediate access … to a lovely basalt reef platform. Enough crashing waves to remind them that this is a place connected to vast ocean … Just camp and a really strong daily routine. Get up in the morning. I'd get them all up at the same time and go for a walk. And usually that would be a quiet walk, and not a long way. We'd just mosey and meander and maybe stop and look at a banksia and talk about it. Just wander them around and kind of wake them up to the place in a really deliberate way. And then back and have some brekkie. And then slow after brekkie. Good time while your brekkie is going down to clean up your tent and actually know where your hat is and that sort of stuff, which for grade threes can be a bit of an episode (chuckles). So, do that and then talk about what we'd like to do for the day. Talk about where do you think we should go. You know, 'It's a bit windy down there but what if we go around the corner kind of thing.' So include them in the kind of planning in the day. And then pack. Say, 'Oh I think we should take some lunch'. So pack a lunch and a water bottle and a hat. And usually you would go, 'Oh, we will take a rain coat just in case.' That 'just in case' ethic is a big part of embedding possibility in the way that they think towards the relationship between gear and experience. So, pack a lunch and off we go and walk all of 200m and sit down. You know if it is a really windy day it is wonderful to have little kids walking … Not a long way … and then find a spot out of the wind to let their little souls settle back again. Have lunch and walk back again. And if you can it's good to walk back into the wind so it gives you the kind of sense of arrival when you get there … Get them to help to get dinner organised. It depends actually. It depends on the dynamic in the group. Sometimes they just really need to play, to immerse themselves in play, and often it will be quite imaginative play at that time of the day. Then draw them together for a pretty early dinner and then tell them a story after dinner, usually an incredibly domestic story. Often I will tell them about a childhood experience of mine and it will often be enlivening in terms of something that's a little bit outrageous or a little bit daft … I think it slowly alerts them to the possibility that there a lots of ways to be in places like this. (Interview 2)

The Latin root of the word education, *educare*, literally means *bringing forth*. This seems to be a good description of the teaching and learning style of the camp. Rather than direct instruction the style of learning is about gently leading the child into a field of possibilities. Subsequent year levels continue to develop the subtle approach outlined above; 'the rhythm is always the same on every trip' (Interview 2). Year level camps gradually expand the students' horizons. 'We do lots of stuff around the Yarra Valley and the watersheds [close to the school], so there is lots of engagement with the very, very immediate local place' (Interview 2). But there is a deliberate shift in year nine, which is the most intensive in terms of number of camping programs, where choices are made about going to a range of locations across Victoria.

## 'Deepening into place'

In year nine a sequence of camping programs sees students experiencing a wide range of distinctively different locations.

> These are places that are the nearest examples of quite marked different kinds of environments … They do some time in the box ironbark forest and they do some time in the limestone and basalt down by the beach. They go to the sandstone country at Grampians and to the Sunset Country and to the red gum forest in Barmah and to the East Gippsland tall forests. They really are remarkably different but characteristic of reasonable spans or areas of Victoria. That is quite deliberate. (Interview 2)

This might be described as a kind of experiential geography, where expanding the students' direct encounter with their broader region is timed with the transitions they are making from childhood into adolescence. Implicit is the understanding that a person can become deeply attached to more than one place. It also teaches that no place should be ignored or taken for granted. Each and every place is considered to be potentially brimful of meaning and value. Places are selected not only because they are geographically distinctive, but also because Arthur and the staff have already established a relationship with the place being visited. What unfolds is, perhaps, a kind of pedagogic role modelling of how to engage with, live in, and value outdoor places.

> I want them to have an understanding that there is something to be known here… Always making sure that they realise that these are our favourite places … we introduce the variety of places that we take them to as some of our favourite places – 'ours' being the collective group of leaders … it's a kind of passive modelling of the fact that we have relationships with these places. These are places that are known to us and loved by us, that we know something about these places. I've never thought about kind of why, but we always do it. Always talk about it … That you can have relationships with places that you favour. And we would often talk as staff in the presence of the kids about, you know, kind of river people and ocean people and that kind of thing. Not as a borrowing of the saltwater people concept of indigenous fellas. But that there are different kinds of places that nourish us differently. (Interview 2)

When asked whether he could describe these kind of approaches to teaching through a particular example, Arthur paused for some time. 'It's hard,' he said. Not because it was hard to describe a particular camping program, but because it was hard for him to choose one loved place over another. After a while, he began to describe in detail how he came to know a place called Raak Plain, and how he teaches there. Raak Plain is in the far north west of Victoria. Most people would skirt its edge driving on the highway from Melbourne to Mildura on the River Murray. Flashing past their car window they would get the impression of endless kilometres of apparently featureless red sand and mallee scrub. It is still, for most Victorians and Australians, a blank space on the map.

> Raak Plain is a place that is a bit of an enigma to a lot of people who visit there. This is west of Hattah. It is an empty place on almost any map that you care to look at. It's an 80,000 acre salt pan, and we camp on the south eastern edge of it in belah ridge country right on the edge of the mallee scrub … We move our camp a bit every year so that we kind of monitor and watch the impact on the country. My first relationship with the place was to meet this extraordinary old man, Harold McArthur, who, at the time that I met him was about 72. Six foot three. Did all his stock work on horseback, crack shot. Lived in that country since he was 11 years old. Started shepherding sheep, [a]

mob of 400 sheep when he was 11 years old for three months at a time – been there ever since. You know he used to go on holidays. Plan a two-week holiday in Queensland and go away and come back after a week cause he missed the place. Probably as close as I have ever come in a whitefella to an indigenous kind of relationship to the place. If the blue mallee weren't flowering at the right time of the year he went to work out why, and he knew five or six stages of ecological relationships … So, who eats what. If the blue mallee weren't flowering he would know the insect that fed on that, and if it wasn't around he would think, 'Well, what are the birds doing that would be eating that insect?' And he would go and look for where he knew that they nested, and if they weren't nesting then he would look at scats and evidence to see what had happened in that cycle. So there was a whole landscape of relationships kind of hovering above the land itself that he was cognisant of. [I] went out there and was utterly enchanted by this old man and his relationship with the place. I was absolutely certain that I needed to take kids out there, and not entirely sure what we were going to do. There's not a lot there (chuckle). But wanted the kids' relationship with the place to be engaged with him and began with the idea of wanting the experience in that place to be kind of ethereal, kind of hovering above the land … We went up there on the night train from Spencer Street, the train stopped at Hattah Platform. The train stopped for just long enough to throw the children and their gear off and then off it went again.

Arthur's story about Harold McArthur living on Raak Plain as an eleven-year-old and the fact that the school students taken there are roughly the same age is not, I think, a coincidence. There is a palpable sense here of deliberate choices being made about how students would arrive, physically and emotionally, at start of the camping experience on Raak Plain. After the noisy, rolling, rollicking journey on the night train they suddenly find themselves 'thrown' into a dark, quiet and undeniably remote location. I have encountered similar situations in my own travels, both alone and with students. You briefly feel suspended between one world, now vanishing down the train tracks, and another. It is a transitory moment and the effect is one of sudden shock with the unfamiliar.

And then Harold picked us up in his cattle truck in the half light and drove us out to the middle of nowhere, to a seemingly nondescript spot and drove off. So, had these kids kind of arrive, having stayed awake 'cause it was exciting on the train a lot … Initially the kids did what most people do in that kind of country and go, 'There's nothing here. What are you thinking? This is ridiculous. What are we going to do while we are here?' No tents. Just put a truck tarp up on in the trees and mostly slept out from under it. Had a fire. And again, just like on the primary trips, established a rhythm in that place. It is an incredible place because the way that our relationship to it works is that we expand out to it in these kind of increasing radiuses. So in the first day we just circumnavigate the camp about a kilometre distant in a loop. Visit the mallee sandhill country, have a look at the bulldog ants and go and look at the belah trees. And lie down under the belah trees and listen to the breeze and the sound on the shore and all those kind of familiar little stories that for me are like mates. You know, you get back there and you go, 'Oh, g'day mate. Whoa, listen to you!'

For Arthur, returning each year to Raak Plain is like catching up with a cherished friend. For the students the relationship is just beginning.

A bit more breeze on a day under a belah tree is just this incredible thrill, and you can see it rippling through the children. It's just incredible. They relate to this place and go 'Oh, this is fantastic.' So, they begin to discover interest and excitement in the minutiae in the country. There are these tiny happenings that become satisfactory. Partly because the place is lacking grand mountain ranges or the crashing of waves or that kind of stuff. They just get there and are confronted. It makes you feel small inevitably, with that huge sky. You know it is a massive sky. It feels like it drops below the horizon on both sides. So we just do a walk around the campsite, and on the next day we do a longer walk out onto the salt plain. Just walk, barefoot, carrying stuff all gear, usually wrapped up in a sleeping bag cover or you now make a backpack out of your raincoat kind of thing. And wander out onto the saltpan and just expand that experience of the place. Make a big thing out of looking back to where we have come from. You don't need to get very far out till you can't see where we have come from. That kind of experience of vastness is just incredible and very confronting when you first get there. But after a couple of days of kind of moseying around the kids get right into it. We go out to this spot, a little island of mallee scrub out in the middle of the thing. It has got a bit of a saltpan out there, and we just play all day. Walk out there in the early morning and walk back as the sun is setting and for me the experience of taking children to this place is about watching them almost sink into the landscape.

You can watch them just immersing, just deepening into the place. For these kids the demands for entertainment are pretty high. They don't put their ipods in their ears on half volume. The world has got to come at them pretty bright and pretty loud. And you watch these kids and they will be kneeling down in the sand lifting the little trap door up on a trap-door spider's nest, looking at this trap-door spider's little space and trying to sit there and wait and watch a trap-door spider come out and grab something. And it's not out of that bloodlust of watching something kill something. It's about the kind of excitement about these incredibly intimate little happenings that are observable in this place. So they just deepen into it. By the last day this place that they thought they would be entirely unimpressed by, has just crept into [them]. It has got under their fingernails in a kind of way. (Interview 2)

That which was strange has become familiar. I think that there are deep lessons about what it takes to begin the process of making connections with country, of taking the first steps to learning to empathise with a place. Students are led, even gently coached, through a deceptively simple journey between the vast immensity of the place and the intimacy of its detail. The place that was silent and empty begins to fill with happenings and stories.

You can see our own footprints from the previous year. So it is an incredibly simple trip to unfold. It's a place that I love because there is incredible richness in the ecological happenings. So there is a real depth of stories to be told. And I really love telling those stories and engaging the kids in that. For me it is really nourishing, because in some places where there is really spectacular happenings, it can be pretty hard to get kids to care much about [the] kind of happenings in trees and that sort of stuff. It is a very nourishing place in that way. (Interview 2)

Stories of the place can be about intimate details or more expansive narratives that connect the students' experiences to more than just their immediate surrounds.

There is a sense to participating in a kind of cultural icon, in terms of the experience of laying under the stars in the vast inland. That inland Australian sky is almost like a character in your experience there. It is a huge part of how you experience that place. To lie down at night time under those stars, it's wonderful, and you do it and realise that you are participating in an experience which has characterised the lives of people throughout Australia's history. There's not a lot of difference lying there now than there was 150 years ago … I adore it because of the depth and longevity of my relationship with that place. I know there are trees that if I go and knock on them during the day a pink cockatoo is going to poke his head out at us. And I know that there is another tree there that if I go and knock on a mallee ring neck is going to poke its head out of a hollow. And there is another tree there that I know if I sit and watch it for ten minutes the flocks of wild budgerigars will come and go from it … I can go there and have an idea of things that are happening and you take with you a kind of knowing, and when that is reciprocated by happenings in that place that is incredibly nourishing in terms of the relationship with the place. I really love it that it is a place that isn't burdened by any of the danger stuff. You could walk barefoot there for two years and nothing is going to happen. (Interview 2)

For Arthur the meaning of Raak Plain is 'incredibly locked into a fabric of stories' (Interview 2). Stories, whether they are ecological, cultural or even personal in their genesis, ultimately are not the possession of any individual. They reflect broader culture traditions as well as the more-than-human world. It is not a one-sided telling either; 'You kind of let the country walk on you.' (Interview 2). Stories come from country and people and, for Arthur,

> The currency of those cultural stories is really important to me. I really know that it is not OK to be a receptacle for them. You have to be a conduit. You receive them and you pass them on, and you recognise the importance and the integrity. (Interview 3)

Arthur believes that such an approach, shared amongst the staff, brings richness and diversity to the program that cannot be manufactured. It can only arise out of long-term associations between staff, students and places.

> The storytelling is distributed. I think that way there is a great deal of richness in that. Certainly the other staff adore returning to the same places, that is something that is universally celebrating the work … and they bring different aspects of joy to the return to places. There are different things that sparkle for them in different moments and different places [and] to see that variation across the staff group is a really rich thing. (Interview 2)

# Conclusion

As we have described earlier in the book, place is best understood as an emerging phenomenon. A place is always in a state of change. It is experienced in particular physical locations and is a combination of meaning that is inherent in that place and the ideas and desires that we bring with us when we go there. To be responsive to this phenomenon requires the educator to connect their knowledge, experience and intentions for the educational encounter with an equally deep knowledge of the learner. In the case of Arthur's school program this occurs across a range of sites throughout Victoria; some very close to the students' homes and some in the far corners of the state. In each camping program the place itself is considered a crucial character in the unfolding story. Keeping the programs 'uncomplicated and not very busy' as Arthur says, creates the space for the constant negotiation between staff, students and place to occur, so that learning is emergent. All of these elements come together in practice. Making the local significant and meaningful involves letting go of some of the grander narratives of outdoor education.

> I don't do things for the social psych reasons and that sort of stuff, but the nourishment to a person's sense of identity arising out of being cognisant of, and able to meet, their own needs are an important part of their own experience in nature ... And we're not as persuaded by all the challenge stuff. That is not a part of it. (Interview 2)

But equally, it involves letting go of another deceptive distraction that often makes it difficult for outdoor educators to be responsive to the educative moment with young learners in outdoor places.

> There is a kind of vortex of practicalities, particularly in outdoor work. It is incredibly easy just to slip into making sure that that has happened so that this can happen. There is a kind of logistical whirlwind, which you can easily be caught in. (Interview 3)

The camps that Arthur and his colleagues conduct seem to have used a different starting point in terms of values and ideas, a different logic, than much typical outdoor programming. What seems like a simplification of the usual requirements of outdoor programming (such as adventurous activity, risk management, the technical demands of equipment and skill acquisition and complex program logistics), might be better understood as a release from the grip of those traditions so that negotiated practice can be pursued authentically.

> [You are] reminding yourself back to what is there to be responded to. What's emerging in the moment, either in the kids … or in the place … the extent to which those kids can be drawn into another level of engagement, another level of deeper experience of that place. Sometimes that is through something practical, like a solo or a slow walk, or just listening, or even just a walk, and other times it's talking to them and reframing what is going on and you can't do that when you are preoccupied by the machinations of the day. (Interview 3)

This is hard, labour intensive work. It requires constant attention to what is unfolding.

> I guess in endeavouring to be open to what is going on in the place and in the children I am also making a deliberate choice to be vulnerable to rising and falling, to what is going on … The kids would never have a sense that they were being progressed through a program, or through a sequence of planned events such that if this doesn't work then the next thing will be coming anyway. The kids are very much aware that we are kind of working it out as we are going along. They perceive themselves to be participants in that … to be agents in that change. (Interview 3)

Without doubt one of the requirements of the educator in being able to work in this way is to have a deep experience and knowledge base with both the learners and the place, and a sense of trust and respect for both. For Arthur and his colleagues this trust and respect starts on the year three camp and continues right through the students' camping experiences at each year level of their schooling. No camp programs are out-sourced. Few of the programs include 'adventurous' activities that require an excessive focus on technical equipment or skill development. The familiarity with the children and the places engaged with on an annual cycle generates an educational space quite different in potential to many typical outdoor adventure programs. John Cameron (2001, 32) has written about the potential contained in this alternative place-responsive approach.

> Open attentiveness, the willingness to suspend judgment and 'listen' to a place, the capacity to reflect on both affective and intellectual responses. These are abilities which are best communicated by the presence and attitudes of the educators themselves – by how they are rather than what they say when they are outdoors with the students. It sets the outdoor educators on just as much a journey as the students; always broadening and deepening their relationships with places.

Such an approach does, however, place quite different demands on the outdoor educator. He or she must continue to learn about both the children who they teach and about the places where they teach them. Staff must be genuinely interested in the students and the outdoor places on a long-term basis. Arthur is quite conscious of some of the processes he employs to respond to both learners and outdoor places. For the learners:

> You are actually actively teaching every individual. So you run through every kid in your mind before you go to sleep and think about where they are at and what is happening for them. Everyday. (Interview 2)

In terms of the outdoor places, Arthur has always sought out role models who have something he senses is significant that he needs to learn about a place. It could be the history of a working life on the land or an aspect of a place's ecology, geology, or botany. These are all parts leading towards a whole. Some of his knowledge comes from books and formal study. But in the main the most valuable learning comes face to face, with both people and places.

> Some part of it is deliberate questioning, but I don't think that is the main thing. I think I have probably become more aware of it as I have got older. I realise that I do watch the world very carefully and in a deliberately kind of inquisitive way. I am watching to learn things … Some part of it definitely comes with ways of being valued as a child. I operate with the belief that I can know and understand most things. (Interview 3)

Arthur and I discussed several important role models he had learned from and that had, in various ways, influenced how he thinks about and practices being in the outdoors with children. And he continues to seek out connections with people in the places that he teaches.

> Part of it is also that I just chat. I just chat to people. Kind of seeking people out … It's a very lovely thing that I would often seek out is to go and spend some time in a particular place with someone to whom that place had enormous meaning, like Harold at Raak Plain. And we've had an incredible network of those people all over Victoria … These people are actually involved in trips wherever I can coax them along, or get them to come and meet us in their tinny, or drive their truck down, or whatever it is. That is certainly my preferred, my favourite way to come to know them. I really love the kind of

intimacy and the slow nature of reading things, coming to know things through literature, but I'd never substitute [it for the] the real experience. (Interview 3)

Bringing together the ability to respond to both children and the unfolding phenomena of a place requires a very different set of skills and values as an educator.

I am conscious of some of what has gone before in terms of what might prevent or draw away from an emerging possibility on a trip. But also all the things that have gone before that might point towards, or be fertile ground, or might be raw materials for another experience. It also means that there is not as much loaded on an individual moment. I don't have one moment in which all the bells and whistles have to go at the same time. There are kids who just are not able to be present in a given moment for all sorts of reasons. They will be a part of it, they will be witness to it, it will be a part of their memory, but it didn't touch them. And I don't have to think that it was my only chance. I have got lots and lots more trips and in some cases those things reside in me as something that is ahead. I can anticipate a trip and know that a particular child is coming on a trip and that this is another opportunity to be with that child in a particular way. I guess I keep mining for the potential for them and a place to meet in the depth of an experience. (Interview 3)

Ultimately, there seem to be two underlying pedagogic priorities in Arthur's work. The first is an unfailing belief in the worth in countering broader societal values about nature. He sees this as vital in providing students with a more optimistic basis on which to nurture their relationship with the natural world.

I think we have made some extraordinary mistakes as a society in the way that we have framed the possibility for a relationship with nature in the broader sense, not just places. And a lot of it has been around fear and danger – this place could kill you and this weather could kill you. And we have lots of that kind of dialogue happening. We've got lots of change for the worse kind; climate change, pollution. So much dialogue associated with the potential for nature to fail us in terms of her sustenance. And all of that rhetoric is already part of what kids bring to the moment of an engagement with a place. We've done so much telling our society to not trust nature in a way … But to me I think part of it is about pursuing a culture of care, pursuing that reciprocal relationship with places. That's about love. It is about loving those places and them finding a way into our heart. (Interview 3)

The other fundamental principle that appears to guide Arthur's teaching is that he believes it is educationally legitimate to craft a rich opportunity for children to learn about the world in a way that comes to them naturally. Experience of this quality, even if momentary, is considered rich in possibility. These encounters are shared between staff and students, places where stories are seen to unfold and are unpredictable in their educational outcomes. They have intrinsic worth. They require children to be inquisitive, to work with their hands and feet in the dirt, attuning themselves to ecological happenings that emerge before them, and within them. Then carefully crafted stories provide engagement with the broader context of culture and the land. Experience, thus enlivened, is exquisite and connected. Collectively, the world becomes knowable precisely because it is experienced as a world made up of particular places.

"I think part of it is about pursuing a culture of care, pursuing that reciprocal relationship with places. That's about love. It is about loving those places and them finding a way into our heart."

# Chapter 9

# Signposts to a Place-Responsive Pedagogy in Outdoor Education

In this book we have argued that outdoor educators' and learners' experiences of the significance of outdoor places are less well understood than is warranted. The pedagogic implications of this omission are important and have significant consequences for outdoor education philosophy and practice. We have proposed that outdoor places are not merely venues or empty spaces, rather they are rich in significance and meaning. Places are a powerful pedagogic phenomenon. However, if educators fail to acknowledge and respond to places as an expression of culture they fail to recognise that places could be other than what they presently are. David Gruenewald (2003a, 627) argues that when we accept places as unproblematic,

> such as the farm, the bank, the landfill, the strip mall, the gated comm-
> unity, and the new car lot – we also become complicit in the political
> processes ... that stewarded these places into being and that continue
> to legitimize them. Thus places produce and teach particular ways of
> thinking about and being in the world. They tell us the way things are,
> even when they operate pedagogically beneath the conscious level.

We have added wilderness, national parks and other environmental reserves to Gruenewald's list of places. Despite appearances, 'natural areas' are also cultural products with complex historical, political and economic forces having influenced their current state and what they may become in the future. The case studies in the previous four chapters have illustrated how outdoor places, and our experiences of them, are shaped by historical events, contemporary land use practices, and current cultural expectations. Not only are these places a product of ongoing human intentions and actions but we come to them full of expectations and desires for what we want them to be. The process of becoming place-responsive has the potential to engage both educators and students in different ways with regards to thinking, knowing and being in places such as the River Murray, Maungatautari, Raak Plain, or coastal Mount Maunganui. Teachers and guides who wish to facilitate outdoor programs that develop place-responsiveness need to be committed to come to know their places deeply.

The educator whose aim is to guide participants towards a responsiveness to a particular place is engaged in what Michael Thomashow (1996) calls 'ecological identity work'. Thomashow offers a perspective that requires a response:

> Ecological identity work requires the ability to overcome both internal and external distractions, achieving a state of mind, a way of being, an approach to life experience, and a philosophy of learning. The challenge is to experience ecological identity everywhere, not just in specific places – contained regions such as nature centers or parks – but in the various domains of everyday life. (p. 179)

Thomashow's 'ecological identity work' is, of course, simultaneously cultural identity work. This is why place is such a powerful concept for educators. David Gruenewald (2003a) also makes a strong case for the 'profoundly pedagogical' importance of place (p. 621). He states that 'places *teach* us about how the world works and how our lives fit into the spaces we occupy. Further, places *make* us: As occupants of particular places with particular attributes, our identity and our possibilities are shaped' (p. 621). We are suggesting that outdoor educators need to understand and pay greater attention to how particular places call us to learn and how this learning may be interconnected from one place to another. For example, from the outdoor journey to our everyday home, or from the school yard to the shopping mall. To rephrase Thomashow, we need to be prepared to do place-work wherever we are if the place is to have any significance for us and if we are to be involved in its future prospects. Otherwise we are just passing through.

We hope we have revealed how problematic some forms of outdoor education are, for both participants and places, when they are underpinned by ideals that stress difference, contrast and novelty from the everyday. The downside of some adventure education and even experiential approaches is that place is silenced as the mere backdrop to human action and this impoverishes opportunities for learning. Practices that promote the distinctiveness of learning and the essential self that will be 'revealed' in the outdoors remain 'out there' in the land of the exotic rather than in the-here-and-now, or in the felt (embodied) complexity of the everyday. The learning that is experienced as being 'out there' is potentially marginalised and tends to stay 'out there'.

We have also demonstrated, through recourse to relevant literature and examples, that a place-responsive outdoor education philosophy and practice is eminently achievable. It involves little, if any, investment in high-tech equipment and reduces the emphasis on risky activities and therefore the cost of ever-increasing risk management compliance. The emphasis for the guide or educator shifts away from technical skills and credentials, to knowing one's place(s) and developing good pedagogic strategies for introducing others to it/them. Outdoor programs could be conducted locally, or in familiar and readily accessible locales more often. As we have discussed, this does not necessarily negate travel to locations further afield. But it shifts the emphasis away from being the exotic visitor to getting 'beneath the skin' of a place by becoming an empathetic traveller. The empathetic traveller is one who also knows their home-place well, and so can judge the similarities and the particularities of places encountered via the journey.

Because place-responsive outdoor education is, by its very nature, specific to particular locales it is not possible to prescribe a generic program, sequence of events, or list of activities. However, we have attempted to draw together four signposts to a place-responsive outdoor education pedagogy that we believe might help point the way. As with the case studies, consideration of how these signposts might apply or need to be adapted to best suit other places, teachers and learners is best left to the reader, and ultimately must be negotiated within the experience of each different place and its peoples. The following signposts gesture towards new pedagogic pathways that bring together the embodied, sensory encounter and the interpretive lifeworlds of participants with outdoor places themselves. The four proposed signposts are:

1. Being present in and with a place.
2. The power of place-based stories and narratives.
3. Apprenticing ourselves to outdoor places.
4. The representation of place experiences.

## Signpost 1: Being present in and with a place

Peter Hay poses a question of relevance to educators who take the challenge of place seriously. It is 'How do we learn our way back into place'? Paraphrasing Bachelard, he states that the 'real' can only be approached 'via a sub-linguistic process of uncritical, childlike wonder' (2003, 273). To encounter the world with this sense of wonder, as if for the first time, is a formidable challenge. For those of us steeped in the Western tradition of enlightened rationalism it is tempting, and somewhat natural, to fall 'back into the confines of [the] intellect' (Lopez 1986, 250). Barry Lopez's demanding questions to himself as a writer —'How can you occupy a place and also have it occupy you? How can you find such a reciprocity?' (1996, 11)— attune us to this pedagogic challenge. The first step in developing reciprocity with a place involves re-engaging with a way of being in the world that perhaps, as adults, we have forgotten, fail to value, or have learned to treat with suspicion. As Lopez (1996) suggests:

> The key, I think, is to become vulnerable to a place. If you open yourself you can build intimacy. Out of such intimacy will come a sense of belonging, a sense of not being isolated in the universe. (p. 11)

It is unlikely that educators, guides or participants will allow themselves to become vulnerable to place(s) if they feel threatened by unknown hazards they imagine will be found there. The rhetoric of being outside one's comfort zone, of danger and risk, is not immutable nor necessarily intrinsic to outdoor education. The present, taken-for-granted definitions of what constitutes outdoor education, are social constructions which can be replaced or complemented by other ways of thinking and acting. The case studies we have presented reveal the value of becoming comfortable in a place and being present. You may recall the response of undergraduate students to the slow, early morning drift in a canoe on the River Murray or Arthur Curl's work with students on Raak Plain when they take the time to simply *be* with a belah tree (and its many occupants) and to listen to the music that it makes. Such experiences provide the opportunity for participants to become fascinated with the sounds, textures, smells and the shifting appearance of a place throughout the day and night. Certainly how learners are introduced to these types of activities and the timing of such encounters relies on judgement and attention to nuance on the part of the educator. Outdoor educators, when thinking about their students, would do well to consider the same questions that the literary critic Jonathan Bate asks about the eco-poets that he reviews in *The Song of the Earth*; 'How are they influenced by climate? In what kind of landscape do they flourish? What are their modes of creating shelter, their relations to other species?' (2000, ix).

As educators it is necessary that we first believe that what happens in an outdoor place is significant and meaningful. This is an education in the senses, a learning to attend to our immediate surrounds. The position advocated here reflects in part the call by some educators (Gardner 1999;

Weil 1959, 2002) for greater focus within education for students to be given the opportunity to develop attentiveness. Tooth and Renshaw (2009) have recently summarised the work of several authors on the purpose and significance of educators working with learners to develop their perceptual acuity to their environment. Paraphrasing Gardner (1999) they suggest that the primary purpose of schools is to develop attentive citizens who have studied the world most carefully and lived in it most thoughtfully. They draw also upon the work of Simone Weil (1959, 2002) who claims that *attention* is the real object of education because only when human beings make the effort to connect to the social and material world around them do they grasp truth and gain deep understanding. Finally, they consider the 'profound attentiveness' proposed by the eclectic biologist Mary Clark (2004). We might add to this group John Cameron's call for experiential educators to practice an 'open attentiveness' with their students.

It may be that encounters with outdoor places, when sensory awareness is heightened to its zenith, will be temporary, momentary, even fleeting. But this does not lessen its educative value. We may learn through repeated efforts to attend to the immediate, the first step in a journey towards connection. This is why philosophers such as Maurice Merleau-Ponty and David Abram have written so extensively on the theme of perception. To experience a meaningful relationship with anything we must first perceive our connectedness with it. Perception, according to Abram (1996a, 52),

> is precisely this reciprocity, the ongoing interchange between my body and the entities that surround it. It is a sort of silent conversation that I carry on with things, a continuous dialogue that unfolds far below my verbal awareness.

In the moment that we perceive our fundamental and constant reciprocity with the world it ceases to be a thing made up of objects. Instead, it becomes an unfolding phenomenon and we come to stand within it, alongside all the other beings, as integrated co-members within the land community (Leopold 1987). As the Canadian outdoor educator Bob Henderson says, we are released to return to the terrain itself.

> What does it mean to be 'OF' a place? This is a question worth holding onto consciously. It is certainly a far cry from let's 'overcome' this route, 'challenge this whitewater,' 'beat this mountain,' 'study the particulars of this setting or phenomena.' Perhaps it is a greater traveller's challenge to be 'still' and come to see really where you are. (Henderson 1995, 33).

Experiencing being present, or even working on being present, does not necessarily involve activities such as drawing, reading, writing, or photographing. It does not involve trying to record or represent the experience in any way. These things come later. It simply involves making the effort to attend to what is meaningful in our immediate surrounds and to increase our levels of awareness. What it requires of participants is stillness, silence and patience. What it requires of educators is a sense of timing and a feel for the possibilities in our immediate surrounds. What it does suggest is the need to take time in and with place(s) rather than rushing or pushing through. This may have an impact on our mode of travel, our choice of activity in-place, and our revisiting of places in different seasons or cycles of learning (see Payne and Wattchow, 2008). What it does challenge is notions of quick 'raids' (Brookes, 1994) that disregard the pedagogical significance of place.

## Signpost 2: The power of place-based stories and narratives

A heightened sensory awareness of our surrounds may be the first step towards connection, but experience is more than our sensory reaction to the world. Experience includes interpretation and reflection; the cognitive sense we make of our situatedness in the world. Our senses are filtered and conditioned through technologies and how we have been enculturated to make meaning from our experiences. Rather than diminish the value of the senses, which is the way of the rationalist, we argue that outdoor educators and learners should attend to them and strive to better understand the cultural meanings they are attaching to them. In relation to the experience of outdoor places an effective and appropriate way to do this, we suggest, is through the power of story and storytelling.

There are several ways that we can think about story and storytelling as outdoor educators. When we hear the word 'story' these days, many of us might imagine a news story 'breaking' in the daily paper or on the TV screen or the web. Or we might have an image of sitting quietly soaking up the narrative of a novel, biography or historical account in a book. Similarly, we might immerse ourselves in a story unfolding on the big screen in a darkened cinema. Story is fundamental to being human. These relatively modern versions of story may be distant relatives of the more ancient and enduring ways that storytelling has been used when people told and listened to stories face to face, passing on subtle cultural and educational messages from one to another.

It is for precisely this reason that stories play a significant role in the experience of places by participants in outdoor education. Lopez (1986) and Abram (1996a) believe that stories can hold the accumulated knowledge of peoples and places and that the act of telling a story, when one had earned the right to do so, is 'to actively preserve the coherence of one's culture' (Abram 1996a, 181). Lopez and Abram have described the significance of story in indigenous oral cultures where lessons contained within stories are passed from one generation to the next. We contend that the use of story in outdoor education, while unable to capture the depth and quality of stories that sustain fully oral traditions, still has a crucial role to play. We are not talking about outdoor educators or guides providing written texts about a place so participants can read them for themselves while camping out. Rather, we are talking about outdoor educators taking up the responsibility to becoming storytellers in the outdoor places that they work.

What stories should outdoor educators tell? What should these stories be about? And, how should they be told? Two examples shed some light on this. First, we will look briefly at how two outstanding environmental historians we have drawn upon repeatedly in this book, George Seddon and Geoff Park, both recently deceased, handled this dilemma. Each faced choices about what to put in and what to leave out in their respective land histories of the Snowy River and the coastal forests of lowland New Zealand. They also had to search for a suitable way to construct their stories. Even though these are examples of written stories they provide some important clues. In the second example, we return to look again at how storytelling was used in some of the case studies as a way of making sense of encounters with outdoor places and as a pedagogic strategy by outdoor educators and learners.

The doyen of place writing in Australia, George Seddon, states in *Searching for the Snowy* (1994) that despite its mythic stature, the river had 'no historical, social or political reality ... There is not even an accepted name for the area' through which it flows (p. xxi). Seddon (1994) credits Banjo Patterson's iconic poem *The Man from Snowy River* as the source of the river's mythic stature. In the poem an unnamed man, as wild and as untamed as the mysterious mountainous Snowy River country from which he came, outrides the horseman of the plains as he recaptures an expensive colt that has escaped to run with the mountain brumbies (wild horses). Of course the myth was further popularised (some would argue the narrative was modified inappropriately) when an interpretation of the poem was made into a feature film for an international audience. Later still, the opening ceremony of the Sydney 2000 Olympics commenced with a lone rider entering the stadium, galloping to centre stage and cracking his stockwhip astride his rearing horse in front of a television audience of many millions. Clad in his akubra hat and 'driza-bone' coat, he was the man from Snowy River reborn for the global stage. He remains, it seems, an evocative and quintessential story in the Australian consciousness.

In *Searching for the Snowy*, Seddon (1994) attempts to tell the story of the river from its source in the Australian Alps to the sea. The Snowy River begins its 500km journey to Bass Strait high on the south-eastern slopes of Australia's highest peak, Mt Kosciusko, at about 1700m above sea level. Within its first 50km it is dammed twice, at Guthega and Jindabyne, where water is redirected into the Snowy Mountains Hydro Electric Scheme. Ultimately this water flows into the Murray. Downstream from the Guthega Power Station the river can run dry at the flick of a switch. Until recently, 99% of the original Snowy River flow did not make it past the Jindabyne dam wall. Beneath the dam wall, the river is a dry course for nearly half of its journey to the sea. Construction on the Snowy Mountains Hydro Electric Scheme began in 1951. It was Australia's largest post-World War II nation building project, and continues to be celebrated as one of the country's greatest engineering achievements. It aimed to simultaneously water the dry inland agricultural districts to the east of the Great Divide, to encourage industrial expansion, provide hydro-electric power, and to promote large-scale immigration from Europe to Australia in the post-war years. Much of Australia's current multi-cultural diversity owes its origins to the Snowy Hydro Scheme. Seddon acknowledges that telling the story of the river is a near impossible task. In searching for the river he finds that there have 'been almost as many rivers as there have been observers, and that is in the end why the river is "incoherent". There can be no single view of it' (Seddon 1994, xxxii). The widest gaps, perhaps, are between our stories of the river as a wild place and the ecological reality of a dammed, diminished and irrevocably changed river.

> It says something for the flexibility of our sense of national identity that many people seem capable of maintaining both sets of values simultaneously regarding the Snowy: they can be proud of our great engineering achievement, and be thrilled by the grandeur of a wild river. (Seddon 1994, xxx)

Seddon (1997) later concluded that part of the problem he faced in telling the story of the Snowy stemmed 'from the linearity of language, where I wanted a polyphonic account' (p. 58). Stories can only be told one at a time.

The geographic sequence, historic accounts, natural history, history of land use and even a history of how we have perceived a place might all contribute to telling the story of a place as complex and contradictory as the Snowy, but we cannot read or hear them all at once (Seddon 1997). Part of the reason for briefly introducing the story of the Snowy is to demonstrate the complexity of the challenge facing the storyteller. All outdoor places are full of stories. Some are settler legends or myths, others are the accounts of scientists and geographers, still others reflect national agendas, and so on. The anthropologist Deborah Bird Rose (1996, 18) reminds us that in a country like Australia 'there is no place where the feet of Aboriginal humanity have not preceded those of the settler'.

The same holds true, of course, for Māori in New Zealand. Every place in these countries is full of stories, layer upon layer. Some are harder than others to uncover. Some are suppressed and silenced, almost gone. Others shout at us. We might stand, metaphorically, on George's shoulders to get a clearer view of the story of the Snowy for example, but ultimately each individual must begin to construct a fuller sense of the whole, for a place, out of the pieces of its many stories.

Geoff Park demonstrates better than any writer we have come across the construction of place-inspired stories. In *Ngā Uruora (The Groves of Life): Ecology and History in a New Zealand Landscape* (1995) Park explores the meaning of New Zealand's remnant lowland forests, most of which have been cleared, fenced and drained for farming and settlement.

> Mention ngā uruora today is like raising something from the dead. Go into a lowland kahikatea forest in Autumn when its koroï are ripening, lie under the towering trees listening to the cacophony of birds and the constant patter of the inedible bits hitting the leaves around you, and you'll know what 'the groves of life' mean. These are ecosystems now, like huia and kākāpō, vanished or down to a few survivors in need of intensive care, their wildness something to marvel at. What did it mean for Māori to lose them and their soils, their best soils, to Europe's settlers? (Park 1995, 15)

The quotation above illuminates two of the three key components of Park's storytelling style. His book is constructed around six journeys, one each to the remnant patches of lowland forest. In each case the story contains descriptions of the physical exploration of the forest, by foot or canoe. These places are of a human-scale, they can readily be walked and paddled. Park also uses only the Māori names for indigenous entities and patterns of life (such as different species of trees, birds, for Māori practices and so on). Park brings a third element into his stories; deep research into the historical records of each place. Each story weaves these three strands into patterns that take the reader deep into the forests themselves. Seddon (1996, 397) concluded that Park had achieved the 'polyphonic account' that he was searching for. The result is a sophisticated storytelling that is 'for New Zealanders about *becoming* New Zealanders' (Seddon 1996, 405). Park's style encapsulates that fact that humans are, as Leopold asserts, co-members of the land community, standing with the other species. We are part of the ecology of a place. But humans are also different in so far as there are 'spiritual, linguistic, historical, regional and national aspects of our senses of identity and belonging' (Bate 2000, x). Stories such as those conveyed by Seddon and Park offer the opportunity to connect ecological sensibility with cultural understanding.

Arthur Curl spoke at length, in the interviews conducted for the case study presented in the previous chapter, about using stories as a pedagogical strategy in outdoor education. The stories that he and his colleagues share are always told in situ and face to face with students. A story is only drawn from the well of stories if, and when, it is appropriate to do so. It might be something as intimate as the life of a singular shell clinging to a basalt reef. Or it might be something as vast as the inland night sky. Background material for some of the stories is gathered through reading historical and contemporary accounts of the places. But many of the stories are also sourced from the many repeated visits through listening to others who know the past and present 'happenings' in a place in detail, and from attending to the place intently. Every opportunity to revisit a particular outdoor place is a seen as a chance to deepen one's knowledge and sense of connection. The River Murray historian Paul Sinclair (2001, 22) wrote; 'stories bring nature into culture and ascribe meaning to places, species and processes which would otherwise remain silent to the human ear'.

In place-responsive outdoor education telling stories, or facilitating others' stories, that connect nature and culture becomes part of the responsibility of being with people in outdoor places. In chapter six we also explained how a community of outdoor learners, including staff, can collaborate to uncover and tell stories about the places they are experiencing. As adult learners they are capable of recognising the ethical considerations and responsibilities that comes with relaying stories about colonisation, dispossession and land use conflicts. We suggest that younger learners are capable of this as well. It must first be modelled sensitively by educators and leaders and then younger learners should be inducted into the role of transmitting cultural knowledge in this way. Storytelling is not a frivolous or fanciful endeavour, it is a serious attempt to connect and make sense of where we are and who we are.

Geoff Park opens *Ngā Uruora: The Groves of Life* with a quotation from Frank Gohlke, the American landscape photographer; 'A landscape whose story is told is harder to dismiss ... At its best, telling the landscape's story can still feel like a sacred task' (Park 1995, 11). There is no hard and fast guide as to what stories to tell and how to tell them. Each story needs to be felt by the educator, or storyteller, to be accurate and worthwhile. A story contains something to be learned that cannot easily or readily be instructed or summarised. Intense interest in the place on the part of the educator will reveal, over time, stories of its history, geography, ecology, land use, and so on. Characters will emerge who encapsulate a story that tells a part of the larger whole. Yet, equally, outdoor educators need to realise that 'every storyteller falls short of a perfect limning of the landscape – perceptions and language both fail' (Lopez 1988, 69). It is a realistic goal for outdoor educators and their students to aspire to work towards understanding the places they experience as much more than the simplistic versions of playgrounds, arenas or backdrops for human action. The power of story has an important role to play here.

> When we cease to demand the truth and realize that the best we can have of those substantial truths that guide our lives is metaphorical – a story ... that the interior landscape is a metaphorical representation of the exterior landscape, that the truth reveals itself most fully not in dogma but in paradox, irony, and contradictions that distinguish compelling narratives. (Lopez 1988, 71)

## Signpost 3: Apprenticing ourselves to outdoor places

The third signpost to a place-responsive pedagogy involves combining the first two. Neither alone is enough.

What is needed is both a felt, embodied encounter with a place and an engagement with knowing the place through various cultural knowledge systems, such as history, ecology, geography, and so on.

According to Abram (1996a), many indigenous hunters would apprentice themselves to the animals that they would track and kill. We would draw a contemporary parallel and suggest that in order to 'know' a place there is a vital need for people to become an apprentice to that place. James Raffan (1992) has a phrase for this, which he terms 'land as teacher'. In such an apprenticeship people draw into balance the tensions always existing between the pre-discursive 'sensorial present' and the interpretive worlds of rational and conscious thought. The division in Western culture between embodied experience and rational interpretation must become reconciled in a place-responsive society. That is, the two aspects which are commonly held apart, need to be brought into correct relationship with each other. To do so would be to enact the legacy of Aldo Leopold's *A Sand County Almanac: And Sketches Here and There* (1987), which models for us, again and again, the elegant human tension between poetic response and rational description. The experience of place is neither one nor the other, but both.

James Raffan's (1992) doctoral thesis, discussed in chapter four, explored how the land may act as teacher in shaping both personal and communal responses to place. Raffan's dissertation was an exploration of how the land did, or did not, act as a teacher in terms of shaping perceptions about the Thelon Reserve as a place for these various diverse groups of people. As a result of the study Raffan (1992, 1993) identified in the data four guiding concepts that constituted how the land acted as teacher. We discussed these at some length in chapter four, but it is worth revisiting these four concepts here, albeit briefly.

This first component that Raffan refers to is the experiential component of a sense of place as the personal link to the land itself through experience. He calls the second component the toponymic sense of place. This refers to the origin and significance of place names and the process of naming places. The third component relates a narrative sense of place and how stories about the land came to be, and the cultural significance of oral traditions, and tales of travelling the land. He describes the land knowledge triangle as an embodiment of three ways of knowing: 'place names, land related stories, and personal experience living, hunting and trapping on the land' (p. 370). The final component Raffan describes is the numinous, a sense of divine presence in spiritual encounters with the land.

The influence of Raffan's canoe journey (mirrored also in Park's explorations) and his poetic and artistic responses to the land and the participants in his study should not be underestimated. People's experiences of places, their spiritual or numinous encounters, the names and naming of outdoor places, and the stories that people both tell and listen to in a place, provide outdoor educators with important clues in thinking about what a place-responsive form of practice might look like.

Part of the work of the outdoor educator then is to craft, through program design, a responsive negotiation between participants and place. Central to this task is the search for pedagogic opportunities or 'moments' that peel back the many masks we make for outdoor places. Outdoor educators are well placed to present a truly integrated curriculum for learners; one where teachers and guides know how to thoughtfully and tactfully combine experiencing particular places with the study of those places. Such a curriculum and pedagogy, one that is committed to an exploration of the ties between experience, interpretation and reflection, and between people and place, has the potential to position outdoor education pedagogy as an exemplar for other teaching areas to follow. A place-responsive pedagogy would require us to become more reliant on local places and peoples, to study a place's histories and ecologies, and constantly couple this with experiencing places through our bodies. We find eloquent exemplars in the works of writers such as Leopold (1987) and Park (1995). It is likely that such a program would require more time for historical and ecological study and creative writing/artistic responses to place, meeting and working with locals who inhabit the region, greater reliance on the local community for resources and knowledge, and consideration of the interconnection between the outdoor place encountered and the participants' home places of residence. We can then extend the questions inspired by Wendell Berry (1987) into a cycle of place-apprenticeship that compels us to respond to places wherever it is that we teach or guide learners.

- *What is here in this place?* What can we seek to learn here through our senses and through our knowledge systems? How do we remain watchful, attentive and listening to this place whilst we are here? Who (human and non-human) lives here? Who relies upon this place? What was its past, how has it changed and what is it becoming?

- *What will this place permit us to do?* What wounds does this place carry? Who cares for this place now? How can we insure that our experiences do not wound this place further? How can our actions help to heal this place?

- *What will this place help us to do?* How does this place sustain us whilst we are here? How do we design an experience that is attuned with this place; that works with it rather than against it?

- *How is this place interconnected with my home place?* How is this place influenced by my home place? How is my home influenced by this place? Can we reveal and experience the threads of these connections? Are there ways of experiencing and knowing this place that return us to the first question when we return to home: What is here in this place?

These are, of course, all rational questions that would seem to seek a rational response. But we have seen repeatedly in this study that this will not be enough. We must remain ever cautious about our propensity to colonise places with our own intentions, desires and rationalisations. We must remain alert to the numinous and the sensual moment when something of place may be revealed that completely surprises us and that we cannot reduce to words. Then, perhaps, we may experience those places that seemed fragmented and isolated as part of a richer, connected mosaic. It is a pedagogical approach where educators position themselves and their learners in the very heart of the tension between *being* and *becoming*.

## Signpost 4: The representation of place experiences

As outdoor educators we should be experts in learners' sensory engagement with the outdoor places, as we outlined above in *Signpost 1: Being present in and with a place*. We also should know how to uncover and cultivate a community of learners who tell worthwhile stories about the place they are experiencing. In *Signpost 2: The power of place-based stories and narratives*, we suggested that outdoor places are brimful of personal, geological, ecological, historical, economic and political stories. Outdoor educators and guides may not be experts in any of these fields. However, through their natural inquisitiveness in the outdoor places where they work, often returning to them repeatedly over the years, they can engage at a meaningful level in these topics with their students. The fact that outdoor educators may be more limited than a professional historian like Geoff Park in uncovering the near complete story of a place, does not diminish the educational value in experiencing the power of place-based stories. In *Signpost 3: Apprenticing ourselves to outdoor places* we drew together signposts *1* and *2* as ways of knowing outdoor places and discussed the questioning frame that we must take with us as we learn about a place with our students. But there is another dimension here in terms of how we encourage students to reflect on and express their subjective response to their experiences.

We wrote earlier about John Dewey's educational vision. Dewey proposed a scientific method whereby students would be faced with a problem and develop a hypothesis in response. They would then test their hypothesis in action and reflect on the results. The final stage would see them develop a generalisable theory that could then be tested against similar problems in the future. Experiential educators have adapted the work of Dewey and others to come up with cyclical models of learning. We have outlined how certain aspects of a simplistic application of such cyclic pedagogies are problematic for a place-responsive approach. One of our chief concerns here was that the often rushed and guided articulations about an experience failed as worthwhile expressions of the participants' subjective encounters. Subjectivity, the felt and imagined experience of the participant, is surely central to the work of outdoor educators.

Despite these problems we see considerable merit in the kernel of Dewey's idea, which is for a sophisticated understanding of the pedagogic relationship between experience, reflection and the learner's world. Considerable inspiration for the development of place-responsiveness has come from the visual and literary arts. In addition, place-responsive design is well supported within schools of thought and practice in architecture. The key to unlocking the potential of place-responsiveness as pedagogic practice extends the relationship of experience and reflection to include the representation of experience.

There are two ways of working with learners in terms of how outdoor places are represented. First, as educators we should be developing learners' critical capacities in interpreting how the place they are learning in has been and is being represented in various forms of cultural media. For example, how has the place been represented in historical documents and can those representations be contested? How has, and is, the place been represented in land management documents, on current maps and charts, in tourism advertising material, and so on? The second way that learners could respond, in terms of representation, is to create their own interpretive works inspired by the place. The representation of experience can take many forms; verbal articulation, prose, poetry, visual art, sculpture, film, song and music, drama, and so on. We have already written about this in relation to story, but other forms of creative representation have proved very effective in terms of shifting environmental values (e.g. Dombrovskis' iconic photographs of the Franklin River or Brian Turner's poetry and prose of central Otago) We have discussed the role of the romantic writers and artists and how they provided the ecological impulse that launched the environmental movement.

Why have outdoor educators largely limited representation of subjective experience to the spoken word in 'debriefing' sessions? In addition, how might outdoor educators engage with the practice of the arts to deepen participants' understandings of their experiences?

When we talk about the relationship between experience, reflection and the representation of experience it is important to point out that we do not see these as discrete entities in a linear relationship. It is better to think of them as overlapping phases, with blurred boundaries, in the same phenomenon – learning to experience and be responsive to an outdoor place. We are already interpreting and reflecting on meaning when we are experiencing. We may continue to reflect later, after the active experience, but reflection on experience is an experience in its own right. Similarly, when we work from our notes or sketches, often long after the active phase of an experience, to produce a literary or artistic work, we are re-engaging and re-immersing ourselves back into the subjective experience of that place. We are not proposing that outdoor educators and learners are aiming to *produce* art, historical accounts or literary products only for their own sake (as might be the case in an Art or History or Literature subject). As we discussed under signpost 2, what is important here is that learners are experiencing *doing* history, geology, ecology, and so on, in the field when they draw on those knowledge systems. The same may be said for the creative arts. In *doing* art and creative writing, educators can guide learners in engaging knowingly with their subjective encounters with a place. Notes, working sketches, photographs and so on can be taken home and become the basis for continued exploration of the experience. Such an approach finds support in John Dewey's (1915) recognition of the centrality and interconnectedness of experiences in learning. 'Experience has its geographical aspect, its artistic and its literary, its scientific and its historical sides. All studies arise from aspects of the one earth and the one life lived upon it … We live in a world where all sides are bound together. All studies grow out of relations in the one great common world' (p. 91).

## Conclusion

There are those who might view outdoor education, as advocated through these signposts as simply a history, ecology or art fieldtrip, rather than as something distinctive with its own body of knowledge and its own pedagogical strategies. While this in its own way is not necessarily damning, it ignores the centrality of embodied experiences which we see as integral to outdoor education. A place-responsive outdoor education cannot be conducted in the classroom, nor can it be effectively implemented if one is in the outdoors and is only 'being active' – the simplistic binary of doing or reflecting on experience overlooks the nuanced, highly contextualised and interconnected webs of people, places and contested meanings of experience.

It is the integration of sensory experiences, in community, and in places, coupled with reflection and representation that make the work of place-responsive outdoor educators distinctive in terms of curriculum and pedagogy. These points of distinction are not exclusive to place-responsive outdoor educators, but collectively they help frame a place-responsive pedagogy. First, the topic of study on any place-responsive outdoor education program is the connections between educators, learners and the place. This involves a sophisticated approach to place on the part of the educator and guides where they work as, at various times, a co-learner, a negotiator, a translator, and a storyteller with deep knowledge about that place, and so on. The objective for the educator is to facilitate an experience of place so that the learner's connections with it might be fostered and they understand the interconnections between individuals, places and communities. People and place(s) are the foundation for curriculum development in this approach. What is taught, and learnt, emerges through interaction rather than being delivered through set activities with pre-determined outcomes. All participants 'become creators of knowledge rather than the consumers of knowledge created by others' (Smith 2002, 593). The second distinction returns us to the concept of experiential learning.

Sensory engagement with place, a critical reflection on the lifeworld of the learner, and attempts to represent the subjectivities of experience are the three foundations of the place-responsive experience. Collectively, they inscribe a circle that models best the pedagogic parameters of a holistic place-experience. Outdoor educators and guides work alongside students on this pedagogic journey. Rather than an experiential learning cycle whose centrifugal force spins the learner outwards into generalisations and abstractions, we see a gradual centripetal movement inwards as educator and learner continue to deepen their experience, knowledge and connection to particular places of significance and meaning. It is an active journey towards belonging. With belonging comes connection and the development of an ethic of care.

Along with Smith (2002), we would urge teachers to become the creators of curriculum that is responsive to their place rather than 'the dispensers of curriculum developed by others' (p. 594) in contexts that may have little or no relevance in the lives of our students. While a unit on rock climbing, as a means to develop communication skills, might be possible in Mount Maunganui or Melbourne (or Boulder Colorado) it fails to take into account the relevance of the varying places that students live. While climbing at the local indoor rock climbing centre might be viewed as a legitimate means to achieve skill advancement and an opportunity to interact with peers, we are left wondering how much is omitted from the experience when serious attempts to understand and respond to culturally-relevant activities are overlooked. By way of example, when writing the case study from Mount Maunganui College both Jane and Erin used terms such as *waka ama* and *whenua*; words that are part of the everyday vocabulary in New Zealand and that require no explanation. Both, however, are laden with meaning and significance, protocols and ritual. It wasn't until Brian read drafts of the chapter that it became how apparent how distant and distinct two seemingly similar 'down-under' cultures can be.

As we have illustrated in the case studies, places have an integral role in the teaching and learning experience. They are the sites of meaning making, the centre of lived experiences. Failure to enact a place-responsive pedagogy in outdoor education has potentially profound implications. As Gruenewald (2003a) argues, a 'lack of attention is disturbing because it impoverishes human experience, conceals from view the correspondence between ideology, politics, and place, and potentially leads to biological and cultural extinctions that we may regret' (p. 645).

Place-responsive outdoor education holds the potential of situating learning within the learner's community through locating activities in the local environment and by also altering the pedagogical approach to that of empathetic insider in journey programs. Admittedly this is no easy task but it does attempt to provide an alternative to the rootlessness, hyper-mobility and globalising forces of current times. As we said at the outset, significant environmental and social challenges will always be felt and responded to, first and foremost, locally.

For outdoor educators and guides this involves both a shift in priorities and expectations. Short term learning objectives based on an overly simplistic view of learners, learning and the places that they learn in will need to be replaced with a different kind of work. As Bate (2000, 23) concludes, 'the practical consequences of that work – social, environmental, political in the broadest sense – cannot be controlled or predicted. They will be surprising, haphazard, indirect, long-term.'

Building a 'better world', through improved self-knowledge or social relationships, encouraging engagement in the democratic process, or countering the effects of environment degradation are all worthy aims for outdoor educators. The difficult question is how do we best go about achieving these? As we have highlighted, 'traditional' approaches to

**"As outdoor educators, developing a sense of connection with places is one of the greatest pedagogical challenges we face."**

outdoor education, via novel activities in wilderness settings, is appealing but is only one, and we would argue somewhat limited, way to achieve these goals. A place-responsive pedagogy offers a counter balance and a different perspective for our field – a field of study and practice that has been constructed within specific historical, social and geographical contexts. A place-responsive pedagogy should not be dismissed as outdoor education 'lite' or 'low strength'. It is not a call to abandon active embodied experiences of a challenging nature. It is, however, a reminder to be responsive to where we are educating and asking questions such as, 'what will this place permit?', 'how is it connected to my home?' It does call into question the placelessness of much outdoor education – both the traditional activity focus and 'do-review-reapply' pedagogy is under the spotlight.

What we are advocating is a re-appraisal of how we conduct outdoor education programs. Rather than being prescriptive or formulaic we are suggesting that these signposts might help guide educators as they develop programmes that are responsive to their students, their community and their places. Becoming and being place responsive offers opportunities to enrich the lives of our students, our communities and our places. As Geoff Park (1995) noted, 'How we inhabit a place can be the most telling expression of how we sense its worth, our intention for it and our connection with it' (p. 21). As outdoor educators, developing a sense of connection with places is one of the greatest pedagogical challenges we face. We contend that the development of a place-responsive pedagogy is essential if we are to develop a sound and forward looking pedagogy that is able to respond to a changing world.

# Notes

## Chapter 1. Personal Narratives: A Place to Start

[1] Michael King was an accomplished and highly regarded (one could say famous) New Zealand historian, biographer, and writer who was associated with The University of Waikato, both as a student and academic.

[2] Pākehā: Traditionally viewed as New Zealanders of European descent (predominantly British). It has been suggested that the term be broadened to include all non-Māori New Zealanders.

[3] OE, colloquial term for overseas experience. A 'rite of passage' for many antipodeans who were able to get a two-year working holiday visa.

## Chapter 3. The Case for Place

[1] Read's three books *Returning to Nothing* (1996), *Belonging* (2000) and *Haunted Earth* (2003) represent a sustained investigation into the attachment to place and significance of place experiences in Australia. Read has explored in depth attachment to place and the grief that results when people become displaced, the complexities of indigenous and settler attachment to the same places, and the possibility of a spirit of place that resides independently of humans.

[2] C. Bell (1996, 34). The author's identity is 'concealed' so as to not immediately permit the reader to identify with the author's country. We have also changed 'New Zealanders' to 'of the population' from the original quote.

## Chapter 6. 'That Feeling of Familiarity': Developing Place-Responsiveness

[1] For full details visit www.maungatrust.org

[2] Three male and two female students. This project complied with the university's ethics regulations. Pseudonyms have been used.

[3] See Tuan's comment in the final paragraph of Chapter 5.

## Chapter 7. Transitions: A Changing Sense of Place

[1] This project is funded by a Teaching and Learning Research Initiative (TLRI) grant 2010–2011. The TLRI seeks to enhance the links between educational research and teaching practices to improve outcomes for learners. www.tlri.org.nz

2    Both the school and teachers reported in this chapter were happy that they be identified.

3    The decile rating is the indicator used to measure the extent to which schools draw pupils from low socio-economic communities. A decile is a 10% grouping. Decile 1 schools are the 10% of schools with the highest proportion of students from low socio-economic communities. Data was obtained from Education Review Office report, July 2008.

4    Boogie board; approximately half-body length buoyant board that swimmers rest their torsos on to surf waves.

5    *Waka ama* are traditional open canoes with an outrigger. Modern versions are constructed of fibreglass and other high tech composites. *Waka* refers to a canoe and *ama* the outrigger. This is popular recreational and competitive activity in New Zealand. The use of *waka ama* is a good example of adopting (and adapting) a traditional mode of transport in a contemporary setting. Tradition records that Māori arrived in Aotearoa via seven *waka* in the great fleet. Anthropologists have suggested that migration occurred over a longer period involving in excess of 40 voyages (http://www.teara.govt.nz/en/canoe-traditions accessed 30 August 2010).

6    *Marae.* Meeting area for *whānau* (family) or *iwi* (tribe), it is the focal point of a settlement. It is an area into which visitors are welcomed and accommodated. The key building being the *wharenui* or meeting house.

7    *Whenua.* Māori term for both land and placenta. The link between the nourishing nature of both definitions is highly significant. It is not uncommon for Māori to return the *whenua* (placenta) to the family's marae to be buried in the *whenua* (land) to which they have long association. The practice of burying the placenta in a place of significance is not uncommon for Pākehā.

8    Education Outside The Classroom (EOTC): Term used in New Zealand to incorporate all learning activities outside the classroom. This might include a visit to a museum or fire station. OE is therefore one part of EOTC.

# References

Abram, D. 1996a. *The Spell of the Sensuous: Perception and Language in a More-than-Human World*. New York: Vintage Books.

Abram, D. 1996b. 'Merleau-Ponty and the voice of the earth'. In *Minding Nature: The Philosophers of Ecology*, edited by Macauley, D. London: The Guilford Press: 82–101.

Adams, W; Mulligan, M., eds. 2003. *Decolonizing Nature: Strategies for Conservation in a Post-Colonial Era*. London: Earthscan.

Andkjaer, S. 2009. 'Outdoor education in New Zealand: A comparative and cultural perspective'. Paper presented at the Fourth International Outdoor Education Research Conference. La Trobe University, Beechworth.

Bate, J. 2000. *The Song of the Earth*. London: Picador.

Beck, U. 1992. *Risk Society: Towards a New Modernity*. Trans. Ritter, M. London: Sage.

Beedie, P. 1994. 'Risk taking: The consensus views'. *Journal of Adventure Education and Outdoor Leadership* 11 (2): 13–17.

Beedie, P. 1995/6. 'Where are the risk takers in outdoor education?: A critical analysis of two current perspectives'. *Journal of Adventure Education and Outdoor Leadership* 12 (4): 10–13.

Bell, A. 2003. 'A narrative approach to research'. *Canadian Journal of Environmental Education* 8 (Spring): 95–110.

Bell, C. 1996. *Inventing New Zealand: Everyday Myths of Pakeha Identity*. Auckland, NZ: Penguin.

Bell, M. 1993. 'What constitutes experience? Rethinking theoretical assumptions'. *Journal of Experiential Education* 16 (1): 19–24.

Berman, D; Davis-Berman, J. 2005. 'Positive psychology and outdoor education'. *Journal of Experiential Education* 28 (1): 17–24.

Berry, W. 1987. *Home Economics*. San Francisco, California: North Point Press.

Berthold-Bond, D. 2000. 'The ethics of "place": Reflections on bioregionalism.' *Environmental Ethics* 22: 5–24.

Berzonsky, M. 2005. 'Ego identity: A personal standpoint in a postmodern world'. *Identity: An International Journal of Theory and Research* 5 (2), 125–136.

Bishop, R; Glynn, T. 1999. *Culture Counts: Changing Power Relations in Education*. Palmerston North, New Zealand: Dunmore Press.

Bolton, G. 1981. *Spoils and Spoilers*. Sydney: Allen and Unwin.

Bonyhardy, T. 2000. *The Colonial Earth*. Melbourne: The Miegunyah Press.

Bonyhardy, T; Griffiths, T. 2002. *Words for Country: Landscape and Language in Australia*. Sydney: University of New South Wales Press.

Boud, D; Keogh, R; Walker, D. 1985. 'Promoting reflection in learning: A model'. In *Reflection: Turning Experience into Learning*, edited by Boud, D; Keogh, R; Walker, D. London: Kogan: 18–40.

Bowers, C. 1993. *Education, Cultural Myths, and the Ecological Crisis: Toward Deep Changes*. Albany: State University of New York Press.

Bowers, C. 2005. *The False Promises of Constructivist Theories of Learning: A Global and Ecological Critique.* New York: Peter Lang.

Brookes, A. 1993. 'Deep and shallow outdoor education: Can we tell the difference?' *The Outdoor Educator* June: 8–17.

Brookes, A. 1994. 'Reading between the lines: Outdoor experience as environmental text.' *Journal of Physical Education, Recreation and Dance* October: 29–33.

Brookes, A. 2000. 'Dwelling in the details: The fallacy of universal nature experience, and the myth of the essential self'. Paper presented at the DEEP seminar on Outdoor Education and Deep Ecology in the 21st century. 14–17 January; Haeverstolen, Rennebu, Norway.

Brookes, A. 2002. 'Lost in the Australian bush: Outdoor education as curriculum'. *Journal of Curriculum Studies* 34 (4): 405–425.

Brookes, A. 2004. 'Astride a long-dead horse: Mainstream outdoor education theory and the central curriculum problem.' *Australian Journal of Outdoor Education* 8 (2): 22–33.

Brown, B; Duncan, F. 1980. *Franklin River Rafters and Bushwalkers.* Hobart: Tasmanian Wilderness Society.

Brown, J; Collins, A; Duguid, P. 1989. 'Situated cognition and the culture of learning'. *Educational Researcher* 18 (1): 32–42.

Brown, M. 2002. 'The facilitator as gatekeeper: A critical analysis of social order in facilitation sessions'. *Journal of Adventure Education and Outdoor Learning* 2 (2): 101–112.

Brown, M. 2003. 'Paraphrases and summaries: A means of clarification or a vehicle for articulating a preferred version of student accounts?' *Australian Journal of Outdoor Education* 7 (2): 25–35.

Brown, M. 2008a. 'Comfort zone: Model or metaphor?' *Australian Journal of Outdoor Education* 12 (1): 3–12.

Brown, M. 2008b. 'Outdoor education: Opportunities provided by a place-based approach'. *New Zealand Journal of Outdoor Education* 2 (3), 7–25.

Brown, M. 2009. 'Reconceptualising outdoor adventure education: Activity in search of an appropriate theory'. *Australian Journal of Outdoor Education* 13 (2): 3–13.

Brown, M. 2010. 'Transfer: Outdoor adventure education's Achilles heel? Changing participation as a viable option'. *Australian Journal of Outdoor Education* 14 (1), 13–22.

Brown, M; Fraser, D. 2009. 'Re-evaluating risk and exploring educational alternatives'. *Journal of Adventure Education and Outdoor Learning* 9 (1): 61–77.

Brown, R. 2004. *Memo for a Saner World.* Camberwell, Victoria: Penguin.

Cameron, J. 2001. 'Beyond dualism: Wilderness, outdoor education and everyday places'. In Education Outdoors: Our Sense of Place, 12th National Outdoor Education Conference Proceedings. Carlton, Victoria: Victorian Outdoor Education Association: 27–32.

Cameron, J. 2003a. 'Responding to place in a post-colonial ear: An Australian perspective'. In *Decolonizing Nature*, edited by Adams, W. M; Mulligan, M. London: Earthscan: 172–196.

Cameron, J, ed. 2003b. *Changing Places: Re-imagining Australia.* Double Bay: Longueville Books.

Caplan, P. 2000. 'Introduction: Risk revisited'. In *Risk Revisited*, edited by Caplan, P. London: Pluto Press: 1–28.

Carr, W; Kemmis, S. 1986. *Becoming Critical: Education, Knowledge and Action Research.* Geelong, Victoria: Deakin University.

Carter, P. 1988. *The Road to Botany Bay*. Chicago: The University of Chicago Press.

Casey, E. 1993. *Getting Back into Place: Toward a Renewed Understanding of the Place-world*. Bloomington: Indiana University Press.

Casey, E. 1996. 'How to get from space to place in a fairly short stretch of time: Phenomenological prolegomena.' In *Sense of Place*, edited by Basso, K H; Feld, S. Santa Fe: School of American Research Press: 13–52.

Cason, D; Gillis, L. 1994. 'A meta-analysis of outdoor adventure programming with adolescents'. *Journal of Experiential Education* 17 (1): 40–47.

Chambers, D. 1984. *Imagining Nature*. Victoria: Deakin University.

Clark, M. 2004. 'Falling in love again'. *ABC Radio National Science Show*. Interview by Alexandra de Blas: 1 May.

Claxton, G. 2002. *Building Learning Power*. Bristol, UK: TLO Ltd.

Cook, L. 1999. 'The 1944 Education Act and outdoor education: From policy to practice'. *History of Education* 28 (2): 157–172.

Cooper, G. 1994. 'The role of outdoor education in education for the 21st century'. *The Journal of Adventure Education and Outdoor Leadership* 11 (2): 9–12.

Cosgriff, M. 2008. 'What's the story? Outdoor education in New Zealand in the 21st century'. *Journal of Physical Education New Zealand* 41 (3): 14–25.

Cronon, W. 1996. *Uncommon Ground: Rethinking the Human Place in Nature*. New York: W.W. Norton & Company.

Crump, B. 1960. *Good Keen Man*. Wellington, New Zealand: Reed.

Cuthbertson, B. 1999. 'Explorations of place: A critical approach to gaining a sense of place in outdoor education training'. Ph.D. thesis, Edmonton: University of Alberta.

Cuthbertson, B; Socha T; Potter, T. 2004. 'The double-edged sword; Critical reflections on traditional and modern technology in outdoor education'. *Journal of Adventure Education and Outdoor Learning* 4 (2), 133–144.

Davidson, L. 2008. 'Tragedy in the adventure playground: Media representations of mountaineering accidents in New Zealand'. *Leisure Studies* 27 (1): 3–19.

Davis-Berman, J; Berman, D. 2002. 'Risk and anxiety in adventure programming'. *Journal of Experiential Education* 25 (2): 305–310.

Dewey, J. 1915. *The School and Society*. Chicago: University of Chicago Press.

Estrellas, A. 1996. 'The eustress paradigm: A strategy for decreasing stress in wilderness adventure programming'. In *Women's Voices in Experiential Education*, edited by Warren, K. Dubuque, Iowa: Kendall Hunt: 32–44.

Ewert, A. W; Garvey, D. E. 2007. 'Philosophy and theory of adventure education'. In *Adventure Education: Theory and Applications*, edited by Prouty, D; Panicucci, J; Collinson, R. Champaign, Illinois: Human Kinetics: 19–32.

Exeter, D. 2001. *Learning in the Outdoors*. London: The Outward Bound Trust.

Fang, Z. 1996. 'A review of research on teacher beliefs and practices'. *Educational Research* 38 (1): 47–65.

Fenwick, T. 2001. *Experiential Learning: A Theoretical Critique from Five Perspectives*. Columbus, Ohio: ERIC Clearinghouse on Adult, Career, and Vocational Education.

Fenwick, T. 2003. 'Inside out of experiential learning: Troubling assumptions and expanding questions'. Paper presented at the Researching Learning Outside the Academy. 27–29 June; Glasgow Caledonian University.

Foley, M; Frew, M; McGillivray, D. 2003. 'Rough comfort: Consuming adventure on the "edge"'. In *Whose Journeys? The Outdoors and Adventure as Social and Cultural Phenomena*, edited by Humberstone, B; Brown, H; Richards, K. Cumbria, UK: Institute of Outdoor Learning: 149–160.

Ford, P. 1981. *Principles and Practices of Outdoor/Environmental Education*. New York, NY: Wiley.

Fox, K. 2008. 'Rethinking experience: What do we mean by this word "experience"?' *Journal of Experiential Education* 31 (1): 36–54.

Fullerton, T. 2001. *Watershed: Deciding our Water Future*. Sydney: ABC Books.

Gair, N. 1997. *Outdoor Education: Theory and Practice*. London: Cassell.

Gardner, H. 1999. *The Disciplined Mind: Beyond Facts and Standardized Test, the K-12 Education Every Child Deserves*. New York: Penguin Putnam.

Geertz, C. 1996. 'Afterword'. In *Senses of Place*, edited by Feld, S; Basso, K. Santa Fe, New Mexico: School of American Research Press: 259–262.

Gentry, K. 2006. 'Introduction: Place, heritage and identity'. In *Heartlands: New Zealand Historians Write about Where History Happened*, edited by Gentry, K; McLean, G. Auckland, NZ: Penguin: 13–26.

Giddens, A. 1991. *Modernity and Self-Identity: Self and Society in the Late Modern Age*. Stanford, California: Stanford University Press.

Gill, N. 1999. 'The ambiguities of wilderness'. In *Australian Cultural Geographies*, edited by Stratford, E. London: Oxford University Press: 48–68.

Gruenewald, D. 2003a. 'Foundations of place: A multidisciplinary framework for place-conscious education'. *American Educational Research Journal* 40 (3), 619–654.

Gruenewald, D. 2003b. 'The best of both worlds: A critical pedagogy of place'. *Educational Researcher* 32 (4), 3–12.

Gruenewald, D; Smith, G. 2008. *Place-Based Education in the Global Age*. New York: Lawrence Erlbaum Associates.

Haluza-DeLay, R. 2001. 'Nothing here to care about: Participant constructions of nature following 12-day wilderness program'. *The Journal of Environmental Education* 32 (4): 43–48.

Haskell, J. 2000. 'Experiencing freefall: A journey of pedagogical possibilities.' Ph.D. thesis, Vancouver, Canada: University of British Columbia.

Hattie, J; Marsh, H. W; Neill, J. T; Richards, G. E. 1997. 'Adventure education and Outward Bound: Out-of-class experiences that have a lasting effect'. *Review of Educational Research* 67: 43–87.

Hay, P. 2002. *Main Currents in Western Environmental Thought*. Sydney: University of New South Wales Press.

Hay, P. 2003. 'Writing place: Unpacking an exhibition catalogue essay.' In *Changing Places: Re-Imagining Australia*, edited by Cameron, J. Double Bay: Longeville Books: 272–285.

Heller, C. 1999. *Ecology of Everyday Life: Rethinking the Desire for Nature*. New York: Black House Press.

Henderson, R. 1995.'Outdoor travel: Explorations for change.' Ph.D. thesis, Edmonton: University of Alberta.

Higgins, P. 1996. 'Outdoor education for sustainability: Making connections'. *Far Out* 1 (4): 4–11.

Higgins, P. 2003. 'Outdoor education in the UK: A journey with an uncertain destination?' In *Whose Journeys? The Outdoors and Adventure as Social and Cultural Construction* edited by Humberstone, B; Brown, H; Richards, K. Penrith, Cumbria: the Institute of Outdoor Learning: 131–145.

Hill, A. 2007. An examination of New Zealand secondary school teachers' beliefs about outdoor education from a critical perspective. Unpublished PHSE 40 Research Report, Dunedin: University of Otago.

Hill, A. 2010a. 'Connection to place as a central theme for sustainable outdoor education'. *New Zealand Journal of Outdoor Education* 2 (4): 26–47.

Hill, A. 2010b. 'Reflections on beliefs and practices from New Zealand outdoor educators: Consistencies and conflicts'. *Australian Journal of Outdoor Education* 14 (1): 30–40.

Holman, D; Pavlica, K; Thorpe, R. 1997. 'Rethinking Kolb's theory of experiential learning in management education'. *Management Learning* 28 (2): 135–148.

Hope, A. 2005. 'Risk, education and culture: Interpreting danger as a dynamic, culturally situated process'. In *Risk, Education and Culture*, edited by Hope, A; Oliver, P. Aldershot. UK: Ashgate: 3–20.

Hope, A & Oliver, P. 2005 'Preface'. In *Risk, Education and Culture*, edited by Hope, A; Oliver, P. Aldershot, UK: Ashgate; ix–xii.

Hopkins, D; Putnam, R. 1993. *Personal Growth through Adventure*. London: David Fulton.

Horne, J. 2005. *The Pursuit of Wonder: How Australia's Landscape was Explored, Nature Discovered and Tourism Unleashed*. Carlton, Victoria: The Miegunyah Press.

Hovelynck, J. 2001. 'Beyond didactics: A reconnaissance of experiential learning'. *Australian Journal of Outdoor Education* 6 (1): 4–12.

Humberstone, B; Brown, H; Richards, K., eds. 2003. *Whose Journeys? The Outdoors and Adventure as Social and Cultural Construction*. Penrith, Cumbria: The Institute of Outdoor Learning.

Hunt, J. 1995. 'Dewey's philosophical method and its influence on his philosophy of education'. In *The Theory of Experiential Education* edited by Warren, K; Sakofs, M; Hunt, J. Dubuque, Iowa: Kendall/Hunt Publishing: 23–32.

Hutchins, E. 1993. 'Learning to navigate'. In *Understanding Practice: Perspectives on Activity and Context*, edited by Chaiklin, S; Lave, J. Cambridge: Cambridge University Press: 35–63.

Hutchinson, D. 2004. *A Natural History of Place in Education*. New York: Teachers College Press.

Ihimaera, W. 1994. 'So what are our dreams and visions?' In *Vision Aotearoa: Kaupapa New Zealand*, edited by Ihimaera, W. Wellington, New Zealand: Bridget Williams: xi–xii.

Irwin, D. 2007–8. 'Educating for sustainability'. *Out and About* 19: 6–8.

Irwin, D. 2010. 'Weaving the threads: Exploring identity through bicultural outdoor education experiences'. *New Zealand Journal of Outdoor Education: Kō Tane Mahuta Pupuke* 2 (4): 67–87

Jackson, J. B. 1984. *Discovering the Vernacular Landscape*. New Haven and London: Yale University Press.

Jarvis, P. 1987. *Adult Learning in the Social Context*. London: Croom-Helm.

Johnson, D. 2004. 'Student perspectives on the impact and transfer of the Camp Mallana experience: A case study.' M.A. thesis, Melbourne: Monash University.

Joplin, L. 1995. 'On defining experiential education'. In *The Theory of Experiential Education*, edited by Warren, K; Sakofs, M; Hunt, J. Dubuque, Iowa: Kendall/Hunt: 15–22.

Kemmis, S. 1985. 'Action research and the politics of reflection'. In *Reflection: Turning Experience into Learning*, edited by Boud, D; Keogh, R; Walker, D. London: RoutledgeFalmer: 139–164.

King, M. 1999. *Being Pakeha Now: Reflections and Recollections of a White Native*. Auckland, New Zealand: Penguin.

King, M. 2003. *The Penguin History of New Zealand*. Auckland, New Zealand: Penguin.

Kolb, D. A. 1984. *Experiential Learning.* Englewood Cliffs, NJ: Prentice-Hall.

Kraft, R. J. 1981. 'A call to action and reflection'. *Journal of Experiential Education* 4 (1): 5–8.

Lakoff, G; Johnson, M. 1980. *Metaphors We Live By.* Chicago: University of Chicago Press.

Lave, J. 1988. *Cognition in Practice.* Cambridge: Cambridge University Press.

Lave, J; Wenger, E. 1991. *Situated Learning: Legitimate Peripheral Participation.* Cambridge: Cambridge University Press.

Lease, G. 1995. 'Introduction: Nature under fire.' In *Reinventing Nature? Responses to Postmodern Deconstruction*, edited by Soule, M.E; Lease, G. Washington: Island Press: 3–15.

Leberman, S; Martin, A. 2003. 'Does pushing comfort zones produce peak learning experiences?' *Australian Journal of Outdoor Education* 7 (1): 10–19.

Leopold, A. 1987. *A Sand County Almanac: And Sketches Here and There.* New York: Oxford University Press.

Lines, W. 1991. *Taming the Great South Land: A History of the Conquest of Nature in Australia.* Sydney: Allen and Unwin.

Lines, W. 2001. *Open Air Essays.* Sydney: New Holland Publishers.

Lippard, L. 1997. *The Lure of the Local: Senses of Place in a Multi-Centred Society.* New York: The New Press.

Loeffler, T. 1999. 'Should modern communication systems (cellular telephones) be used in the wilderness? No'. In *Controversial Issues in Adventure Education: A Critical Examination*, edited by Wurdinger, S; Potter, T. Dubuque, Iowa: Kendall/Hunt: 78–85.

Lopez, B. 1986. *Arctic Dreams: Imagination and Desire in a Northern Landscape.* London: Picador.

Lopez, B. 1988. *Crossing Open Ground.* New York: Charles Scribner's Sons.

Lopez, B. 1996. 'A literature of place'. *US Society and Values* August: 10–12.

Lopez, B. 2003. 'The language of animals.' In *A Place on Earth: An Anthology of Nature Writing from Australia and North America*, edited by Tredinnick, M. Sydney: University of New South Wales Press: 160–166.

Loynes, C. 1998. 'Adventure in a bun'. *Journal of Experiential Education* 21 (1): 35–39.

Loynes, C. 2002. 'The Generative Paradigm'. *Journal of Adventure Education and Outdoor Learning* 2 (2): 113–125.

Luckner, J. L; Nadler, R. S. 1997. *Processing the Experience: Strategies to Enhance and Generalize Learning.* 2nd ed. Dubuque, Iowa: Kendall Hunt.

Lugg, A. 1999. 'Directions in outdoor education curriculum'. *Australian Journal of Outdoor Education* (4) 1: 25–32.

Lugg, A. 2004. 'Outdoor adventure in Australian outdoor education: Is it a case of roast for Christmas dinner?' *Australian Journal of Outdoor Education* 8 (1): 4–11.

Lynch, P. 2006. *Camping in the Curriculum: A History of Outdoor Education in New Zealand Schools.* Lincoln University, New Zealand: PML Publication.

Lynch, P; Moore, K. 2004. 'Adventures in paradox'. *Australian Journal of Outdoor Education* 8 (2): 3–12.

Macauley, D., ed. 1996. *Minding Nature: The Philosophers of Ecology.* New York: The Guilford Press.

Macdonald, D. 2002. 'Critical pedagogy: What might it look like and why does it matter?' In *The Sociology of Sport and Physical Education*, edited by Laker, A. London, Routledge: 167–189.

Macdonald, D., & Kirk, D. 1999. Pedagogy, the body and Christian identity. *Sport, Education and Society* 4 (2): 131–142.

Macfarlane, R. 2003. *Mountains of the Mind: A History of Fascination*. London: Granta Books.

Marshall, P. 1992. *Nature's Web: Rethinking our Place on Earth*. London: Cassell.

Martin, B; Cashel, C; Wagstaff, M; Breunig, M. 2006. *Outdoor Leadership: Theory and Practice*. Champaign, Illinois: Human Kinetics.

Martin, P. 1992. 'Future directions for outdoor education: Are they worth the costs?' *The Outdoor Educator* December: 19–23.

Martin, P. 1994. 'Future directions for outdoor education.' *Journal of Adventure Education* 10 (3): 16–19.

Martin, P. 1995. 'New perspectives of self, others and nature'. *Australian Journal of Outdoor Education* 1 (3): 3–9.

Martin, P. 1998. 'Education, ideology and outdoor leadership education'. *Australian Journal of Outdoor Education* 3 (1): 14–20.

Martin, P. 1999. 'Outdoor recreation and outdoor education: Connections and disconnections.' *Journeys* 4 (4): 9–15.

Martin, P. 2005. 'Human to nature relationships through outdoor education'. In *Outdoor and Experiential Learning: Views from the Top*, edited by T. Dickson; T. Gray; B. Hayllar. Dunedin: Otago University Print: 28–52.

Martin, P; Priest, S. 1986. 'Understanding the adventure experience'. *Journal of Adventure Education* 3 (1), 18–21.

Martin, P; Thomas, G. 2000. 'Interpersonal relationships as a metaphor for human-nature relationships.' *Australian Journal of Outdoor Education* 5 (1): 39–46.

Mason, B. 1984. *The Path of the Paddle: An Illustrated Guide to the Art of Canoeing*. Toronto: Key Porter Books.

Mason, B. 1988. *Song of the Paddle: An Illustrated Guide to Wilderness Camping*. Toronto: Key Porter Books.

Massey, D. 1994. *Space, Place, and Gender*. Minneapolis: University of Minnesota Press.

Massey, D. 1995. 'Migration, globalization and place'. In *A Place in the World? Places, Cultures and Globalization* edited by Massey, D; Jess, P. Oxford: The Open University: 45–85.

Massey, D. 2005. *For Space*. London: Sage.

Matthews, E. 2002. *The Philosophy of Merleau-Ponty*. Chesam: Acumen.

McAvoy, L. 1999. 'Rescue-free wilderness areas'. In *Adventure Programming*, edited by Miles, J C; Priest, S. State College, Pennsylvania: Venture: 325–329.

McKenna, M. 2002. *Looking for Blackfella's Point: An Australian History of Place*. Sydney: University of New South Wales Press.

McRae, K. 1990. *Outdoor and Environmental Education: Diverse Purposes and Objective*. South Melbourne: McMillan.

Mehan, H. 1996. 'Beneath the skin and between the ears: A case study in the politics of representation'. In *Understanding Practice: Perspectives on Activity and Context*. edited by Chaiklin, S: Lave, J. Cambridge: Cambridge University Press: 241–268.

Meinig, D. 1979. *The Interpretation of Ordinary Landscapes*. New Haven: Oxford University Press.

Merleau-Ponty, M. 2002. *Phenomenology of Perception*. Trans. Smith, C. London: Routledge.

Miles, J. C; Priest, S., eds. 1990. *Adventure Education*. State College, Pennsylvania: Venture Publishing.

Morley, D; Robins, K. 1993. 'No place like Heimat: Images of home(land) in European culture'. In *Space and Place: Theories of Identity and Location*, edited by Carter, E; Donald, J; Squires, J. London: Lawrence and Wishart: 3–31.

Mortlock, C. 1984. *The Adventure Alternative*. Milnthorpe, UK: Cicerone Press.

Mulligan, M; Hill, S. 2001. *Ecological Pioneers: A Social History of Australian Ecological Thought and Action*. Cambridge: Cambridge University Press.

Mullins, M. 2007. 'Ways of knowing the river: A guides-in-training perspective'. Master of Education thesis, Melbourne: Monash University.

Muir, J. 1911. *My First Summer in the Sierra*. Boston: Houghton Mifflin Company.

Nash, R. 1982. *Wilderness and the American Mind*. New Haven: Yale University Press.

Nast, H; Pile, S., eds. 1998. *Places through the Body*. London and New York: Routledge.

Nerlich, M. 1987. *Ideology of Adventure*. 2 vols. Minneapolis: University of Minneapolis.

Nettleton, B. 1993. 'A perspective of outdoor education: Nature as a friend'. *The Outdoor Educator* September: 17–21.

Nicol, R. 2002a. 'Outdoor education: Research topic or universal value? Part One'. *Journal of Adventure Education and Outdoor Learning* 2 (1): 29–41.

Nicol, R. 2002b. 'Outdoor education: Research topic or universal value? Part Two'. *Journal of Adventure Education and Outdoor Learning* 2 (2): 85–99.

Nicol, R. 2003. 'Outdoor education: Research topic or universal value? Part Three'. *Journal of Adventure Education and Outdoor Learning* 3 (1): 11–27.

Nicol, R; Higgins, P. 1998. 'A sense of place; A context for environmental outdoor education'. In *Celebrating Diversity: Learning by Sharing Cultural Differences*, edited by Higgins, P; Humberstone, B. Buckinghamshire Chilterns University: European Institute for Outdoor Adventure Education: 50–55.

Norberg-Schulz, C. 1980. *Genius Loci: Toward a Phenomenology of Architecture*. New York: Rizzoli.

ODENZ. 2009. Accessed 29 June 2009. Available from http://outdoorednz.co.nz/about-odenz/default.asp

Onore, C., & Lubetsky, B. 1992. 'Why we learn is what and how we learn: Curriculum as possibility'. In *Negotiating the Curriculum: Educating for the 21st Century*, edited by Boomer, G; Lester, N; Onore, C; Cook, J. London: Falmer: 253–265.

Orr, D. 1992. *Ecological Literacy: Education and the Transition to a Postmodern World*. Albany: State University of New York Press.

Orr, D. 1994. *Earth in Mind: On Education, Environment and the Human Prospect*. Washington, DC: Island Press.

O'Neill, D. 2005. *Ancestral Streams: Notes from the Murray Valley*. Narre Warren South: Bookhenge Press.

Palmer, J; Suggate, J; Robottom, I; Hart, P. 1999. 'Significant life experiences and formative influences on the development of adults' environmental awareness in the UK, Australia and Canada'. *Environmental Education Research* 5 (2): 181–200.

Panicucci, J. 2007. 'Cornerstones of adventure education'. In *Adventure Education: Theory and Applications*, edited by Prouty, D; Panicucci, J; Collinson, R. Champaign, Illinois: Human Kinetics: 33–48.

Papprill, J. 2009. 'Preparing the ground for a sustainable future'. *Out and About* 22: 14–16.

Park, G. 1995. *Ngā Uruora (The Groves of Life): Ecology and History in a New Zealand Landscape*. Wellington: Victoria University Press.

Park, G. 2006. *Theatre Country: Essays on Landscape and Whenua*. Wellington: Victoria University Press.

Payne, P. 2000. 'Embodiment and action competence'. In *Critical Environmental and Health Education*, edited by Jensen, B; Schnack, K; Simovska, V. Copenhagen: The Danish University of Education, Research Centre for Environmental and Health Education: 185–208.

Payne, P. 2002 'On the construction, deconstruction and reconstruction of experience in 'critical' outdoor education.' *Australian Journal of Outdoor Education* 6 (2): 4–21.

Payne, P; Wattchow, B. 2008. 'Slow pedagogy and placing education in post-traditional outdoor education'. *Australian Journal of Outdoor Education* 12 (1): 25–38.

Pinn, J. 2003. 'Restor(y)ing a sense of place, self and community'. In *Changing Places: Re-imagining Australia*, edited by Cameron, J. Double Bay: Longueville Books: 38–47.

Plumwood, V. 2003. 'Decolonizing relationships with nature'. In *Decolonizing Nature*, edited by Adams, W.M; Mulligan, M. London: Earthscan: 51–78.

Preston, L; Griffiths, A. 2004. 'Pedagogy of connections: Findings of a collaborative action research project in outdoor and environmental education'. *Australian Journal of Outdoor Education* 8 (2): 36–45.

Price, J. 1996. 'Looking for nature at the mall: A field guide to the Nature Company'. In *Uncommon Ground: Rethinking the Human Place in Nature* edited by Cronon, W. New York: W W Norton and Company: 186–202.

Priest, S. 1986. 'Redefining outdoor education: A matter of many relationships'. *Journal of Environmental Education* 17 (3), 13–15.

Priest, S; Gass, M. A. 1997. *Effective Leadership in Adventure Programming*. Champaign, Illinois: Human Kinetics.

Prouty, D; Panicucci, J; Collinson, R., eds. 2007. *Adventure Education: Theory and Applications*. Champaign, Illinois: Human Kinetics.

Raffan, J. 1992. 'Frontier, homeland and sacred space: A collaborative investigation into cross-cultural perceptions of place in the Thelon Game Sanctuary, Northwest Territories'. Ph.D. thesis, Kingston, Ontario: Queen's University.

Raffan, J. 1993. 'The experience of place: Exploring land as teacher'. *The Journal of Experiential Education* 16(1): 39–45.

Read, P. 1996. *Returning to Nothing: The Meaning of Lost Places*. Cambridge: Cambridge University Press.

Read, P. 2000. *Belonging: Australians, Place and Aboriginal Ownership*. Cambridge: Cambridge University Press.

Read, P. 2003. *Haunted Earth*. Sydney: University of New South Wales Press.

Relph, E. 1976. *Place and Placelessness*. London: Pion Limited.

Relph, E. 1985. 'Geographical experiences and being-in-the-world: The phenomenological origins of geography'. In *Dwelling, Place and Environment: Towards a Phenomenology of Person and World*, edited by Seamon, D; Mugerauer, R. Martinus Nijhoff Publishers, Boston: 15–31.

Relph, E. 1992. 'Modernity and the reclamation of place'. In *Dwelling, Seeing, and Designing: Toward a Phenomenological Ecology*, edited by Seamon, D. State University of New York Press: New York: 25–40.

Rigby, K. 2004. *Topographies of the Sacred: The Poetics of Place in European Romanticism*. University of Virginia Press: Charlottesville and London.

Ringer, M. 1999. 'The facile-itation of facilitation? Searching for competencies in group work leadership'. *Scisco Conscientia* 2: 1–19.

Rose, D. B. 1996. *Nourishing Terrains: Australian Aboriginal Views of Landscape and Wilderness*. Canberra: Australian Heritage Commission.

Rose, D. B. 2002. *Country of the Heart: An Indigenous Australian Homeland*. Canberra: Aboriginal Studies Press.

Rose, D. B. 2004. *Reports from a Wild Country: Ethics for Decolonisation*. Sydney: University of New South Wales Press.

Rousseau, J. J. 1762. *Émile, ou de l'éducation*. Frankfort.

Schama, S. 1995. *Landscape and Memory*. London: Fontana.

Schoel, J; Prouty, D; Radcliffe, P. 1988. *Islands of Healing: A Guide to Adventure Based Counselling*. Hamilton: Project Adventure.

Seaman, J. 2007. 'Taking *things* into account: Learning as kinaesthetically-mediated collaboration'. *Journal of Adventure Education and Outdoor Learning* 7 (1): 3–20.

Seaman, J. 2008. 'Experience, reflect, critique: The end of the "learning cycles" era'. *Journal of Experiential Education* 31 (1): 3–18.

Seamon, D. 1979. *A Geography of the Lifeworld: Movement, Rest and Encounter*. New York: St. Martin's Press.

Seddon, G. 1972. *Sense of Place*. Perth: University of Western Australia Press.

Seddon, G. 1994. *Searching for the Snowy: An Environmental History*. St. Leonards, New South Wales: Allen and Unwin.

Seddon, G. 1996. Oh brave new world. *Meanjin* 55: 395–409

Seddon, G. 1997. *Landprints: Reflections on Place and Landscape*. Cambridge: Cambridge University Press.

Seddon, G. 2005. *The Old Country: Australian Landscapes, Plants and People*. Cambridge: Cambridge University Press.

Seidman, I. 1998. *Interviewing as Qualitative Research: A Guide for Researchers in Education and the Social Sciences*. New York: Teachers College Press.

Sharp, N. 2002. *Saltwater People: The Waves of Memory*. Sydney: Allen and Unwin.

Sinclair, P. 2001. *The Murray: A River and its People*. Carlton South: Melbourne University Press.

Smith, G. 2002. 'Place-based education: Learning where we are'. *Phi Delta Kappan* April: 584–594.

Soper, K. 1995. *What is Nature? Culture, Politics and the Non-Human*. Oxford: Blackwell.

Soule, M; Lease, G., eds. 1995. *Reinventing Nature: Responses to Postmodern Deconstruction*. Washington: Island Press.

Stan, I. 2009. 'Recontextualizing the role of the facilitator in group interaction in the outdoor classroom'. *Journal of Adventure Education and Outdoor Learning* 9 (1): 23–43.

Stewart, A. 2003a. 'Encountering landscapes: An exploration of environment specific learning on an extended journey'. M.A. thesis, Hobart: University of Tasmania.

Stewart, A. 2003b. 'Encountering landscapes: An exploration of environment specific learning on an extended journey.' In *Whose Journeys? The Outdoors and Adventure as Social and Cultural Construction*, edited by Humberstone, B; Brown, H; Richards, K. Penrith, Cumbria: the Institute of Outdoor Learning: 311–328.

Stewart, A. 2003c. 'Reinvigorating our love of our home range: Exploring the connections between sense of place and outdoor education.' *Australian Journal of Outdoor Education* 7(2): 19–24.

Stewart, A. 2004a. 'Canoeing the Murray River (Australia) as environmental education: A tale of two rivers.' *Canadian Journal of Environmental Education* 9: 136–147.

Stewart, A. 2004b. 'Decolonising encounters with the Murray River: Building place responsive outdoor education'. *The Australian Journal of Outdoor Education* 8 (2): 46–55.

Stone, D; Stone, S. 1996. *Touring Murray River Country: Mountains to the Sea*. Lilydale, Victoria: Pioneer Design Studio.

Sturt, C. 1833. *Two Expeditions into the Interior of Southern Australia, during the years 1828, 1829, 1830, and 1831: With Observations on the Soil, Climate, and General Resources of the Colony of New South Wales*. 2 vols. London: Smith, Elder and Co.

Sutherland, A. 2009. 'Blumine Island project has far-reaching outcomes'. *Out and About* 22: 19–22.

Tacey, D. 1995. *Edge of the Sacred: Transformation in Australia*. North Blackburn: Harper Collins.

Tacey, D. 2000. *Re-Enchantment: The New Australian Spirituality*. Sydney: Harper Collins.

Tacey, D. 2003. 'Spirit place.' In *Changing Places: Re-Imagining Australia*, edited by Cameron, J. Double Bay: Longueville Books: 243–248.

Tanner, T. 1980. 'Significant life experiences: A new research area in environmental education'. *Journal of Environmental Education* 11 (4): 20–24.

Thiele, C. 1963. *Storm Boy*. Adelaide: Rigby.

Thiele, C. 1965. *February Dragon*. Adelaide: Rigby.

Thomashow, M. 1996. *Ecological Identity: Becoming a Reflective Environmentalist*. Cambridge, Massachusetts: The MIT Press.

Thoreau, H. 1854. *Walden and 'Civil Disobedience'*. New York: Penguin.

Tinning, R. 2002. 'Toward a "modest pedagogy": Reflections on the problematics of critical pedagogy.' *Quest* 54: 224–240.

Tooth, R; Renshaw, P. 2009. 'Reflections on pedagogy and place: A journey into learning for sustainability through environmental narrative and deep attentive reflection'. *Australian Journal of Environmental Education* 25: 95–104.

Tuan, Y. 1974. *Topophilia: A Study of Environmental Perception, Attitudes, and Values*. New Jersey: Prentice Hall.

Tuan, Y. 1977. *Space and Place: The Perspective of Experience*. Minneapolis: University of Minnesota Press.

Vella, J. 2002. *Learning to Listen, Learning to Teach*. San Francisco, CA: Jossey-Bass.

Vince, R. 1998. 'Behind and beyond Kolb's learning cycle'. *Journal of Management Education* 22 (3): 304–319.

Walsh, V; Golins, G. 1976. *The Exploration of the Outward Bound Process*. Denver, Colorado: Colorado Outward Bound School.

Walter, E. 1998. *Placeways: The Theory of Human Environment*. Chapel Hill and London: The University of North Carolina Press.

Warren, K. 1999. 'Unpacking the knapsack of outdoor experiential education: Race, gender, and class sensitive outdoor leadership'. Ph.D. thesis: Union Institute.

Watson, I. 1990. *Fighting over the Forests*. Sydney: Allen & Unwin.

Wattchow, B. 1998. 'River… I Follow River'. *Journeys: The Journal of the Victorian Association of Outdoor Education* 3 (2): 20–24.

Wattchow, B. 2001a. 'Outdoor education as the experience of place'. Paper presented at the 12th National Outdoor Education Conference. 15–18 January; La Trobe University, Bendigo, Australia.

Wattchow, B. 2001b. 'A pedagogy of production: Craft, technology and outdoor education'. *Australian Journal of Outdoor Education* 5(2): 19–27.

Wattchow, B. 2004. 'Many voices speak the river: Education in an adventure-river-landscape'. *Educational Insights* 9 (1). Available from: http://www.ccfi.educ.ubc.ca/publication/insights/v09n01/articles/wattchow.html

Wattchow, B. 2005. '"Belonging to proper country": Australian outdoor education as experiencing relationships in place'. In *Outdoor and Experiential Learning: Views from the Top*, edited by T.J. Dickson; T. Gray; B. Hayller. Dunedin: Otago University Print: 13–27.

Wattchow, B. 2006. 'The experience of river places in outdoor education: A phenomenological study'. Ph.D. thesis, Melbourne: Monash University.

Wattchow, B. 2007. 'Playing with an unstoppable force: Paddling, river-places and outdoor education'. *Australian Journal of Outdoor Education* 11(1): 10–20.

Wattchow, B. 2008. 'Moving on an effortless journey: Paddling, river-places and outdoor education'. *Australian Journal of Outdoor Education* 12 (2): 12–23.

Wattchow, B. 2010. *The Song of the Wounded River*. Port Adelaide, South Australia: Ginninderra Press.

Weigert, A; Gecas, V. 2005. 'Symbolic interactionist reflections on Erikson, identity, and postmodernism'. *Identity: An International Journal of Theory and Research* 5 (2): 161–174.

Weil, S. 1959. *Waiting on God*. Trans. Craufurd, E. London: Harper Collins.

Weil, S. 2002. *The Need for Roots: Prelude to a Declaration of Duties towards Mankind*. New York: Routledge.

Wolfe, B; Samdahl, D. 2005. 'Challenging assumptions: Examining fundamental beliefs that shape challenge course programming and research'. *Journal of Experiential Education* 28 (1): 25–43.

Wurdinger, S. 1997. *Philosophical Issues in Adventure Education*. 3rd edn. Dubuque, IA: Kendall Hunt.

Zink, R; Leberman, S. 2003. 'Risking a debate-redefining risk and risk management: A New Zealand study'. *New Zealand Journal of Outdoor Education: Kō Tane Mahuta Pupuke* 1 (2): 63–76.

Zink, R; Boyes, M. 2006. 'The nature and scope of outdoor education in New Zealand schools'. *Australian Journal of Outdoor Education* 10 (1): 11–21.

Zweig, P. 1974. *The Adventurer: The Fate of Adventure in the Western World*. Princeton, NJ: Princeton University Press.